Sustainable Management of Japanese Entrepreneurs in Pre-War Period from the Perspective of SDGs and ESG

Masaatsu Takehara • Naoya Hasegawa

Sustainable Management of Japanese Entrepreneurs in Pre-War Period from the Perspective of SDGs and ESG

palgrave
macmillan

Masaatsu Takehara
Hosei University
Tokyo, Japan

Naoya Hasegawa
Hosei University
Tokyo, Japan

ISBN 978-981-15-6506-9 ISBN 978-981-15-6507-6 (eBook)
https://doi.org/10.1007/978-981-15-6507-6

This Palgrave Macmillan imprint is published by the registered company Springer Nature Singapore Pte Ltd.
The registered company address is: 152 Beach Road, #21-01/04 Gateway East, Singapore 189721, Singapore

Aiming to Be Companies Selected by Future Generations

One of the key management issues for modern companies is how to address social issues, especially issues raised by the Sustainable Development Goals (SDGs). For example, climate change is one of the 17 goals of the SDGs. After the Paris Agreement came into effect in 2016, companies around the world are accelerating their efforts to decarbonize their business. The Paris Agreement and the SDGs reject energy resource–intensive business models. Companies are now required to restructure their management structures and business models from the perspectives of ESG: E (environment), S (society), and G (governance).

The SDGs are a "challenges list" for the global community, and it includes both risks and opportunities. The essence of business is to solve problems in society. Managers are expected to have the ability to grasp opportunities within the issues raised by the SDGs and develop them into new businesses.

When we look into the history of Japanese companies, there are many entrepreneurs who tried to solve social issues through their business. The entrepreneurs featured in this book are examples of finding opportunities from social issues. Their philosophy and the SDGs share many elements.

This book features 13 Japanese entrepreneurs who made a significant contribution to the development of society from 1868, when modernization in Japan began, to the 1950s, after World War II. They worked on solving social issues at that time through their businesses and succeeded in creating social value (solving social issues) and economic value (development of their businesses). They anticipated the integration of solving social issues into corporate management, which is currently advocated in the SDGs. Their trajectories provide a wealth of practical knowledge necessary to survive in a changing society and have many lessons for modern companies that are expected to contribute to the achievement of SDGs.

The following is an overview of how modern companies should be managed under this new paradigm. The authors think reading this overview in advance will help readers have better understanding of key messages each chapter presents.

Philosophy of SDGs: Toward a World Where No One Is Left Behind

Sustainable Development Goals (SDGs) are a set of international development goals described in the 2030 Agenda for Sustainable Development which was adopted by the UN Sustainable Development Summit in September 2015. The SDGs built on the success of Millennium Development Goals (MDGs). SDGs consist of 17 goals and 169 targets to be tackled and achieved from 2016 to 2030. The SDGs aim at realizing a world that "leaves no one behind".

The main theme of the MDGs was human development in developing countries such as poverty reduction and promoting education and health. On the other hand, the SDGs have 17 goals and 169 targets that address key issues in economic, social, and environmental fields, such as sustainable economic growth, elimination of inequalities, and measures against climate change. In addition, the SDGs apply not only to developing countries, but to all countries, including developed countries.

The words "sustainable development", used in the Sustainable Development Goals (SDGs) as a key phrase, have been widely used since the 1987 Brundtland Commission report introduced the concept of sustainable development. Sustainable development is defined as development that meets the needs of the present generation without compromising the ability of future generations to meet their own needs. The word "sustainability" is also often used.

Prior to the Brundtland report, "Limits to Growth", published by the Club of Rome in 1972, shocked the world by predicting that food shortages, resource depletion, and increased environmental pollution would cause economic collapse and that humanity would eventually head for catastrophe. The Club of Rome's assertion that an economy based on infinite use of the earth's natural capital is not sustainable is reflected in the philosophy of the SDGs.

After the Earth Summit held in Rio de Janeiro in 1992, sustainability came to be used in two ways: the sustainability of the global environment and the sustainability of society. Since the Earth Summit, sustainability has become a global common value.

The Earth Summit adopted the Framework Convention on Climate Change, the Convention on Biological Diversity, the Statement of the Principles of Forestry, and Agenda 21 as measures to realize sustainability. With regard to tackling the climate change, based on the Framework Convention on Climate Change, global agreements on reducing greenhouse gas emissions from the Kyoto Protocol to the Paris Agreement have been formed.

At the United Nations Conference on Sustainable Development (Rio+20) held in 2012, discussions began on strengthening the green economy and formulating the SDGs. A green economy is an economic system that promotes sustainable growth while properly conserving the ecosystem from which humanity benefits.

Sustainable economic growth is an important issue in the SDGs. Therefore, businesses are expected to play a more important role than they did in the MDGs. Former United Nations Secretary-General Ban Ki-moon said, "Business is a key partner in achieving the SDGs. Business can contribute to it through its core businesses".

Rather than committing to all 17 SDGs goals, companies are expected to address the challenges associated with their business activities. Tackling the issues of the SDGs through business leads to the creation of new opportunities.

Global Trends in Responsible Management

To look back on the historical development of the relationship between businesses and society, it is useful to review examples from the UK and the EU.

In the UK in the 1980s, the Thatcher administration (1979–1990) implemented policies to promote deregulation and free competition to turn around social and economic stagnation. Thatcher's policies were successful in revitalizing the economy, but widened the gap between rich and poor, creating a new problem of social exclusion.

To tackle this problem, the Blair administration, which took charge of British politics from 1997 to 2007, set social inclusion as a policy vision and tried to close the gap in British society. Social inclusion meant all groups of people within a society felt valued and important, and they were given the opportunity to realize decent work. This idea shares the same underlying ideas with the SDGs which aim at realizing a society that leaves no one behind.

In Europe in the 1990s, as problems of youth unemployment and social exclusion became serious, companies were expected to play a more active role to address these social problems. In the UK, as part of its social inclusion policy, the Blair administration promoted various measures to encourage businesses to fulfill corporate social responsibility (CSR). In fact, the administration appointed a new cabinet minister to be in charge of promoting CSR and integrated CSR into government policy. By making CSR part of its corporate strategy, the UK government encouraged companies to tackle social issues.

In 2011, the EU changed its definition of CSR from "corporate voluntary action to take social and environmental considerations into business activities and building relationships with stakeholders" to "The responsibility of enterprises for their impact on society". The EU decided to implement a policy to drive businesses to create shared value (social value and economic value) while mitigating the negative effects of business activities.

Companies have been required to create innovative products and services that meet the needs of diverse stakeholders based on a long-term strategy that incorporates CSR. The corporate management which aims at increasing corporate value while addressing social issues through business is what companies are expected to address in regard to the SDGs.

Creating Shared Value

The SDGs emphasize the achievement of three aspects in a well-balanced and integrated manner. They are sustainable economic growth, the realization of a world where no one is left behind, and environmental protection centered on countermeasures against climate change. Compared with MDGs, businesses are expected to play a more active role to contribute to the achievement of SDGs.

Many businesses succeeded because they created products and services that solved social issues. However, many social issues are still left unsolved because social systems such as regulations are not well developed, or social systems exist but they are not properly functioning. So, new businesses can be created by identifying opportunities within these social issues and trying to solve them.

In 2011, Michael Porter advocated the concept of creating shared value (CSV), arguing that companies should work on CSV. This is the idea that new businesses are created by companies finding potential opportunities among social issues and developing solutions that contribute to solving them.

CSV is different from CSR in that CSR is not always tied to the core business of a company. What companies are expected, in order to achieve the SDGs, is to solve social issues through business and contribute to sustainable economic growth in the world. It is essentially synonymous with CSV, which aims to solve social issues and create economic opportunities.

A business case that anticipated an approach to SDGs and CSV was taken by Honda Motor. In 1970, the US Congress passed the Clean Air Act of 1970 (often called the Muskie Act) to regulate automobile exhaust emissions to address the growing problem of air pollution. However, three major US auto manufacturers opposed the legislation. It was the CVCC engine developed by Honda which passed the strict standards for the first time among world auto manufacturers. This wasn't long after Honda entered the automobile business. Honda's engineers firmly believed that "exhaust gas problems must be solved as our corporate social responsibility", and with Honda's core competence of excellent engine manufacturing technology, it actually contributed to mitigating the air pollution.

When companies engaged in CSR, it had an aspect of the redistribution of wealth, especially in corporate philanthropic activities, but now, when addressing the SDGs, companies are expected to simultaneously create social value and economic value. In Honda's case, what Honda did was creating shared value: they successfully created social value (their newly developed CVCC engine contributed to mitigating the air pollution problem in the USA) and economic value (Honda's compact cars with CVCC engines were purchased by many US consumers).

Decarbonization Era Is Changing Business

In 2015, there were two events that set the course for the global society: SDGs and the Paris Agreement. The SDGs were adopted at the UN Sustainable Development Summit and the Paris Agreement was adopted at COP21.[1]

The Paris Agreement set the goal of keeping global temperature rise by the end of this century well below 2° Celsius above pre-industrial levels and to pursue efforts to limit the temperature increase further to 1.5° Celsius. Achieving this goal requires reducing greenhouse gas emissions to virtually zero by the second half of this century.

According to the Intergovernmental Panel on Climate Change (IPCC), if cumulative CO_2 emissions exceed three trillion tons, the average global temperature will rise by 2° Celsius. Humanity has already emitted about two trillion tons of CO_2, and to achieve the goal set in the Paris Agreement, cumulative CO_2 emissions must be kept within the remaining one trillion ton. At the current pace, CO_2 emissions are expected to reach one trillion tons within the next 30 years, so we have to slow down the pace.

Estimated potential CO_2 emissions from fossil fuels currently buried underground are about 2.86 trillion tons. Of that amount, to achieve the 2° Celsius target, only one trillion ton of CO_2 is usable, so the remaining 1860 billion tons of fossil fuels can no longer be used. In this way, fossil fuels that can no longer be mined are called "stranded assets" because they are assets whose value are significantly impaired by changes in the market and social environment. For this reason, increasing numbers of investors around the world, the institutional investors in particular, are quickly avoiding the investment in coal-related companies. This is called "divestment". (More details are discussed in the next section.)

With the effect of the Paris Agreement, businesses are accelerating their efforts to reduce greenhouse gas emissions from their business activities. Advanced companies are introducing new key performance indicators (KPIs) such as "decoupling", which aims at achieving economic growth while reducing CO_2 emissions, and return on carbon (ROC), which is the operating income per unit of CO_2 emissions.

Companies are required to achieve sustained growth. In order for companies to survive and grow in the era of decarbonization, it is necessary for businesses not only to reduce CO_2 emissions but also to gain new business opportunities and increase profitability. In the past, return on equity

(ROE) has been considered an important management indicator, but in the new era of decarbonization, businesses will be evaluated on how much profit they made while achieving decarbonization.

Accelerating ESG Investment and Growing Importance of Non-financial Information

The Principles for Responsible Investment (PRI), announced by the United Nations in 2006 and signed by institutional investors around the world, ask signer investors to avoid short-termism (pursuit of short-term profits) and help investee companies realize sustainable growth through long-term investment.

The PRI require the integration of the non-financial elements of the environment (E), society (S), and governance (G) into the selection process of the investee companies, in addition to the financial elements. Investing in accordance with PRI is called ESG investment.

Institutional investors around the world are accelerating ESG investment with the announcement of the SDGs and the effect of the Paris Agreement. ESG investment is expected to play an important role in accelerating the greening of the economy.

Although financial information is useful for forecasting short-term business performance, in ESG investments that select investee companies from a longer-term perspective, non-financial information such as long-term vision, business strategy, and potential risks is more important. With the spread of ESG investment, an increasing number of companies are integrating financial and non-financial information and issuing integrated reports that disclose the future vision and strategy.

Financial Markets Drive Decarbonization

There are two approaches to ESG investment: positive screening and negative screening. In positive screening, investors set their own ESG criteria and invest in companies that have a high score for the criteria. In negative screening, they exclude specific companies or industries that do not meet criteria.

A recent example of negative screening for ESG investment is excluding coal-related companies and power companies which are involved in coal-based thermal power generation. This move is specifically called divestment.

For example, in 2015, the Government Pension Fund Norway, known for its active ESG investments, announced that they would divest companies that earned 30% or more of their business revenue from coal-related businesses. These included several Japanese power companies generating coal-based thermal power. A business model that relies on fossil fuel combustion deteriorate the climate, one of the 17 challenges of the SDGs, so the Norway fund called for changing the business model. Also, the business model that relies on fossil fuel combustion will no longer be feasible due to the tightening of emission regulations, and the risk of losing corporate value will increase. In the long term, the impact of climate change on business is expected to increase, so the European institutional investors are divesting to reduce the risk of climate change.

In 2017, the German environmental NGO Urgewald published the Global Coal Exit List (GCEL), which covers coal-related industries from coal mining to coal-fired power generation. The Urgewald stated that the GCEL aimed to capture the world's coal industry as a whole and served as an information source and a divestment tool for the finance sector.

In September 2019, the Principles for Responsible Banking (PRB) were launched, and 131 banks signed globally. The PRB requires banks to invest and lend in line with the SDGs and the Paris Agreement. In addition, the Sustainable Insurance Principles, formulated in 2012, require insurers to integrate ESG issues in their risk management. Responding to this principle, major insurance companies such as Axa, Allianz, and Swiss Reinsurance stepped up their engagement with companies to reduce their dependence on coal and have already stopped underwriting and investing in coal-fired power plants. It is expected that institutional investors, banks, and insurers who are expanding engagement with companies through ESG will accelerate the decarbonization of business and eventually have positive long-term results for society.

Businesses Required by a Sustainable Society

The SDGs and the Paris Agreement are accelerating the changing business environment surrounding companies. For one thing, investors and stakeholders have become more interested in long-term value creation processes that cannot be seen only by financial information disclosed by companies.

In response to this move, the International Integrated Reporting Council (IIRC) published the International Integrated Reporting

Framework in 2013. An integrated report is a communication tool that explains the value creation process of a company from both financial and non-financial information. In recent years, an increasing number of companies issue integrated reports based on this framework.

According to the IIRC, intangible assets accounted for only 17% of the market value of US S&P 500 stocks in 1975. However, in 2009, the proportion of intangible assets rose to 81%.

The fact that intangible assets account for the majority of corporate value implies the growing importance of non-financial factors that do not usually appear in financial information. Examples of intangible assets include corporate philosophy such as mission and vision, quality of managers, employee abilities and motivation, and the relationship between business strategies and the SDGs. Therefore, it is becoming difficult to interpret the long-term value creation process of a company only by analyzing the company's financial information.

The SDGs are highlighting social issues for humanity that need to be solved by 2030. Therefore, the philosophy of the SDGs is future-oriented. Companies are required to have back casting thinking that considers the issues and strategies to be tackled, based on what it should be like in 2030. In that case, there is a limit in explaining the future "what should be" using only financial information that only shows the results of past management. Therefore, companies are required to convey to stakeholders a long-term value creation story that integrates sustainability. In fact, global companies such as Unilever and Marks & Spencer use their long-term value creation story to engage investors and stakeholders.

Now, ESG and SDGs have become a common language connecting companies and their stakeholders. It is considered that a company that communicates financial and non-financial information in a unified manner will win the sympathy of investors who expect future value of the company and millennials who are highly interested in the SDGs. For companies to achieve long-term value creation, it is essential for them to gain empathy and trust from various stakeholders through constructive dialogue by effectively utilizing integrated reports.

Rebuilding Trust

As described in detail in Chaps. 1 and 2 in this book, during the Meiji era (1868–1912), when modernization began in Japan, Sumitomo, one of major industrial conglomerates, caused smoke pollution. It was caused by the sulfur dioxide gas generated from a Sumitomo-owned copper smelting plant at the Besshi Copper Mine in Ehime Prefecture.

To address this problem, Teigo Iba, the second president of Sumitomo, under the philosophy of "Jiri-Rita-Koshi-Ichijo" (means Sumitomo's profit [self-interest] and the profit to society [altruistic profit] needed to be integrated), threw off objections and took drastic measures against the problem including relocation of smelters to uninhabited islands and large-scale reforestation. Iba is regarded as a pioneer in CSR in Japan.

Masaya Suzuki, who succeeded Iba, advocated a policy of not emitting harmful substances from the copper smelting process and succeeded in producing chemical fertilizers from sulfur dioxide, which otherwise would have caused smoke damage. Suzuki not only solved the environmental problem, but also linked it to industrial innovation. There are many things we can learn from Iba and Suzuki who promoted businesses in harmony with the public interest.

The 2018 Edelman Earned Brand study reveals that nearly two-thirds of consumers around the world now buy on belief. These belief-driven buyers will choose, switch, avoid, or boycott a brand (=company) based on where it stands on the political or social issues they care about.[2]

Now the time has come when companies will be asked by society how they respond to the SDGs and the Paris Agreement. It is indispensable for companies' growth to gain empathy and support from their stakeholders through proactive efforts on social issues.

However, many social issues are becoming more and more complex; therefore, companies alone cannot solve these problems. So the multi-stakeholder partnerships are increasingly important. In order for companies to leverage their strengths and contribute to the SDGs, it is imperative that companies cooperate with external organizations and create new value by combining different knowledge.

Businesses need to keep in mind that profits (tangible assets) they earn depend heavily on intangible assets, such as trust and empathy from their stakeholders. Companies are now required to rebuild business models that contribute to solving social issues such as the SDGs and gain trust and empathy from their stakeholders.

Tokyo, Japan — Masaatsu Takehara
Tokyo, Japan — Naoya Hasegawa

SDGs comparison table

Category			*Economy*		*Social*							*Environment*						*Governance*		
			8	*9*	*1*	*2*	*3*	*4*	*5*	*11*	*12*	*6*	*7*	*12*	*13*	*14*	*15*	*10*	*16*	*17*
【*17 goals of SDGs*】																				
Part I	Chapter 1	Teigo Iba	○	○			○	○						○			○	○		○
Management by philosophy	Chapter 2	Masaya Suzuki	○	○			○	○						○			○	○		○
Part II	Chapter 3	Ryoichiro Okada	○	○	○			○		○	○							○		○
Integration of economy	Chapter 4	Meizen Kinpara	○	○			○	○		○				○			○	○		
and morality	Chapter 5	William Merrell Vories	○				○	○	○	○								○	○	○
Part III	Chapter 6	Jokichi Takamine	○	○			○						○					○	○	○
Value creation through	Chapter 7	Sakichi Toyoda	○	○	○						○							○		○
innovation	Chapter 8	Michio Suzuki	○	○	○						○							○		○
	Chapter 9	Shojiro Ishibashi	○	○			○	○			○							○		○
Part IV	Chapter 10	Magosaburo Ohara	○	○	○		○	○	○	○	○							○	○	○
Management that enhanced human capital	Chapter 11	Tsurukichi Hatano	○	○	○		○	○	○	○	○							○	○	○
Part V	Chapter 12	Kenkichi Kagami	○	○			○				○							○	○	○
Creating social solutions	Chapter 13	Tsuneta Yano	○	○			○				○							○	○	○

Note: SDGs Goal 12 is "Ensure sustainable consumption and production patterns" so we compared each entrepreneurs' management with the Goal 12 from the viewpoints of both environment and society

Notes

1. COP stands for Conference of the Parties, referring to the countries that have signed up to the 1992 United Nations Framework Convention on Climate Change. The COP in Paris is the 21st such conference.
2. https://www.edelman.com/earned-brand

Acknowledgments

This book is the research results of the Study Group on Entrepreneur's History at Hosei University, Japan. In history, entrepreneurs faced many kinds of crises and opportunities, where they made various tough, sometimes ultimate decisions. The significance of studying business history is to learn these entrepreneurs' decisions and choices. There are many lessons in past cases that are still valid in modern society. One of the great benefits that companies can learn from history is that they can find common points between the past and the present, and apply those lessons to business management. We believe that the lessons we can learn from entrepreneurs in this book will be helpful for modern companies which are expected to contribute to solving social problems through business.

In publishing this book, we would like to extend our deep appreciation to the members of the Hosei University Study Group on Entrepreneur's History for their constructive advice. We also thank the Hosei University Research Institute for Innovation Management for their support in the operation of the study group and partial funding for proofreading of the manuscripts. In addition, we thank Hosei University's Faculty of Sustainability Studies to which authors belong, for supporting a portion of proofreading of manuscripts.

We are greatly thankful to Dr. Lori A. Forman. She took time in her busy schedule to read all the chapters of this book and gave us important feedback and suggestions. Thanks to her outstanding knowledge about Japan and Japanese companies and excellent skill for academic writing, the book was made readable. We are also thankful to Dr. Atsuko Watanabe, our colleague at Hosei University. She provided a variety of helpful advice on preparing for publication.

Last but not least, we are particularly grateful to Jacob Dreyer and Anushangi Weerakoon at Palgrave Macmillan and entire production team of Spi Global in India.

Contents

List of Figures

List of Tables

PART I

Management by Philosophy

CHAPTER 1

Teigo Iba: A Pioneer of Management Aimed at Creating Shared Value

Teigo Iba (1847~1926) (Source: Sumitomo Historical Archives)

Achievement of Teigo Iba and related SDGs

Economy			* Modernization of Sumitomo Zaibatsu (industrial conglomerate) * Reform of Besshi Copper Mine
Society	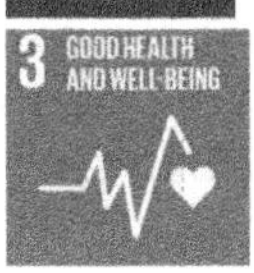		* Fundamental solution of smoke problem * Promotion of Education (Osaka Commercial Training Institute)

(*continued*)

M. Takehara, N. Hasegawa, *Sustainable Management of Japanese Entrepreneurs in Pre-War Period from the Perspective of SDGs and ESG*, https://doi.org/10.1007/978-981-15-6507-6_1

(continued)

Environment	12 RESPONSIBLE CONSUMPTION AND PRODUCTION	15 LIFE ON LAND	* Relocation of smelter to Shisaka-jima island * Implementation of large reforestation plan in Besshi * Development of infrastructure for forestry business
Governance	10 REDUCED INEQUALITIES	17 PARTNERSHIPS FOR THE GOALS	* Practice of management based on management philosophy * Promotion of external talents * Establishment of Sumitomo Bank

Source: Created by authors

1 Introduction

In Japan, two major pollution incidents occurred as a result of developing copper mines. These two incidents were called "Besshi in the west and Ashio in the east". "Ashio in the east" refers to the Ashio copper mine, which Ichibee Furukawa started to manage from 1877. The Ashio Mining pollution incident became a serious social problem which shocked Japanese society in the Meiji period (1868–1912).

The Ashio Mining pollution incident occurred at the Ashio copper mine located near the Watarase-gawa River in Tochigi Prefecture and Gunma Prefecture during the nineteenth to twentieth centuries. Furukawa introduced Western-style smelting methodology, but this methodology released sulfur into the atmosphere during the smelting process. The sulfur released combined with oxygen to make sulfur dioxide, and this caused major damage to the forest in the mountains and to crops (Kamioka 1971, 10–11).

On the other hand, "Besshi in the west" refers to the Besshi copper mine located in Niihama, in Ehime Prefecture. The mine was consistently managed by Sumitomo between 1690 and 1973. In 1884 Sumitomo established a Western-style furnace in Niihama and the smoke damage from sulfurous acid gas generated from the smelting process of copper expanded rapidly.

Teigo Iba, then the second president and CEO of the Sumitomo Zaibatsu (industrial conglomerate), assumed the post of general manager of the Besshi copper mine and took the lead in solving the smoke problem which was occurring. Iba faced various criticisms and pressures from inside and outside of the company, but with a long-term vision he fundamentally tried to solve the mining pollution problem through the relocation of its smelter and large-scale foresting.

Today, with more than 100 years having passed since the pollution problem at the Besshi copper mine, modern society is suffering from global problems such as climate change and the depletion of resources caused by excessive economic activities obsessed with a profit-oriented business philosophy. Both public and private sectors are working on various initiatives in an attempt to achieve sustained economic growth while addressing global problems.

The economic mechanism dominating global society does not incorporate the means of controlling a profit-oriented business philosophy based on the theory of capital. To correct the sense of values of modern companies which excessively prioritize profit-making, a new approach needs to be adopted to integrate the creation of both social values and economic values for complicated global problems such as climate change, the loss of biodiversity, and the degradation of the ecosystem.

This problem D. H. Meadows raised by saying "The burden to the earth and nature humans are giving will exceed the limits that they can absorb unless humans change the way of economic activity" has not yet been solved; rather, it is currently further deteriorating (Meadows, 178–183).

This situation has not changed from when Iba faced a mining pollution problem 100 years ago. In this global society many environmental and social problems are left unsolved. To turn this situation around, it is necessary for a new relationship between business and society to be constructed.

Iba passed away before seeing a complete solution to the mining pollution problem, but we can learn a lot from his business views and how they focus on the relationship with society. His remark "We persistently esteem reality, but we must not be captured by reality. Always pursuing our ideal, we must think beyond reality" (Suehiro 2000, 103) teaches us Iba's consistent attitude. He did not stick to short-term profit but tried to optimize the relationship between business and society with a long-term view.

We who live today's world must work on constructing a sustainable society which is backed by a sense of ethics aiming at protecting the global environment and at the optimization of a civil society.

Iba is said to be a pioneer of corporate social responsibility (CSR) in Japan. We can see many common elements between Iba's management philosophy, which meant trying to balance business activities while conserving the natural environment, and modern society's expectation that people should have decent lives in a sustainable environment. In this chapter, we will look back on Iba's philosophy and business activities in order to reconsider its meaning for us in the modern era.

2 Younger Days

In 1847 Teigo Iba was born in Omi-Hachiman City, Shiga Prefecture. Iba learned Sinology and swordplay from the time of his infancy and became a guard protecting the Kyoto Imperial Palace under the Meiji government. His duties included guarding the Kyoto Imperial Palace and Kyoto city. It was a dangerous mission. He was risking his life as there was the possibility of a counterattack by the remaining forces of the Tokugawa Shogunate.

In 1871 the Ministry of Justice was established by government reform. In 1873, Iba, who was promoted to the position of a judge, was assigned to the newly established Hakodate court and worked in that office until 1876. Before he was assigned to the Hakodate court, Iba learned civil law and criminal law from Professor Boissonade[1] of the University of Paris, who had been invited from France and was serving as a legal adviser for the Japanese government (Kamiyama 1960, 101).

In 1877, Iba was appointed as a judge in the Osaka High court. When he was assigned to Osaka, Takamori Saigo, who took up arms in revolt against the Meiji government, was defeated in the Seinan War (the last civil war in Japan)[2] and died. After the Seinan War, the spirit to create a new country and the freehearted atmosphere which had been vibrant right after the Meiji Restoration were beginning to be lost by the government.

Iba, who respected liberty, always tried not to disturb the liberty of others, and he did not like his own liberty being disturbed by others either. It was unbearable for a man like him to work in the shrinking atmosphere rampant in the Japanese government. In 1879, the then 32-year-old Iba resigned from his position as judge and returned to his hometown in Shiga Prefecture.

3 Joining Sumitomo

3.1 Saihei Hirose

After resigning as a judge, Iba called on Saihei Hirose (1828–1914) (Fig. 1.1). Hirose was Iba's uncle and he was then the president of Sumitomo.

Here let's look back at the Sumitomo family and its involvement with the copper refining business. The history of Sumitomo goes back to Masatomo Sumitomo (1585–1652), who ran a pharmacy in Kyoto in the seventeenth century. A document he wrote on business wisdom, titled "Monjuin-shigakisho", detailed the importance of esteeming honesty, carefulness, and sureness.

Masatomo Sumitomo thought that the purpose of business was not just profit-making but to polish the character of the person engaged in the business. To practice business based on morality has been the business philosophy inherited by the Sumitomo conglomerate.

The Sumitomo family received approval to develop the Besshi copper mine[3] from the Shogunate in 1691 and entered the copper mining business. Since then, Sumitomo has contributed to Japan's modernization for over 283 years until 1973 (Showa-era year 48).

The Besshi copper mine was supposed to be requisitioned by the newly established government following the Meiji Restoration. However, Hirose explained Sumitomo's firm commitment to develop the Besshi copper mine and the difficulty of mine management and argued that it served the national interest for Sumitomo to continue to manage the Besshi copper mine. Hirose's persuasion worked, and the Meiji government approved the continuation of Sumitomo's right to manage the Besshi copper mine in 1868 (Fig. 1.2).

Fig. 1.1 Saihei Hirose. (Source: Sumitomo Public Relations Committee)

Fig. 1.2 The Besshi Copper Mine (1881). (Source: Suehiro Shokei 2005, p. 34)

3.2 The Decision to Join Sumitomo

Hirose recommended Iba join Sumitomo when he resigned as a judge. Hirose explained the businesses of Sumitomo and the trends of industry, and emphasized the significance of contributing to the nation through business. Iba gave in to Hirose's persistent persuasion and determined to join Sumitomo. The biggest reason why Iba decided to join Sumitomo was Sumitomo's corporate philosophy, which emphasized that Sumitomo's profit (self-interest) and the profit to society (altruistic profit) needed to be integrated. (In Japanese this philosophy is called "Jiri-Rita-Koshi-Ichijo".)

In 1880, Iba assumed the post of general manager at the Osaka head office with exceptionally good treatment. Behind Hirose's selection of Iba for this position, there was Hirose's strong expectations concerning Iba's rich experience and ability. Working for Hirose, Iba learned the details of Sumitomo's business until 1894 when he was assigned to the Besshi copper mine as general manager. While he was under Hirose, Iba was involved with the establishment and the management of various companies and schools including Osaka Boseki (established in 1882 and currently Toyobo Co., Ltd.), Osaka Shosen Company (established in 1884 and currently Shosen Mitsui), and Osaka Commerce School (established in 1880 and currently Osaka City University).

Iba stated his company management policy as follows: "The situation surrounding a company changes at every moment. The president sincerely thinks about the sound development of the company and plans an adequate management policy, and we must do our best to prevent the business strategy from failing on the way. This will lead to benefits both for the company and its stockholders" (Kamiyama 1960, 126).

In addition, when Osaka Shosen, a merchant ship company which Sumitomo helped to establish, had business problems and fell into financial difficulties, Iba argued against the idea of a withdrawal from the management of the company by making the following remark:

> If the business performance of our group company is not going well, we should make more efforts to help them turn around their business. Strengthening a mutual relationship when a business is going well and cutting the relation when a business is not going well is a bad idea. We have no right to talk about a stock company with this kind of thinking. If the top management is not managing the company properly, then we should replace them with a more appropriate executive and change the management. This is one of the advantages that the stock-company system has. (Kamiyama 1960, 127)

On the other hand, Iba was also fully aware of the importance of the shareholder as stakeholder and made the following remarks: "The top management of a company must always understand how the minority shareholders feel. So, we always need to make efforts to pay a dividend to minority shareholders unless this makes a significant impact on the foundations of the company" (Nishikawa 1990, 233). Iba's words get right to the point of a stock company as a main constituent in realizing public interest.

In Japan the Financial Services Agency announced the principles of responsible investors (the Japanese Stewardship Code) in February 2014. The Stewardship Code is a norm introduced to stipulate principles that institutional investors in the UK are expected to follow. The Stewardship Code is based on the idea that institutional investors have the responsibility of linking the long-term sustained growth of the investee companies to the development of the entire economy. Therefore, they should play an active role in realizing this purpose.

The responsibility of institutional investors is to maximize the investment return of the consignor who entrusted the investment (known as fiduciary duty: the duty of a fiduciary to act in the best interests of the beneficiary). However, in recent years, investors have tended to sacrifice the long-term growth of the investee companies and pursue a short-term profit. This trend is called short-termism and is considered obstructive to the healthy growth of a company and the sustainability of the entire society. In the UK, to correct short-termism by institutional investors, the Stewardship Code was introduced in 2010.

Iba's idea, which expressed business responsibility as a shareholder, clearly describes the ideal state of institutional investors which the Stewardship Code aims for. His idea shows that supporting the growth of a company with a long-term view is responsible behavior as a fiduciary of management.

4 The Modernization of the Besshi Copper Mine and the Occurrence of Smoke Pollution

4.1 The Introduction of Modern Mining Technology

Saihei Hirose who served as the general manager of the Besshi copper mine came to know the existence of modern mining technology from a French mining engineer. The Besshi copper mine had been ruined after many years of mining activities. Hirose came to think that he had no other option but to utilize modern technology to restore the copper mine business, which was a key industry for Sumitomo (Takehara 1992, 67).

A scientific investigation of the entire Besshi copper mine was conducted by a French engineer from 1873 (Meiji-era year 6) and a prospectus for the Besshi copper mine was published. Based on the proposals in the prospectus, as a first business plan in 1876 Hirose aimed for (1) development of the inclined shaft extending toward the east, (2) construction of a motor road between Besshi and Niihama, (3) construction of a Western blast furnace, and (4) development of a hydrometallurgical process for copper.

The hydrometallurgical process is a technique for collecting the copper settled in a water solution. The water emitted from the copper mine would include a small amount of copper and sulfuric acid and this contaminated mining water would bring damage to crops downstream and to human health. If the hydrometallurgical process was introduced, an anti-pollution effect was hoped for with harmful pollutants produced in the copper mining process removed from the contaminated water. As shown in chart 1, when the newly established furnace started to operate with the introduction of Western-style smelting, a substantial reduction of production costs and an improvement of labor productivity were realized (Table 1.1).

Table 1.1 Cost reduction as a result of the improvement of smelting methodology

	Old-fashioned refinement	*Western-style refinement*	*Reduction (%)*
Charcoal consumption (kg)	5831	2501	57.1
Burned ore (kg)	13,331	10,373	22.2
Manpower (person)	30	12	60.0
Operating time (hours)	88	40	54.5

Source: Takeda, 28 (revised by the author)

Table 1.2 shows changes in the output of copper from the main copper mine during the Meiji period.

Until 1884, when the Ashio copper mine took over the lead, the Besshi copper mine was the largest copper producer in the country.

With a series of modernization policies for the Besshi copper mine led by Hirose, Sumitomo laid the foundation for new business growth. In 1891, Hirose revised the Sumitomo family's existing precept and announced a new management philosophy (Takehara 1992, 70).

It included the following three key points:

(1) Sumitomo esteems trust in business.
(2) Sumitomo does not chase "Furi" (quick profits) even if it faces changes in the business environment or changes in revenue or profit.
(3) Sumitomo will ensure the sustainable growth of the Besshi copper mine, which is Sumitomo's core business.

It was trust from society that Sumitomo cherished most. Sumitomo thought that trust was not gained by the large or small sum of the assets the company had, but rather it depended on the philosophy of the organization and the character and behavior of its employees. In other words, we must not forget that trust in business is an intangible asset and that the tangible assets of wealth are the result of the accumulation of intangible assets. It appears that the reason why Iba joined Sumitomo after he left the government was that he was fascinated by the management philosophy which Hirose declared. Even though the job was offered by his uncle, Hirose, Iba would not have joined Sumitomo if the company's corporate

Table 1.2 Copper output in major copper mines in Japan

Copper Mine	*Besshi*		*Yoshioka*		*Ashio*		*Kusakura*		*Arakawa*		*Ogoya*		*Total Copper Output (t)*
Year	*Copper output (t)*	*Share (%)*	*Copper output (t)*	*Share (%)*	*Copper output (t)*	*Share (%)*	*Copper output (t)*	*Share (%)*	*Copper output (t)*	*Share (%)*	*Copper output (t)*	*Share (%)*	
1868	421.8	26.5	49.8	3.1	0.0	0.0	0.0	0.0	0.0	0.0	0.0	0.0	1592.4
1870	474.0	29.2	24.6	1.5	0.0	0.0	0.0	0.0	0.0	0.0	0.0	0.0	1620.6
1874	490.8	28.1	133.2	7.6	0.0	0.0	0.0	0.0	0.0	0.0	0.0	0.0	1748.4
1875	558.0	31.1	109.8	6.1	0.0	0.0	0.0	0.0	0.0	0.0	0.0	0.0	1792.8
1876	513.6	31.1	12.6	0.8	0.0	0.0	0.0	0.0	0.0	0.0	0.0	0.0	1651.8
1877	808.8	37.4	77.4	3.6	55.8	2.6	93.0	4.3	0.0	0.0	0.0	0.0	2161.2
1878	1029.0	44.2	11.4	0.5	49.8	2.1	108.6	4.7	0.0	0.0	0.0	0.0	2325.6
1879	990.6	41.3	15.0	0.6	90.6	3.8	172.2	7.2	0.0	0.0	0.0	0.0	2395.8
1880	1094.4	42.9	52.2	2.0	92.4	3.6	172.8	6.8	0.0	0.0	12.0	0.5	2551.8
1881	744.6	28.5	54.6	2.1	173.4	6.6	190.8	7.3	301.2	11.5	22.8	0.9	2616.0
1882	1178.4	34.5	57.0	1.7	293.4	8.6	444.0	13.0	225.6	6.6	93.0	2.7	3420.6
1883	1024.8	23.8	73.8	1.7	654.0	15.2	1016.4	23.6	244.2	5.7	168.0	3.9	4311.0
1884	1035.6	16.8	131.4	2.1	2308.2	37.5	1084.2	17.6	243.0	3.9	228.0	3.7	6160.8
1885	1507.2	17.4	367.2	4.2	4131.6	47.7	1031.4	11.9	235.2	2.7	256.2	3.0	8659.8
1886	1407.0	17.5	344.4	4.3	3631.2	45.2	814.8	10.1	319.2	4.0	394.2	4.9	8042.4
1887	1466.4	19.3	292.2	3.8	2991.6	39.4	802.2	10.6	390.0	5.1	518.4	6.8	7593.0
1888	1588.8	22.3	333.6	4.7	2464.2	34.5	651.0	9.1	386.4	5.4	580.8	8.1	7137.6
1889	1641.6	17.6	478.8	5.1	4115.4	44.2	682.8	7.3	662.4	7.1	589.2	6.3	9303.6
1890	1834.2	15.6	600.0	5.1	5844.0	49.7	827.4	7.0	835.2	7.1	679.2	5.8	11,754.0

Source: Takeda, 31(revised by the author)

philosophy had not eschewed from chasing quick profits and doing business solely for private interest. Sumitomo's corporate philosophy, which Hirose established, and Iba's ability to conceptualize management, enabled various problems involving the Besshi copper mine to be solved.

4.2 Occurrence of Smoke Pollution

The modernization of the Besshi copper mine advanced by Sumitomo did not meet with understanding from the local residents. The construction of a Western-style furnace in Niihama was carried out without listening to the inhabitants of local towns and villages (Kamioka 1971, 265). When the mine railroad between Besshi and Niihama opened in 1893 and the smelting business expanded, the damage to crops by the sulfur dioxide generated from the smelting process of the copper spread. Table 1.3 shows the concern over smoke pollution and the trend of the supervisory authorities.

In those days, the smelting work of copper in the Besshi copper mine was conducted in the Takahashi smelter in mountain areas. In 1889, the Soubiraki smelter in Niihama began full-scale operation and the center of smelting moved from the Besshi mountains area to the coastal region in Niihama (Fig. 1.3). As the smelting quantity increased, damage from smoke pollution caused by sulfur dioxide emitted from the smelter rapidly expanded, bringing large-scale damage to the fields and forests in the mountains.

In 1893, a representative of the farmers brought the matter of smoke pollution to the attention of the prefectural office. The Niihama village office then requested the Sumitomo branch in Niihama to look into the cause of the pollution. The Sumitomo branch reported that the cause of the damage was not from smoke pollution but from insects, and the prefectural office accepted this Sumitomo report and publicly announced it. This gave rise to strong opposition from the farmers (Suehiro 2000, 73). In 1894, the Sumitomo Osaka head office decided on a new executive appointment which meant transferring Iba from the position of general manager of the Osaka head office to general manager of the Besshi copper mine. Iba moved to Besshi himself and confronted the various problems around the Besshi copper mine.

Iba needed to solve the following three problems:

(1) The damage from smoke in Besshi mountain areas caused by the sulfur dioxide generated from smelting.

Table 1.3 Record of negotiations with farmer victims damaged by smoke pollution

Year	*Move*
1894	The damaged farmers negotiated with the owner of the mining over the compensation for damage and the detoxification. The damaged farmers petitioned the Osaka mine inspection office and Ehime prefecture for their relief.
1895	The wheat cropping was severely damaged. The damaged farmers demanded direct negotiations with general manager of the Besshi copper mine and collided with the police force. The representative of local landowners involved met with Kichizaemon Sumitomo in Osaka. The establishment of the joint investigating committee on the smoke pollution was agreed, but it was not realized as the general managers of Besshi copper mine opposed.
1897	The rice cropping was severely damaged Village mayors and the representative of local landowners in Besshi areas petitioned the Ehime prefecture for their relief. The damaged farmers petitioned the Minister of Agriculture and Commerce for the moving of the furnace and the establishment of the facility to remove pollution completely. The Osaka mine inspection office and the agricultural experimental station in the Ministry of Agriculture and Commerce conducted investigation and acknowledged the smoke pollution and damage. The Ehime prefectural assembly resolved and proposed "Proposal of the investigation about the damage from the smoke from the Besshi mine Niihama furnace" to the Minister for Home Affairs.
1898	The government confirmed that the smoke pollution damaged the public interest of the farmers in the related areas. The Osaka mine inspection office ordered Sumitomo the following corrective actions: • The move of refinery to Shisaka-jima (island) • Ban on smelting copper ore in Niihama • The remodeling of chimney.

Source: Kamioka (1971, 266) (revised by the author)

(2) The environmental destruction caused by deforestation of mountain forests for fuel and mine timber (Fig. 1.4).
(3) The damage from smoke pollution caused by the sulfur dioxide emitted from the copper refinery in the Niihama coastal zone.

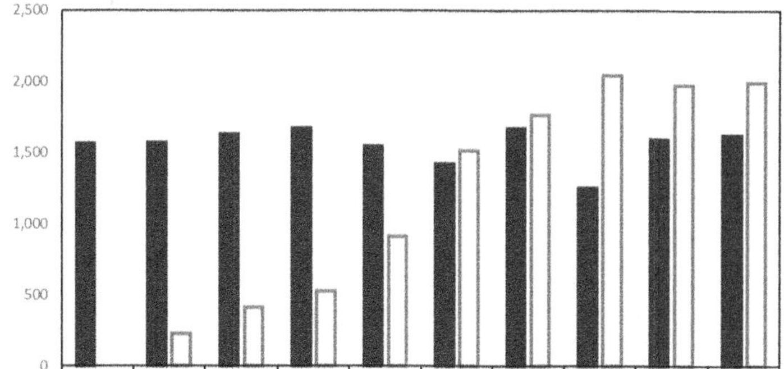

	1890	1891	1892	1893	1894	1895	1896	1897	1898	1899
■Besshi [Takahashi smelter]	1,561	1,571	1,628	1,670	1,543	1,419	1,673	1,253	1,595	1,621
□Niihama [Soubiraki smelter]		230	415	529	916	1,514	1,767	2,049	1,972	1,993

Fig. 1.3 The copper output of the Besshi-Niihama refinery. (Source: Suehiro 2000, 73 [Revised by the author])

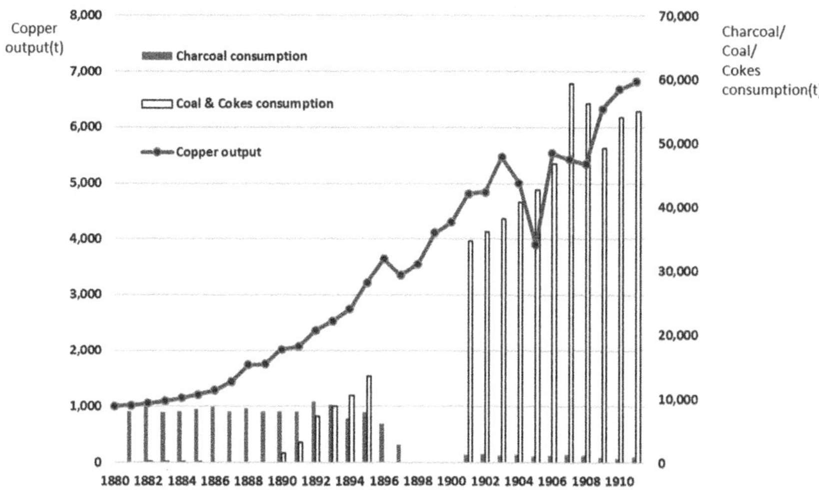

Fig. 1.4 Changes in the copper output and fuel consumption at the Besshi copper mine. (Note: The following data is not available: charcoal [1898–1900], coal and coke [1886–1890; 1896–1900]. Source: Suehiro 2000, 81 [Revised by the author].)

At the Besshi copper mine the output of copper increased rapidly with the introduction of Western-style technology, and the demand for timber for generating energy for smelting also increased rapidly. At the Besshi copper mine, forest management based on a long-term plan was not implemented. Therefore, haphazard deforestation prevailed in the wake of an increase in the demand for firewood, charcoal, and mine timber.

From the viewpoint of environmental protection, it was desirable to abolish smelting in the Besshi mountain areas and to promote reforestation, but this meant that the smelting process was to be concentrated on the Soubiraki smelter in Niihama. As any emission reduction of sulfur dioxide was not yet realized, even if the environmental pollutants in the Besshi mountain areas were to be moved to the Niihama area, it was clear that the damage from smoke pollution in the area of Niihama would increase.

Iba decided on the complete relocation of the Soubiraki smelter to solve this problem. The candidate site was Shisaka-jima, an uninhabited island located 20 km off the coast of Niihama. In 1895, Iba prepared the relocation of the refinery by secretly purchasing Shisaka-jima island in his name. Iba was thinking that the termination of the Soubiraki smelter in Niihama could not be avoided in order to solve the smoke pollution problem. There were only two alternative options: reinforcing the Takahashi smelter in the Besshi mountain area or a complete relocation to Shisaka-jima island. Thinking of forest damage, reinforcing the Takahashi smelter in the Besshi mountain area was impossible. To solve the smoke-problem and to restore the natural environment in the Besshi mountains, the relocation of the refinery to Shisaka-jima island was the only alternative.

Construction for relocation of the refinery to Shisaka-jima island began in 1897 (Meiji-era year 30). In 1899, during this construction period, the Takahashi smelter suffered devastating damage caused by a mudslide from a typhoon and each facility at the Besshi copper mine was forced to be moved to Niihama. In 1905, operations on Shisaka-jima island began. Iba had great expectations for the Shisaka-jima smelter. Everyone believed that the relocation of the smelter would solve the smoke problem, but it failed to live up to peoples' expectations. The sulfur dioxide emitted from the smelter on Shisaka-jima island did not diffuse on the sea. Depending on the weather status, it brought smoke damage to even wider regions than during the Soubiraki smelter times. The situation was totally unexpected for all the parties involved.

Iba could not fundamentally solve the smoke pollution while he was alive. Masaya Suzuki, who succeeded Iba to become the third president of Sumitomo, made a sincere effort for the relief of victims of the smoke damage and promoted technical improvements aimed at solving the smoke pollution. It was in 1939 that the smoke-pollution problem was completely solved. Thirty-four years had passed since the smelter was relocated to Shisaka-jima island.

4.3 Environmental Protection Activities at the Besshi Copper Mine

In addition, to restore the mountains at Besshi which had been made bare, Iba implemented large-scale reforestation. To stop further deforestation, Iba decided to switch the source of fuel from charcoal to coal. Iba fully understood that forestry was indispensable for the infrastructure of the mining business, and it was an industry which played an important role in the preservation of the country through the management of river systems and the development of agriculture, forestry, and fisheries.

Iba separated the "mountain section" from the civil engineering department to have them work solely on the foresting and logging business. Sumitomo began a deliberate forestry business by inviting experts to assist (Sumitomo Forestry Company, Ltd. 1999, 10–111). In 1894, an average of 60,000 trees were planted annually at the Besshi copper mine. Iba planned to increase the numbers of trees planted to two million annually and this went ahead.

Right after Iba began full-scale reforestation activities, a large flood hit the Besshi copper mine in August 1899.[4] Heavy rain from a typhoon was the direct cause of this but it was clear that the indiscriminate deforestation in the mountains expanded the damage. It is said that Masaya Suzuki (later to become the third president of Sumitomo), who succeeded Iba to assume the post of general manager of the Besshi copper mine, strongly promoted reforestation activities as a lesson learned from the flood damage.

In his later years, Iba used to talk about the foresting business at Besshi by saying, "what can be called the 'true business' for Sumitomo is the foresting business. Other businesses do not have to continue" (Nishikawa 1990, 111). Iba aimed at serving the interests of the entire society beyond the scale of a commercial company. Iba's management philosophy coincides in many parts with Sustainable Development Goals (SDGs).

5 A Management Philosophy Intending Sustainability

5.1 Management Gaining Sympathy from Society

Based on its corporate philosophy (termed "Jiri-Rita-Koshi-Ichijo" in Japanese), Sumitomo promoted business in a manner that benefited Sumitomo, the nation, and society. Under this corporate philosophy, while correctly considering profit seeking for the company, Iba insisted that the means to make a profit must be conducted in a morally responsible way.

The human desire to pursue wealth driven by selfishness must be controlled by a sense of morality and an altruistic mindset. Management based on moral responsibility means that management should abandon short-term profit and give higher priority to morality when business brings unfavorable consequences to society, even in the case of a highly profitable business. Through such management, a company can win trust from society. It may be difficult for the sustainability of corporate management to be realized without the trust of society. Adam Smith said in his books *The Theory of Moral Sentiments* (1759) and *An Inquiry into the Nature and Causes of the Wealth of Nations* (1776) that with regard to any selfish acts (economic activity) it is the "impartial spectator" who feels sympathy and can realize public interest (Fig. 1.5).

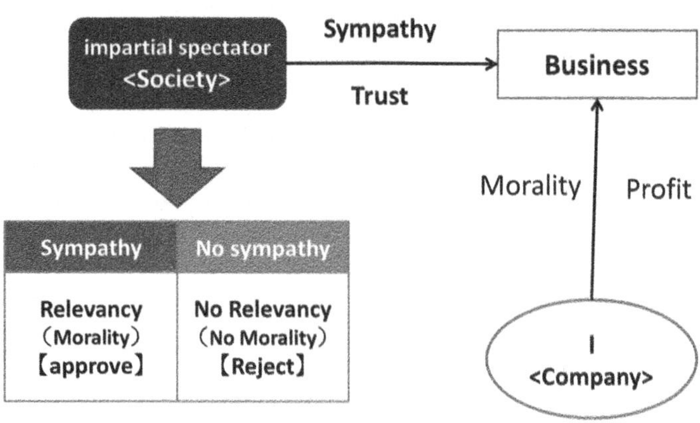

Fig. 1.5 Adam Smith's business ethics. (Source: The author)

In other words, Smith said that people's selfish acts (economic activity) should not be interfered with unless "impartial spectators" feel sympathy for interference, and this is how unexpected maximum public benefits will be generated, being led by an invisible hand. Smith requested that those who do business ask the "impartial spectators" inside their heart if they feel sympathy about business acts.

It was in the Meiji period when companies emerged as the main business players in Japan. For companies, the "impartial spectator" is civil society. Needless to say, a company cannot exist without sympathy from society. Humans are selfish and managers have a mission to pursue profit and lead their organization to prosperity. However, excessive profit seeking is likely to result in losing society's trust and to endanger even the continuation of the organization.

Of course, Iba was neither a person who pursued only ideals without thinking of profit nor someone who sacrificed ideals for profit. We can perceive from his words the difficulty of deciding what should be done and what should not be done in the realization of Sumitomo's spirit of "Jiri-Rita-Koshi-Ichijo", that is, the manner in which Sumitomo's profit (self-interest) and profit in society (altruistic profit) need to be integrated.

5.2 *The Social Responsibility of Managers*

Iba stated "The most important work for a manager is to have the best successor and to choose the best time to hand his work over to his successor". Masaya Suzuki, who was an official of the Ministry of the Interior, accepted Iba's invitation to join Sumitomo in 1896. Inheriting Iba's philosophy, Suzuki worked on a fundamental solution to the Besshi copper mine smoke-pollution problem.

It can be said that the management ethics or the characteristics of the company are none other than a reflection of the character of the top management. Iba entrusted Suzuki, whom he appointed as his successor with full power over Sumitomo's business, and he never interfered in Suzuki's management. It can be said that Iba is an executive without peer who retired at the right time in Japan's enterprise history.

Modern society faces many problems. Globalization and innovation have accelerated economic growth, but serious environmental and social problems have emerged. To address global environmental problems and the exhaustion of natural resources, the construction of a sustainable society supported by an advanced social and economic sense of ethics is

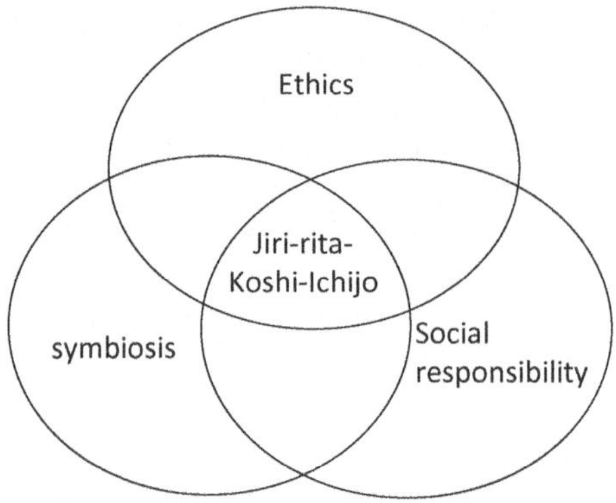

Fig. 1.6 The management philosophy of Teigo Iba. (Source: The author)

indispensable. Facing these circumstances, management concepts such as corporate governance, CSR, and CSV are drawing broad attention, and animated discussion is reviewing the relation between companies and society.

Sumitomo's business philosophy, aimed at benefiting the whole of society, and the actions it took for a fundamental solution to the smoke-pollution problem in the Besshi copper mine, share common conceptual elements with CSR and CSV, ideas which modern companies are being asked to adopt and integrate into their corporate management. It can be said that Iba's philosophy and actions, as introduced in this section, were ahead of his time in that he tried to realize a sustainable society in which economic value and social value were created in a harmonized way (Fig. 1.6).

In writing this chapter, the authors received a grant for English proofreading from the Hosei University Research Institute for Innovation Management.

Notes

1. In 1880, Tokyo School of Law, which is now Hosei University, was established by Dr. Gustave Emile Boissonade of the University of Paris and his students.
2. The large-scale anti-government rebellion caused by Takamori Saigo and members of his shizoku (families or persons with samurai ancestors) in Kagoshima Prefecture in 1877.

3. A copper mine located in the foot of a mountain area in Niihama City, Ehime Prefecture.
4. The fatalities from the Besshi major flood damage exceeded 500.

References

Fujimoto, Tetsuo. 1993. *Besshi and Sumitomo in the Meiji Era*. Ochanomizu Shobo.

Iba, Teigo. 1904. *Shoso to Rosei "Jistugyo-no-Nihon Vol.7 No.4"*.

Kamioka, Namiko. 1971. *Pollution of Modern Japan*. Shin-Jinbutsu-Oraisha.

Kamiyama, Makoto. 1960. *Iba Teigo*. Nichigetsu-sha.

Kimoto, Shoji. 1971a. *Shisaka-jima (First volume) (Second volume)*. Kodansha.

Kimoto, Shoji. 1971b. *Shisaka-jima: Human records on Pollution and conquest ((First volume) (Second volume))*. Kodansha.

Meadows, Donella H. 1972. *Limits of Growth-Rome Club" Human Crisis Report*. Diamond Inc.

Miyamoto, Mataji. 1988. *The Establishment of Sumitomo Bank and Sadayoshi Tanabe. Sumitomo Archives Bulletin No. 18*. Sumitomo Archives.

Niihama-city Hirose Historical Memorial Museum. 2007. *Besshi Copper Mine Connected to the World*. Niihama-city Hirose Historical Memorial Museum.

Nishikawa, Shojiro. 1990. *Yu Ou*. Tosho Shuppansha.

Seoka, Makoto. 1998. *Management Philosophy of Modern Sumitomo*. Yuhikaku Publishing.

Smith, Adam. 1759. *The Theory of Moral Sentiments*.

Smith, Adam. 1776. *An Inquiry into the Nature and Causes of the Wealth of Nations*.

Suehiro, Teruaki. 1990a. *Sumitomo in the Meiji Restoration period (1) The process of modern mining policy and establishment of the mining rights in the Besshi copper mine. Sumitomo Archives Bulletin No. 20"* Sumitomo Archives

Suehiro, Teruaki. 1990b. *Sumitomo in the Meiji Restoration period (2) The process of modern mining policy and establishment of the mining rights in the Besshi copper mine. Sumitomo Archives Bulletin No. 21*. Sumitomo Archives.

Suehiro, Teruaki. 1991. *Saihei Hirose's speech on top of the Besshi mountain and the business spirit of Sumitomo. Sumitomo Archives Bulletin No.22*. Sumitomo Archives.

Suehiro, Teruaki. 2000. *Teigo Iba who tackled environmental challenges of the Besshi Copper Mine in the 19th century. Sumitomo Archives Bulletin No. 31*. Sumitomo Archives.

Suehiro, Teruaki. 2005. *The footsteps of Kohei Hirose and Teigo Iba*. Niihama-city Hirose Historical Memorial Museum.

Suehiro, Teruaki. 2008. *Sumitomo's move in the age of modern enterprises. Sumitomo Archives Bulletin No. 39*. Sumitomo Archives.

Suehiro, Teruaki. 2011. *Sumitomo General manager Masaya Suzuki's joining Sumitomo and Nobuaki Makino. Sumitomo Archives Bulletin No. 42.* Sumitomo Archives.

Suehiro, Teruaki. 2013. *A biographical sketch of Teigo Iba -Pioneer of Environmental Measures.* Niihama-city Hirose Historical Memorial Museum.

Sumitomo Metal Mining Co., Ltd. 1991. *History of Sumitomo Besshi Copper Mine.* Sumitomo Metal Mining Co., Ltd.

Sumitomo Archives. 2014. *Sumitomo History, First volume, second volume.* Shibunkaku Publishing.

Sumitomo Forestry Co., Ltd. 1999. *History of Sumitomo Forestry Company.* Sumitomo Forestry Co., Ltd.

Takeda, Haruto. 1987. *History of Copper Industry in Japan.* The University of Tokyo Press.

Takehara, Fumio. 1992. *Management of Sumitomo in Modern Times. Sumitomo Archives Bulletin No. 23.* Sumitomo Archives.

Tanaka Shozo Complete Works Compilation Committee. 1977. *Tanaka Shozo Complete Works Vol. 8.* Iwanami Shoten, Publishers.

Yamamoto, Kazuo. 2009. *Sumitomo Head Office (Second volume)" "Sumitomo Archives No. 40.* Sumitomo Archives.

CHAPTER 2

Masaya Suzuki: Management Through "Itoku-shori", Aiming for a Sustainable Society

Masaya Suzuki (1861–1922). (Source: Suzuki Masaya Biography Complication Committee)

Achievement of Masaya Suzuki and related SDGs

Economy			* **Business diversification** * **Establishment of Sumitomo Electric** * **Establishment of Sumitomo Metal Industries/Sumitomo Light Metal Industries** * **Establishment of Sumitomo Chemical**

(*continued*)

M. Takehara, N. Hasegawa, *Sustainable Management of Japanese Entrepreneurs in Pre-War Period from the Perspective of SDGs and ESG*, https://doi.org/10.1007/978-981-15-6507-6_2

(continued)

Society	3 GOOD HEALTH AND WELL-BEING	4 QUALITY EDUCATION	* Fundamental solution of smoke problem * Establishment of vocational training center * Strengthened employee education
Environment	12 RESPONSIBLE CONSUMPTION AND PRODUCTION	15 LIFE ON LAND	* Commercialization of artificial fertilizer production * Nationwide reforestation activities * Expansion of forestry business
Governance	10 REDUCED INEQUALITIES	17 PARTNERSHIPS FOR THE GOALS	* Establishment of business philosophy * Promotion of external talents * Reorganization into a limited partnership

Source: Created by authors

1 Critical Biography of Masaya Suzuki

1.1 *The Early Life and Younger Days*

Masaya Suzuki was born in the present-day Miyazaki Prefecture on February 24, 1861. It is said that he grew up receiving a strong influence from his father and three elder brothers. His brother Satoo became a diplomat after he graduated from a school which later became the Faculty of Law at the University of Tokyo. Satoo held posts as the Japanese Ambassador to Sweden, Ambassador to Belgium, and Ambassador Extraordinary in Austria. He served as the Counsellor Plenipotentiary at the Paris Peace Conference in 1919 (Taisho-era year 8).

In 1869, Masaya Suzuki entered a Hanko (domain school) named Meirindo and learned the study of Japanese classical literature (Kokugaku), Sinology, and English for four years until the school was closed due to the reform of the educational system. In 1876, Masaya entered Keimei Prefectural School in Kanazawa. In the year following his entrance to Keimei School, the Seinan War took place. Suzuki's father, who refused to cooperate with the rebel army, died in prison. Suzuki went to Tokyo to get help from his brother Satoo as he was not able to return to his hometown due to the chaos of the war.

In September 1883, Suzuki entered Tokyo Imperial University. Among his classmates in the university there were prominent men such as Senkichiro Hayakawa[1] (Mitsui Zaibatsu [financial combine]), Kitokuro

Ikki[2] (Minister of Education, Minister of Home Affairs), and Kosai Uchida (Minister of Foreign Affairs). In 1887 (Meiji-era year 20), Suzuki entered the Ministry of Home Affairs on graduating from the Tokyo Imperial University.

1.2 Days in the Ministry of Home Affairs

When Suzuki entered the Ministry of Home Affairs, the Minister was Aritomo Yamagata. In 1889, Suzuki was assigned to Matsuyama as an Ehime prefectural clerk. In 1890, a festival was held to celebrate 200 years of the Besshi copper mine in Niihama, Ehime Prefecture. Suzuki, who was working for the Ehime prefectural government, was invited to the festival as a guest. This was his first encounter with Sumitomo-company people.

In 1890, Suzuki transferred to Osaka as an Osaka prefectural official. Following the festival in Niihama, the Sumitomo head office in Osaka held a similar festival to celebrate 200 years of the Besshi copper mine. Suzuki was once more invited to this festival as a guest and made the following remark: "Sumitomo's management of the Besshi copper mine is ethical and has won the sympathy of local people".

Suzuki transferred to Gifu Prefecture in 1893, but within only six months he was again transferred to the Patent Bureau of the Ministry of Agriculture and Commerce.

In 1894, Saihei Hirose, Sumitomo's first president, retired. Hirose contributed to the development of the Sumitomo family for over 57 years, during which he rescued the Besshi copper mine from the crisis of its requisition by the new Meiji government. Teigo Iba, who succeeded Hirose, worked for a solution to the smoke problem in the Besshi copper mine under Sumitomo's corporate philosophy, termed "Jiri-Rita-Koshi-Ichijo" in Japanese.

Iba is evaluated highly as a pioneer who promoted CSR in Japan. Iba practiced management which was not aimed at pursuing a short-term profit but was always conscious of making a balance between public and private interest. In addition, Iba noticed Suzuki as a talented figure who could lead Sumitomo in the future.

1.3 Joining Sumitomo

As previously mentioned, Ehime Prefecture and Osaka Prefecture, where Suzuki worked, were places which had close connections with Sumitomo.

Through his management of the Besshi copper mine, Suzuki deepened his understanding of the management concept and business philosophy of Sumitomo and developed a friendship with Saihei Hirose and Teigo Iba.

Iba, who had succeeded Hirose as the second president of Sumitomo, did not like top-down management; rather, he esteemed decision-making through discussion at the board of directors meeting. To strive for new business while developing Sumitomo's existing business, it was indispensable for the company to recruit and train people who had good judgment and a high capability. Iba accelerated his efforts to recruit talent from outside of the company.

Through his deepening interaction with Suzuki, Iba came to have complete trust in him as a person who could manage diversified businesses and achieve sustainable growth with a good understanding of Sumitomo's management philosophy. In 1896, on accepting the offer from Iba, Suzuki decided to join Sumitomo. At that time he was 36 years old. The reason why Suzuki determined to join Sumitomo was that he sympathized with Sumitomo's management philosophy based on "Jiri-Rita-Koshi-Ichijo". Suzuki told Iba of his willingness to join Sumitomo if his adherence to the mindset of making a profit by virtue (Itoku-Shori) was accepted. Suzuki's thinking was in full agreement with Sumitomo's business philosophy of not to pursuing short-term profit.

Iba, who designated Suzuki as his successor, used to be a judge. Iba disliked any unfair personnel management and favoritism. Iba's uncle, Saihei Hirose, had strongly recommended that Iba should join Sumitomo. The biggest reason why Iba decided to join Sumitomo was his attachment to Sumitomo's management philosophy of putting public interest first. Iba and Suzuki, who both decided to join Sumitomo after resigning as government officials, had a lot in common.

Iba had a strong feeling of trust in Suzuki, a man who shared his business mindset. Suzuki, living up to Iba's expectations, solved the smoke-pollution problem at the Besshi copper mine. He then led the modernization of Sumitomo's business while at the same time enhancing its spirit.

1.4 General Manager at the Besshi Copper Mine

In those days Sumitomo implemented organizational reform, and Teigo Iba, who was on the board of directors as well as general manager of the Besshi copper mine, took a practical position in top management.

Fig. 2.1 The Soubiraki smelter. (Source: Niihama City Hirose Memorial Museum 2007)

With the series of modernization measures Saihei Hirose implemented, copper production at the Besshi copper mine substantially increased. In Niihama a Western-style Soubiraki smelter was constructed and started its full operation from 1888.[3] When the Besshi mine railway was connected to Niihama in 1893,[4] carrying capacity improved dramatically and as a result copper production substantially increased. The completion of the Soubiraki smelter and the railroad moved the center of the smelting work from the mountain area in Besshi to the coastal zone in Niihama (Fig. 2.1).

On the other hand, such a rapid increase in copper smelting caused smoke pollution. A large amount of sulfur dioxide was produced from the copper smelting process and this caused a great deal of damage to the crops in the area. Smoke injury at the Besshi copper mine, together with mining pollution (contaminated water) at the Ashio copper mine, became incidents of full-scale industrial pollution which Japan experienced for the first time.

In 1894, to tackle the smoke problem, Sumitomo decided on an unusual personnel change, namely that Iba should be transferred from General Manager at the Sumitomo head office to General Manager of the Besshi copper mine. Iba took up the post at the Besshi copper mine and confronted various problems.

In those days, exhaust desulfurization technology was not yet established, so it was difficult to remove sulfur dioxide from the smelting process. Therefore, Iba made a decision to purchase Shisaka-jima, an uninhabited island located 20 km off the coast of Niihama, and to move the Soubiraki smelter to the island. In 1896, the establishment of the Shisaka-jima smelter began under Iba's instruction.

After returning to Japan from an inspection tour of Western countries (the USA and Europe) in 1898, Suzuki became a director and vice-president of Sumitomo's head office. The following year, in 1899, Suzuki also took up the post of General Manager of the Besshi mine, as Iba's successor, and spent about three years in Niihama until 1902.

1.5 Inaugurated as Sumitomo's President

In 1904, Suzuki, who was serving on the board of directors and as general manager of the Sumitomo head office, was made Sumitomo's president upon Iba's retirement (Table 2.1). At that time Iba was 58 years old and Suzuki was 44 years old. Iba left the following comment and is said to have been very satisfied with the fact that he left the management of Sumitomo in the hands of the younger Suzuki: "Although the aged have a responsibility to help and guide the young, they try to use their experience aggressively and have the young blindly obey them. As a result, the challenging spirit of the young is crushed, and their courses are closed. The most damaging thing to the progress and development of a business is not the negligence of the young but the existence of the aged" (Iba 1904, 165).

The main issues Suzuki tackled as the president of Sumitomo were (1) a fundamental solution to the smoke-pollution problem at the Besshi copper mine, (2) deepening the business philosophy and diversification of business, and (3) modernization of the organization.

Suzuki believed that Iba's decision to relocate the copper refinery to Shisaka-jima island would fundamentally solve the smoke problem. However, ironically, the relocation to Shisaka-jima island resulted in the wider spread of smoke damage. What was most painful to Suzuki was the fact that Sumitomo's business was actually hurting local residents. Gaining profit at the expense of the local residents was against Sumitomo's business philosophy of "Jiri-Rita-Koshi-Ichijo".

Based on Sumitomo's business philosophy, Suzuki set out a policy of taking whatever actions were possible to solve the smoke-pollution problem fundamentally. The dispute with the victims of smoke pollution calmed down as the following agreement was concluded: setting a limit on the quantity of smelting; an operational limitation to the summer when

Table 2.1 List of Sumitomo Presidents

	Tenure of office	*Took office/Retired*	*Years*	*President*
First	1877	Took office	17	Saihei Hirose
	1894	Retired		
Blank period	1894	–	6	Teigo Iba
	1900			
Second	1900	Took office	4	Teigo Iba
	1904	Retired		
Third	1904	Took office	18	Masaya Suzuki
	1922	Retired		
Fourth	1922	Took office	3	Kinkichi Nakata
	1925	Retired		
Fifth	1925	Took office	5	Kankichi Yukawa
	1930	Retired		
Sixth	1930	Took office	11	Masatsune Ogura
	1941	Retired		
Seventh	1941	Took office	5	Shunnosuke Furuta
	1946	Retired		

Source: The author

the smoke damage was more likely to occur; and the payment of compensation for damages.

In 1939 (Showa-era year 14), a neutralization factory (Petersen-type sulfuric acid plant) was completed at the Shisaka-jima island smelter. With this new facility, the smoke problem which had started in September 1893 finally reached a complete solution after 46 years.

1.6 Deepening of the Management Philosophy

Suzuki made the following remark: "A person who engages in the business of Sumitomo needs to understand the correct reason for things, esteem morality and gain trust from society. If the duties of the morality cannot be achieved in a business conducted by Sumitomo, that business should be abolished" (Masaya Suzuki Biography Compilation Committee 1961, 140). Under its corporate philosophy of "Jiri-Rita-Koshi-Ichijo", Sumitomo made it an essential part of its business to carry out its duties not as a mere private enterprise but as a state organization (a public entity).

The history of the Sumitomo family began with Masatomo Sumitomo (1585–1652), who ran a pharmacy in Kyoto in the seventeenth century.

"Monju-in-Shiigaki", which Masatomo Sumitomo left behind, was the essence of the business philosophy of Sumitomo: that is, the view of management that the purpose of business is not just making a profit but refining one's personality and practicing business based on morality. It was Saihei Hirose, the first president of Sumitomo, who established this as Sumitomo's business philosophy. This philosophy was passed on to Suzuki from Iba and further deepened.

1.7 Diversification of Business and Modernization of the Organization

In 1911, Sumitomo Wire Manufacturing was established and the manufacturing of high-voltage cables for telephones and electric power started for the first time in the country. Sumitomo Copper Rolled Products, which was established in 1897, started to manufacture jointless steel tubes, responding to demand from the navy.

In those days, artificial fertilizer was produced as a result of the technological innovation employed to collect the sulfur dioxide which had been the cause of smoke pollution at the Besshi copper mine. To start the full-scale manufacturing of artificial fertilizer, Sumitomo entered the chemical industry by establishing manure manufacturing in 1931. The company later became Sumitomo Chemical. In that same year, Osaka Hokkou (North Port) Inc. was also established, with a view to the business expansion of Osaka Bay through harbor improvement and the development of the coastal industrial zone. The company later became Sumitomo Corporation.

Sumitomo had had a family tradition of esteeming technology since its foundation, and therefore it achieved magnificent results at the Besshi copper mine by introducing modern mining technology. Suzuki inherited this family tradition, and actively introduced modern technologies from foreign countries. Businesses such as wire, copper rolled products, and artificial fertilizer were created as the result of technological innovations based on scientific knowledge. It is possible to say that the characteristic of Sumitomo's business in Suzuki's time was avoiding the pursuit of short-term profit and expanding business through the introduction of modern technologies.

In 1921, Suzuki reorganized Sumitomo from being an independent business proprietor into a limited partnership. Among other zaibatsu (industrial conglomerates) in Japan, the Mitsubishi zaibatsu established the Mitsubishi Limited partnership in 1893 and separated the personal assets of the Iwasaki family and the management of Mitsubishi's business. The Mitsui zaibatsu established a holding company, the Mitsui unlimited partnership in 1909, and separated the personal assets of the Mitsui family and the management of Mitsui's business.

In the case of Sumitomo, the new Sumitomo limited partnership was established to improve the governance of Sumitomo head office in the wake of the expansion and diversification of the business. Five executives had management rights: Tomoito Sumitomo, Tadateru Sumitomo, Masaya Suzuki (President), Kinkichi Nakata (board of directors), and Kankichi Yukawa (board of directors). Tomoito Sumitomo, who was the head of the Sumitomo family, had three children, but they did not have a voice in Sumitomo's business management (Asao-Sumitomo Archives 2014, 222–223). Sumitomo's limited partnership had a unique structure of governance in that a majority of the executives were non-family members. The reason why such a liberal organization was realized was because Tomoito Sumitomo, the head of the Sumitomo family, had complete trust in Suzuki.

1.8 Suzuki's Later Years

In 1922 Suzuki suffered a cerebral hemorrhage while in a car heading for a branch of Sumitomo Bank. He became paralyzed over the left side of his body by this stroke. After receiving medical treatment for a few days in a room of the Sumitomo Bank, he took some rest at his home in Tokyo. It was four months after he first became ill that Suzuki returned to his home in Kobe.

In line with Hirose and Iba, Suzuki was always thinking that he wanted to make Sumitomo's forestry business the last bastion of the company. He said, "I want to develop forestry extensively, and if by any chance the other businesses decline, I want to make forestry the last fortress of Sumitomo's business" (Masaya Suzuki Biography Compilation Committee 1961, 185).

Having become ill, Suzuki determined to resign as the president of Sumitomo. His faithful service to Sumitomo had lasted 26 years, for 19 of which as president he had shouldered the responsibility of management in many areas of the Sumitomo's business. It can be said that Suzuki certainly lived up to the expectation of Iba who entrusted him the future of Sumitomo.

In 1922, Suzuki had another cerebral hemorrhage in his home and became paralyzed over the right side of his body. He was trying to recuperate at home but developed pneumonia, which then became fatal. He passed away at the age of 62.

2 Analysis of the Essence of Masaya Suzuki's Management

2.1 *The Fundamental Solution to the Smoke-Pollution Problem at the Besshi Copper Mine*

In those days the technology for removing sulfur dioxide from smoke was not established. To deal with the smoke problem, the only possible solution was moving the smelter to a place far away from agricultural land. With the relocation of the smelter to Shisaka-jima island which Iba decided on, everyone hoped that the smoke problem would be completely solved (Fig. 2.2).

Cutting short his participation in an inspection tour of Europe and America, Suzuki came back to Japan. Then he became General Manager of the Besshi Copper Mine as Iba's successor in 1899. Suzuki accelerated the construction of the smelter on Shisaka-jima island. The move was completed in 1905 after many twists and turns. During that time, Suzuki was appointed General Manager of the Sumitomo head office in 1902, so he returned to Osaka.

Fig. 2.2 The Shisaka-jima smelter. (Source: Niihama City Hirose Memorial Museum 2007, page 18)

When a test operation at the Shisaka-jima smelter began in 1904, an occurrence of smoke pollution was reported from a village on the opposite shore from the island. When the smelter began its full operation the following year, complaints about the damage from smoke pollution further increased (Fig. 2.3).

At first, Sumitomo rejected the complaints from the farmers by saying that the cause of their crop damage was not smoke but insects. But Sumitomo could not ignore the mounting voices of the farmers and it requested Tokyo Imperial University to conduct an investigation into the cause of the smoke pollution. The university concluded that the cause of the smoke pollution was sulfur dioxide emitted from the Shisaka-jima smelter.

The damage from the smoke further expanded after 1908, and protests and opposition movements mounted by victimized farmers became more intense. In 1909, the farmers submitted a petition for rescue to the Imperial Diet. Smoke pollution at the Besshi copper mine became a political issue together with other mining-pollution problems such as the Ashio copper mine, the Kosaka copper mine, and the Hitachi mine.

Fig. 2.3 The actual state of smoke injury. (Source: Niihama City Hirose Memorial Museum 2007, page 18)

In 1909, Suzuki negotiated with representatives of the farmers to solve the smoke problem. He proposed that instead of Sumitomo paying compensation to individual farmers, it would provide the necessary capital for farmers to improve their farming and eventually increase their income. Suzuki also said, "If the technology to remove sulfur dioxide is developed, even if it costs more than the total amount of compensation, Sumitomo is sure to introduce such technology". However, the farmers hardened their attitude as they thought the amount of damage Sumitomo calculated was too small, and negotiations broke down.

In 1910, the smoke problem became a political issue again. In that year, for the first time, a conference to discuss compensation for smoke pollution was held at the Ministry of Agriculture and Commerce. As a result of the conference, they made a contract which stipulated the payment of compensation and the upper limit for annual copper production at the Shisaka-jima smelter. This contract was renewed as many as eleven times until 1939, when new technology which enabled the complete removal of sulfur dioxide from the smelting process was established. When combining the compensation and donations, the total amount Sumitomo spent during this time reached as much as 8.5 million yen. The duty to pay reparations, as well as the cap on the production of copper, caused serious harm to the business of Sumitomo.

On the other hand, Suzuki did not make any individual compensation payments to the farmers; instead, he invested all the funds for compensation in the improvement of agriculture and forestry. Suzuki's investment succeeded, enabling the planting of rice and wheat that had resistance to smoke, and the planting of saplings that had resistance to sulfur dioxide. The reason why Suzuki eliminated the option of individual compensation was his firm belief that "No-Kou-Heishin" should be promoted. "No-Kou-Heishin" means that both agriculture and the mining industry should be promoted simultaneously. What Suzuki aimed at was making a mechanism by which both local communities and companies could realize sustainable growth. It is possible to say that Suzuki's view is essentially based on the same sense of value as CSV, which has drawn so much attention in modern society.

2.2 *Establishment of Sumitomo's Business Philosophy*

The biggest reason why Iba designated Suzuki as his successor was, he was confident Suzuki was a person who could take over Sumitomo's business philosophy and fulfil the company's responsibility to society as a corporate manager.

The first Sumitomo president, Saihei Hirose, made efforts toward the establishment of a business base for the company through the modernization of the Besshi copper mine. In 1891, Hirose expressed the management philosophy of Sumitomo in the three following three articles:

(1) Sumitomo esteems trust in business.
(2) Sumitomo does not chase "Furi" (quick profits) even if it faces changes in the business environment or changes in revenue or profit.
(3) Sumitomo will ensure the sustainable growth of the Besshi copper mine, which is Sumitomo's core business.

Hirose esteemed trust from society. The founder of Sumitomo, Masatomo Sumitomo, described the business philosophy of Sumitomo as "Monju-in-Shiigaki".[5] Masatomo Sumitomo explained that (1) what needs to be esteemed for a successful business are honesty, carefulness, and steadiness, and (2) the purpose of business is not just making a profit but refining one's personality and practicing business based on morality.

If we interpret Masatomo Sumitomo's teaching in today's context, it shows that the trust which a company is given from society is not judged by the size of assets it has, but rather by its business philosophy, based on social responsibility, and the character and behavior of its employees. In other words, the teaching of Masatomo Sumitomo is that we must not forget that trust is an intangible asset in business, and the accumulation of wealth (tangible assets) produced by these intangible assets of trust is the central concept of Sumitomo's business philosophy.

The teaching expressed in (1), which is that trust is everything in business, leads to the second teaching (2), which is that employees of Sumitomo must not pursue short-term profits. Pursuing a short-term profit is an act contrary to the business mind of Sumitomo, which aims to promote business to the benefit of society. When business has the purpose of enhancing public interest in society, then business can gain trust from society. That trust becomes the foundation of business development.

Article (3) reconfirmed the importance of the Besshi copper mine for the Sumitomo business. Without the Besshi copper mine, there was no future for Sumitomo. When thinking about the long-term development of the copper business under Sumitomo's corporate philosophy,

"Jiri-Rita-Koshi-Ichijo" was essential for the sustainable development of Sumitomo.

Deepening Sumitomo's business philosophy which Hirose and Iba built, Suzuki practiced their ideas in Sumitomo's businesses, including the Besshi copper mine. Suzuki said, "Making progress and innovation is necessary for us, but our business philosophy of 'not pursuing short-term profit' and 'pursuing the business that benefits society' will not change".

What Suzuki concentrated on most was to promote and develop human resources. Even if we set up a rule backed by a noble philosophy, it is human beings who understand and practice that rule. Suzuki thought that developing staff who had a sound moral sense would lead to practicing Sumitomo's business philosophy effectively.

The business philosophy of Sumitomo is well embodied in their forestry business. Iba expanded the scale of the reforestation business to restore bare mountains in the Besshi area. In his last days, Iba said, "To me, what can be called the 'true business' for Sumitomo is the foresting business. Other businesses do not have to continue" (Nishikawa 1990, 111). Suzuki further developed the forestry business Hirose and Iba had concentrated on, and when Sumitomo's limited partnership was established in 1921, he put the forestry business under the direct control of the head office. In Suzuki's time Sumitomo's forestry business expanded into Hokkaido, Kyushu, and the Korean Peninsula (Fig. 2.4).

Suzuki stated as follows: "Because mining is causing environmental destruction, we must make compensation. When considering mining damage to the nation's land, we must do the work of protecting our land. For this reason, reforestation of the mountains is the most suitable. Forests in mountains protect land and offer great benefits to river system management and flood control" (Masaya Suzuki Biography Compilation Committee 1961, 183).

Fig. 2.4 Besshi Copper Mine before foresting (1881). (Source: Shoukei Suehiro 2005, page 34)

Moreover, as we can see, Suzuki stated that he wanted to make the forestry business the last bastion of Sumitomo if other businesses declined. From these words, we can feel Suzuki's strong consideration of and commitment to the forestry business.

2.3 People Are the Most Important Resource

Suzuki thought that those who engage in Sumitomo's business must understand the reason for things, esteem morality, and gain trust from society. Therefore, he attached importance to the training of staff who would eventually inherit the business philosophy of Sumitomo. Iba stated, "The most important thing in our work is to have the best successors and to choose the right time to hand our work over to those successors" (Iba 1904, 165).

The type of people Suzuki sought had all of the following four qualities: honesty, diligence, capability, and health. Even if a person's ability was excellent, that was not sufficient if the other three qualities were lacking.

Suzuki conducted job interviews by himself and asked candidates various questions. He even spent three hours to interview just one student. Suzuki left the following remark: "I don't mind even if business is interrupted as a result of my absence for a week. It would be a temporary loss. However, if we fail to recruit an excellent talent, the loss is immeasurable" (Masaya Suzuki Biography Compilation Committee 1961, 153). Suzuki's remark clearly shows that he sought staff who had both a sense of value and the morality to lead Sumitomo in the future.

Suzuki also concentrated on employee education. He told young Sumitomo employees that Sumitomo's policy on human resources was never based on one-sided elements, such as an academic record, and therefore appointments and promotions were conducted fairly (Masaya Suzuki Biography Compilation Committee 1961, 157). By saying so, he encouraged them to continue their efforts and to have hope for their futures.

Suzuki also established a vocational school in 1915 as part of Sumitomo's social activities aimed at rescuing the poor. At Sumitomo, various discussions were conducted about the business of providing relief for the poor. As a result, they reached the conclusion that the best option for Sumitomo was to provide vocational training to the children of the poor. The objective of establishing a vocational school was to provide low-income people with the necessary knowledge and skills for them to contribute to the development of industry in Japan (Masaya Suzuki Biography Compilation Committee 1961, 283–284). Suzuki felt dissatisfied with school education in those days in that it overemphasized cramming knowledge into students and as a result it was not effectively bringing up promising human beings who could play an active part in society. Suzuki's management philosophy shares many underlying ideas with the SDGs, which attract attention in modern society.

Notes

1. Senkichiro Hayakawa (1863–1922) joined Mitsui Bank after he worked for the Ministry of Finance and the Bank of Japan. He held positions such as Representative Director of Mitsui Bank.
2. Kitokuro Ichiki (1867–1944) served as the Minister of Education and the Minister for Home affairs during the second Okuma administration.
3. The Soubiraki smelter was completed in 1884 (Meiji-era year 17).
4. The Besshi mining railroad was composed of the lower-part railroad (10 km) in Niihama and upper-part railroad (5.5 km) in the mountainous areas.
5. "Monju-in-Shiigaki" means that the basics of business is to gain trust from society based on the teachings of Buddhism.

References

Asao, Naohiro, Sumitomo Museum. 2014. *Sumitomo History, Volume 2.* Tokyo: Shibunkaku Publishing.

Iba, Teigo. 1904. "Young and Old", *Business Japan Vol. 7 No. 4.* Tokyo: Jitsugyo-no-Nihon-Sha.

Kamiyama, Makoto. 1960. *Teigo Iba.* Tokyo: Nichigetsusha.

Kimoto, Shoji. 1970. *Shisakajima (Book1) (Book2).* Tokyo: Kodansha.

Masaya Suzuki Biography Compilation Committee. 1961. *Masaya Suzuki.*

Niihama City Hirose History Memorial Museum. 2007. *Besshi Copper Mine Connected to the World.*

Nishikawa, Shojiro. 1990. *Yu-Ou.* Tokyo: Tosho-Shuppansha.

Seoka, Makoto. 1998. *Management Philosophy of Modern Sumitomo.*

Suehiro, Shoukei. 2005. *The History of Saihei Hirose and Teigo Iba.* Tokyo: Niihama City Hirose Historical Memorial Museum.

Sumitomo Archives. 2008a. *Sumitomo Archives Bulletin No.39.*
Sumitomo Archives. 2008b. *Sumitomo Archives Bulletin No.42.*
Sumitomo Forestry Co., Ltd. 1999. *History of Sumitomo Forestry Company.*
Sumitomo Metal Mining Co., Ltd. 1991. *History of Sumitomo Besshi Copper Mine.*
Takeda, Haruto. 1987. *History of the Copper Industry in Japan.* Tokyo: The University of Tokyo Press.

PART II

Integration of Economy and Morality

CHAPTER 3

Ryoichiro Okada: Aiming for Integration of Economy and Morality

Ryoichiro Okada (1839–1915). (Source: Dai Nippon Hotokusha)

Achievement of Ryoichiro Okada and related SDGs

Economy	 	* Economic independence of local communities * Spinning industry (Enshu Futamata spinning company) * Banking (asset bank)

(*continued*)

M. Takehara, N. Hasegawa, *Sustainable Management of Japanese Entrepreneurs in Pre-War Period from the Perspective of SDGs and ESG*, https://doi.org/10.1007/978-981-15-6507-6_3

(continued)

Society		* Educational (Kihoku Gakusha/Kakegawa Nogakusha) * The first principal of prefectural Kakegawa Junior High School * Training entrepreneurs * Promotion of management based on Hotoku thought
Governance		* Value standard that integrated economy and morality * Acceptance of modern enlightenment thought * Advocacy of "Zaihon Tokumatsu" principle

Source: Created by authors

1 Ryoichiro Okada's Thoughts on Morality

Ryoichiro Okada was born in 1839, in Kakegawa City, Shizuoka Prefecture, as the eldest son of Saheiji Okada. Father Saheiji educated Ryoichiro thoroughly since his childhood. In 1854, Okada's father made Ryoichiro an apprentice to Sontoku Ninomiya.[1] His father ran Dai Nippon Hotokusha, a nationwide organization to spread Ninomiya's "Hotoku Thought". Since Sontoku emphasized practical science, Ryoichiro worked hard on agriculture every day and experienced the practice of economic recovery in rural areas. At the same time, he learned the Sontoku's theoretical system by copying his books.

In 1876, Ryoichiro became the second president of Dainippon Hotokusha succeeding his father. In his efforts to disseminate the philosophy of Hotoku thought, he focused on the "Suijo".[2] Okada stated that the knowledge should be given to those who lack knowledge and a surplus of one's own resources should be given to those who were economically difficult because the spirit of "Suijo" (literally means concession) is a precious power given only to humanity (Fig. 3.1).

Citing a case of Fujisaburo Suzuki, who was a leading expert in Japan's sugar business, Okada pointed out that the practice of "Suijo" was

Fig. 3.1 Daito Nippon Hotokusha Auditorium. (Source: Dai Nippon Hotokusha)

important for the success of the business. Looking back on the scandals of modern companies in recent years, many companies deceived society because they prioritized corporate profits. If we interpret modern CSR (corporate social responsibility) based on Okada's philosophy, CSR is the practice of "Suijo"—a concession to stakeholders—and its result will lead to companies' profits.

In Japan, after the Meiji Restoration, the capitalist economy rapidly penetrated and industrialization advanced due to the industrial development policy. Okada's philosophy included "Kinken" (working hard and reducing unnecessary expenses), "Bundo" (limiting the spending within a predetermined range of income), and "Suijo" (leaving financial resources for future generations' needs). And at the same time, he emphasized economic independence of the individual. When he became the president of Omikoku Hotokusha, Okada showed three major principles: "Rittoku", "Chifu", and "Kaichi". "Rittoku" means morality, and "Chifu" is the economy. The unity between morality and economy is an important teaching of Okada's master Sontoku Ninomiya. Okada advocated

"Zaihon-Tokumatsu" (economy first, morality later) principle and argued that economic independence is important for the practice of virtue. In addition to morality and economy, Okada repeatedly emphasized the importance of education ("Kaichi" in his words).

In fact, during the Meiji period (1868–1912), funds produced through people's "Kinken" (hard work) and "Suijo" (conceded or transferred) were spent on creating new industries. However, Okada thought unless this hard work and transfer were backed by morality, economic activity would end up just making money. Economy and morality cannot be integrated forever. Recognizing that a large amount of money was required for developing new industries in Japan in Meiji period, Okada had a different mindset from private banks that focused only on commercial finance.

Okada presented "Zaihon-Tokumatsu principles" in his book *Hokoku-Fukoku Theory*. "Zaihon-Tokumatsu principles" was an idea that an economic foundation was necessary to practice social responsibility. Some of the disciples of Sontoku Ninomiya criticized Okada's Zaihon-Tokumatsu principles. However, Okada understood the need for rapid development of capitalist economy and industrial development in Japan and emphasized economic independence in his activities of disseminating Hotoku thought.

Okada accepted the social change after the Meiji Restoration and aimed at the fusion of the capitalist economic system and Hotoku thought. Okada created the "Zaihon-Tokumatsu principles" from this idea. By adding new values to Ninomiya Sontoku's philosophy of Hotoku thought in response to changes in civil society, Okada's "Zaihon-Tokumatsu principles" permeated into the Enshu region (a region centered on Hamamatsu City, Shizuoka Prefecture) and became a philosophical backbone that supported entrepreneurial activities in that region.

Regarding Kaichi (education), one of Okada's three remaining principles, he emphasized the need to acquire knowledge at all ages, and made education a major factor in reaching wealth (economy).

Okada focused on acquiring advanced Western knowledges at the school he founded (Kihoku Gakusha), while maintaining the spirit of Sontoku Ninomiya's practical science. The Meiji Restoration greatly changed Japanese society and he witnessed the economic power of other countries. Therefore, while emphasizing agricultural production, Okada realized that if Japan adhered to the traditional economic doctrine of promoting agriculture (called physiocracy), it could not be independent politically or economically.

In the Enshu region, the number of part-time farmers increased after the Meiji Restoration. The development of commerce and industry progressed mainly in Hamamatsu area, and farmers started to engage in commerce and industry in addition to agriculture.[3] Table 3.1 shows the change in the ratio of full-time farmers and part-time farmers. Since the middle of the Meiji era, part-time farmers accounted for about 40%. Under such circumstances, Okada was gradually aiming for regional economic development centered on commerce and industry rather than an economy so reliant on agriculture.

Okada emphasized the idea that economic independence leads to moral practice. Okada's assertion of economic independence promoted the economic independence of small farmers at the beginning of his activities, and in the Meiji period, it developed into the nurturing of modern industries through banking.

The promotion of economic independence and industrial promotion policies based on Okada's philosophy of "Zaihon-Tokumatsu" had a major impact on the foundation of entrepreneurial activities in the Enshu region (currently Shizuoka Prefecture). After the Meiji Restoration, farmers who were liberated from feudal systems came to have the ability to establish their own economic base by engaging not only in agriculture but also in commerce and industry.

Farmers and craftsmen increased their interest in entrepreneurial activities and awareness of participation in society through the philosophy of

Table 3.1 Ratio of full-time and part-time farmers

Year	*Full-time (%)*	*Part-time (%)*
1884	60.3	39.7
1887	61.8	38.2
1892	54.4	45.6
1897	54.1	45.9
1902	63.4	36.6
1916	50.1	49.9
1923	47.6	52.4

Source: Hamamatsu Historic Site Survey Committee (1977) "Enshu Industrial and Cultural History" on page 473 (Authors revised)

"Zaihon-Tokumatsu" and commercial and industrial projects which Okada promoted based on the Hotoku thought.

Hotoku thought cultivated professional ethics based on ingenuity in the farmers and made them aware that they could become a leading part for social change through business activities.

Examples of this can be seen in the activities of Sakichi Toyoda (founder of Toyota Motor Corporation) and Michio Suzuki (founder of Suzuki Motor Corporation), who produced automatic looms. Business activities in Enshu region were carried out mostly by farmers, carpenters, and craftsmen, and few were from economically rich classes. They accurately understood users' needs and worked on steady technological development, and finally succeeded in developing an innovative automatic loom machine. Toyoda and Suzuki did not monopolize the patents and utility models they acquired, but made them belong to their companies. The wealth generated from the accumulation of knowledge was reinvested in the next technological development. This is exactly the practice of "Suijo" (concession) that Okada advocated.

The common qualities of entrepreneurs in Enshu region were (1) the emphasis on the development of high value–added products through innovation generated from self-help efforts and (2) the fulfillment of social responsibility through their business activities. Economic independence was a prerequisite for practicing virtue through business activities. They accepted self-sacrificing works toward economic independence, becoming social leaders through their success as entrepreneurs.

Hotoku thought Okada propagated was created in his quest for a socioeconomic system that integrated Hotoku thought as capitalist economy rapidly penetrated Japan. The philosophy of "Zaihon-Tokumatsu" that Okada advocated urged farmers and those involved in commerce and industry to have awareness as economic agents. Having those people recognize the social significance of economic activities in the process of promoting economic independence by working hard paved the way for people in Enshu area as entrepreneurs.

2 Acceptance of Modern Enlightenment Thought

Okada's thought was greatly influenced by the Western enlightenment thought introduced in Japan in the early Meiji era. The people who influenced him were Masanao Nakamura and Amane Nishi, who were active as core members of Mei-rokusha, which was Japan's first modern academic society. After the Meiji Restoration, Fuchu Gakumonjo (school) and Numazu military academy were founded by former vassals of the Tokugawa Shogunate who moved to Shizuoka. Both Nishi and Nakamura were engaged in education for a short period of time. Nishi taught at Numazu military academy and Nakamura taught at Fuchu school.[4]

Nakamura translated two Western books into Japanese: *Self-Help; with Illustrations of Character and Conduct* by Samuel Smiles and *On Liberty* by John Stuart Mill. These two books had a great influence on the modernization of Japan. The Japanese translation of *Self-Help; with Illustrations of Character and Conduct* was used as a textbook at an elementary school in the Meiji period. Okada was introduced to modern Western thought through Nakamura's book. He also received direct guidance from Nakamura. Nakamura also made a statement that acknowledged Okada's activities to spread Hotoku thought.

Okada stated in his book *Tanzan-Ronshu* as follows:

> I read Bentham's book and I was glad that there was something in common between utilitarianism and Hotoku thought. Christianity teaches that "love your neighbor as you love yourself".

It is the same as the idea of "Suijo" (concession). Bentham pursues theory and Hotoku pursues practice, but both shared the same essence.[5] Okada was strongly aware of the common elements of utilitarianism and the idea of Zaihon-Tokumatsu philosophy and confessed that he positively accepted utilitarianism.

In the UK, the Industrial Revolution developed capitalism and formed civil society. Utilitarianism in the UK was born behind a social change due to the Industrial Revolution. For capitalists who led the Industrial Revolution, the challenge was how to reconcile their own interests with those of others. Utilitarianism was a realist idea that tried to capture the position of capitalists positively by considering the well-being of individuals from the standpoint of society as a whole.

While John Stuart Mill acknowledged Bentham's principle of utilitarianism, he argued that the standard of good and bad of action was not the happiness of the individual performing the action, but the happiness of all the individuals involved. Mill found the ideal of utilitarianism in the Jesus' teaching of loving neighbors, "Let others do what I want and Love your neighbor as yourself". Utilitarianism requires actors to overcome selfishness. Okada stated that "Suijo" in Hotoku thought was nothing but the pursuit of altruistic happiness symbolized by the love of neighbors in Christianity.

The idea of utilitarianism was introduced to Japanese society through Samuel Smiles' *Self-Help; with Illustrations of Character and Conduct. Self-Help* was translated as a Japanese title *Saikoku Risshihen* by Masanao Nakamura. The book became the best-selling book with one million copies issued throughout the Meiji period.

The saying "Heaven helps those who help themselves" instilled a spirit of self-reliance in people who lived in the Meiji period. Sakichi Toyoda, founder of Toyota Motor Corporation, was said to have been strongly influenced by Hotoku thought. His management philosophy had much in common with the philosophy of Samuel Smiles.[6]

Self-Help explained that the happiness of life would be realized by maximizing the happiness of the people of society through hard work, drawing on the numerous entrepreneurial activities that supported the Industrial Revolution. *Self-Help* showed the possibility of independence of farmers who had been repressed under the feudal system.

In the rapidly changing socio-economic system in Japan after the Meiji Restoration in 1868, Okada transformed the philosophy of Hotoku thought from traditional agricultural ethics to the management philosophy of modern industries centered on commerce and industry by incorporating utilitarianism into the interpretation of the Hotoku thought.

Nakamura denied measuring the value standard of action with a quantitative measure of the secular success of the actor. In other words, Nakamura, from the standpoint of utilitarianism advocated by Mill, emphasized the notion of the actor and argued that the achievement of qualitatively high spiritual well-being was important.

The attitude of seeking the standards of the right and wrong of the act from the point of view of the actor is also recognized in the Hotoku thought. Sontoku Ninomiya, the proponent of the Hotoku thought, made the following statement: "It is not the original purpose for people to hope to succeed in life by learning. If you learn and have your own abilities, you will naturally be enriched from the heaven. Never seek a social status by yourself". Thus, it is considered that the philosophies of Nakamura and Ninomiya about self-help are very close.

Thoughts of Ninomiya and Okada and the thoughts shown in the *Self-Help* had a lot in common, and the spirit of self-help was widely accepted without resistance in the Enshu region where Hotoku thought had permeated.

As we described earlier, Hotoku thought greatly influenced the management philosophy of Sakichi Toyoda. Another entrepreneur who succeeded in incorporating Hotoku philosophy into business was Saburo Suzuki. Suzuki succeeded in the sugar production business. He was born in 1855 in the northern part of the Enshu region. At the age of 28, he developed a manufacturing method for rock sugar and established Japan Refined Sugar Co., Ltd. and Taiwan Sugar Co., Ltd. Suzuki was also known as an excellent inventor, earning 159 patents for his inventions.

Suzuki realized the effectiveness of Hotoku thought when applied to business. As a result, he put it into practice in the sugar production business and made a huge success.

Suzuki was a mediocre merchant who lived in mountain village, but he practiced corporate management based on Hotoku thought and expanded his business with the spirit of self-help. The Hotoku thought, which became popular for the relief of poor farmers, developed into a new entrepreneurial management philosophy with the success of Toyoda and Suzuki.

The Zaihon-Tokumatsu philosophy that Okada proposed was influenced by utilitarianism and significantly expanded the traditional area of the Hotoku thought that remained within the framework of farmers' self-reliance. The Zaihon-Tokumatsu philosophy enabled Hotoku thought to link with modern industries.

3 Okada's Activities as a Social Entrepreneur

3.1 Educational Work

Educational works occupied an important position in Okada's activities. The core of Okada's educational works in Kakegawa was Kihoku Gakusha (school). Kihoku School was a private school established in 1877 by Okada. "Kihoku" was the name of area in China which was known for its production of fine horses. It implies Okada's strong will to foster competent talents.

All the students at the Kihoku school were required to live in the dormitories and the school focused on English education with Hotoku thought as the foundation of its education. All the textbooks in foreign languages were ordered from overseas. There was an influence of utilitarianism behind the school's emphasis on English studies.

In the Naval Academy entrance examination conducted in 1885, thirteen students from Shizuoka Prefecture took the examination. The Naval

Academy entrance examination was one of the most prestigious and difficult examinations with an emphasis on English, and only two out of thirteen passed. The two who passed were from Kihoku school.[7]

Kihoku school had a curriculum centered on English studies and the study of Chinese classics. The following were main textbooks used in English studies.[8]

- Peter Parley, *Universal History*
- George Payn Quackenbos, *Elementary History of the United States*
- Samuel Griswold, Goodrich, *A History of BRITAIN*
- Francis Wayland *The Elements of Political Economy*

At Kihoku school, there were about 20 students at the time of its opening and 50–60 students at its prime. In English classes, original books about Western history and economics, for example, were used as textbooks. From school's English-focused education policy, we can infer that Okada aimed at nurturing human resources who could adapt to drastically changing Japanese society after the Meiji Restoration while cherishing Hotoku thought. Okada developed educational activities at Kihoku school, keeping in mind the new positioning of Hotoku thought in a new capitalist economic society in Japan.

Recognizing the changes in society where the key industry in Japan was shifting from agriculture to commerce and industry, Okada focused on education centering English studies to develop leaders in the industry while using values of Hotoku thought as the educational philosophy (Fig. 3.2).

Fig. 3.2 Kihoku school. (Source: Dai Nippon Hotokusha)

3.2 *Banking*

The banking business in Japan began in 1874 at an asset lending office established by Okada. Recognizing the need for a financial institution to accumulate private capital and supply funds to promote the industry, he aimed to establish an asset lending office. Okada established a semi-private asset lending office, and as a general manager (senior position above the president), he provided loans for the purpose of emergency response, relief for the poor, and reconstruction of devastated villages.

In 1893, when the bank ordinance was promulgated, the asset lending office had to be converted to a regular bank. As a result, the asset lending office was converted into an asset bank. This asset bank later became current Shizuoka Bank.

Okada's purpose was to promote developing new industries in Japan through the transfer ("Suijo" in his words) of benevolent funds to make the ordinary people economically independent. This purpose came out of his strong awareness that there were technical gaps between Western countries and Japan and that in order for Japan to become independent, it was necessary to enhance its industrial and economic power.

Okada's aggressive activities of promoting industrial development during the modern industrial period were in line with the Meiji government's industrial policy, and that was one of the factors that led to the great development of the Hotoku thought he was promoting in the Meiji period.

Today, microfinance is attracting attention as a method for promoting economic independence of the poor. Microfinance is generally defined as "small-scale finance aimed at reducing poverty for the poor and low-income groups".[9]

Founded by Dr. Muhammad Yunus in Bangladesh, Grameen Bank became an internationally recognized microfinance institution. Microfinance is an innovative financial mechanism that enables people in severe poverty to engage in private businesses, become economically independent by earning income, and eventually get out of poverty.

Comparing Okada's banking business with microfinance, it can be evaluated that Okada's banking business was essentially an act of anticipating microfinance. Asset lending stations were based on the idea of giving away surplus funds to the local community and the next generation, that is, the concept of "Suijo" (means concede or transfer). The funds were sourced from hard work of employees of Okada's Hotoku company. Okada first helped people get out of poverty through his banks and provided the opportunity to become financially independent.

In the Meiji period, Shizuoka Prefecture had an extremely large number of banks and bank-like companies nationwide, of which the Enshu region accounted for 62.5% of Shizuoka Prefecture with 115 banks.[10] In the Enshu region, because of the influence of Hotoku thought, farmers engaged in commercial agriculture such as tea and cotton, which had relatively higher cash value than rice. As a result, with the technical improvement and the development of the cotton fabric industry, there was a high demand for financing. In addition, because the landowner class with funding capacity was relatively small in the region, small and medium landlords and merchants mutually provided funds to establish financial institutions.[11]

3.3 Spinning Industry

In 1883, Okada established the Enshu Futamata Spinning Company in Futamata, Toyota-gun, Shizuoka Prefecture (now Futamata-town, Tenryu-ku, Hamamatsu City). The company was established as one of the ten spinning companies that received support from the Meiji government.[12] It had a small-scale spinning with 2000 spindles using the waterpower of the Tenryu River.[13]

Okada made the following statement regarding the industrial promotion:

> A person who starts a business in the industrial field must have the purpose of contributing to society, not for his own selfish demands. Failure to start a business is inherent, but there will be people who will succeed the company. Watts, Stevenson and Arkwright, who were the leaders of the industrial revolution, succeeded in greatly advancing the industry by inheriting and developing the technology and will of their predecessors'.[14]

Okada stressed the social significance of entrepreneurial activities, and pointed out that for creating industries, it was indispensable for banks to provide financial support and develop human resources to be entrepreneurs. He explained this by showing the example of entrepreneurial activities during the Industrial Revolution in the UK.

The Enshu Futamata Spinning Company ceased to operate before fully achieving its objectives of self-reliance of the local economy and protection of the cotton-producing farmers. However, Okada's entrepreneurial activities raised the vocational awareness of farmers and opened the way to modern industries.

Okada actively promoted the Hotoku thoughts with the aim of realizing the independence of the local economy by fostering local industries. This became a social movement and penetrated the Enshu region, producing entrepreneurs with a sense of social mission, mainly among farmers and craftsmen. This ultimately led to forming a foundation for fostering a modern industry centered on the cotton textile industry.

4 The Significance of "Zaihon-Tokumatsu" Thought

Looking at the actual state of entrepreneurship in Shizuoka Prefecture during the Meiji period, the Enshu region accounted for 42% of all the entrepreneurs in Shizuoka Prefecture.[15] Shizuoka Research Institute (1992) pointed out that this region's success in producing entrepreneurs was greatly influenced by business promotion activities and practical guidance through educational activities by Okada and other Hotoku activists.[16]

Regarding the relationship between regional characteristics and entrepreneurship, Nakagawa (1981) analyzed that all management entities are created by certain historical and social factors and do not exist independently of these historical or social factors.[17]

Okada was an undoubtedly social entrepreneur who wanted to build a sustainable community in the wake of major changes in Japanese society. Okada's value as a social entrepreneur lay in building an infrastructure for a socio-economic system that created continuous solutions.

"Zaihon-Tokumatsu" principle that aimed at the integration of economy and morality formed a unique social and cultural temperament in the Enshu region. Even after Hotoku thought lost its social indoctrination power, it was handed down to the Enshu region as an ethical deep consciousness and fostered an entrepreneurial spirit with the color of M. Weber's "capitalism spirit".

Okada's "Zaihon-Tokumatsu" philosophy and social entrepreneurial activities were aimed at nurturing modern industries and utilizing moral values of Hotoku thought, in order to respond to the rapid development of capitalist economy in Japan after the Meiji Restoration. It was characterized by activities targeting a wide range of community members including farmers, merchants, and craftsmen.

With the collapse of feudal society, people's behavior changed from organizational based to individual based, and competition became a new social order. As a result, in Japanese society during the Meiji period, success in life became a powerful ideology.

In contrast, Okada's philosophy cultivated values in the Enshu region that respected entrepreneurial activities with moral values and the acquisition of wealth as a result of their actions. Competition between companies for the purpose of creating social value was accepted, and various innovations were actually created. Examples of such competition between companies can be seen from the enormous number of patents and utility models in the textile industry in the Enshu region.

Okada succeeded in adapting to the new social values after the Meiji Restoration by adding utilitarian elements to the pre-modern philosophy of the Hotoku thought. The core of Okada's thought was virtue: human wealth and the prosperity of the nation were not the purpose of itself, but only as a result of fulfilling morality. On the other hand, on the premise that man's responsibility was to increase virtue through labor, he accepted without any limitation the accumulation of wealth and prosperity as a result of labor (Fig. 3.3).

There is a phrase, "Putting new wine into fresh wineskins". Zaihon-Tokumatsu principles that Okada promoted were new wineskins that went beyond the traditional framework of Hotoku thought. In the era when the socio-economic environment was changing drastically, if Hotoku thought had stuck to the old thought, it would have been buried in society. Okada's Zaihon-Tokumatsu principles succeeded in converting Hotoku thought from the guiding principles in agricultural society to the guiding principles in modern industrial society. This is clear from the fact that

Fig. 3.3 Dai Nippon Hotokusha Moral gate and economic gate (The words "moral" and "economy" are written at the entrance gate respectively). (Source: Dai Nippon Hotokusha)

Zaihon-Tokumatsu principles were a factor in producing a large number of entrepreneurs from the Enshu region and that many entrepreneurs in Japan used these principles as the foundation of their management philosophies and corporate ethics.

Notes

1. Sontoku Ninomiya (1787–1856) was a Japanese agricultural leader and philosopher in the nineteenth century. Ninomiya was born into a farmer's family and lost his parents at a young age, but he worked hard to study and rebuild a ruined family. Later, he helped restore villages throughout the country. Ninomiya's thoughts and actions spread throughout Japan as Hotoku thought, affecting many people, including entrepreneurs and politicians.
2. "Suijo" (concession) is one of four Sontoku's philosophies. Other three are "Kinben" (hard work), "Shisei" (sincerity), and "Bundo" (computational general equilibrium).
3. Hamamatsu Historical Site Survey Society [1977], p. 473.
4. Haraguchi and Umino [1982], pp. 26–30.
5. Okada [1909], p. 185.
6. Hirakawa [2006], pp. 171–272.
7. Horiuchi, Ryo [1998], p. 1.
8. Horiuchi, Ryo [1998], p. 32.
9. Felder [2005], p. 33.
10. Ogino [1999], p. 24.
11. Okada and Honma [1971], p. 41.
12. The Meiji government planned to establish ten private spinning mills to encourage the spinning industry.
13. The number of employees was about 100.
14. Okada [1931], pp. 946–947.
15. Shizuoka Research Institute [1992], p. 208.
16. Shizuoka Research Institute [1992], p. 190.
17. Nakagawa [1981], pp. 21–25.

References

Felder, Naoko [2005] "Introduction to Microfinance-A New Business Model to Save the World from Poverty" Diamond, Inc.

Hamamatsu Historical Site Survey Committee [1977] "The History of Industry and Culture in the Enshu region".

Haraguchi, Kiyoshi and Umino, Fukutoshi [1982] "One Hundred Years of Shizuoka Prefecture-One Hundred Year History of its People" Yamakawa Shuppansha Ltd.

Hasegawa, Naoya [2005] "Michio Suzuki: A Man Who Created Suzuki" Mie University Press.

Hirakawa, Sukehiro [2006] "Heaven helps those who help themselves: Masanao Nakamura and Saigoku Risshi Hen "Nagoya University Press.

Horiuchi, Ryo [1997] "A brief history of Dai Nippon Hotokusha" Dainippon Hotokusha.

Horiuchi, Ryo [1998] "Kihoku Gakusha" Dainippon Hotokusha.

Nakagawa, Keiichiro [1981] "Introduction to Comparative Management History", University of Tokyo Press.

Ogino, Satoshi [1999] "History of Banks in Shizuoka Prefecture, "Shizuoka Culture No. 56", Shizuoka Prefecture Culture Foundation.

Okada, Kazuki and Homma, Yasuo [1971] "Development of Regional Industries and Regional Banks" "Kinyu Keizai (Financial Economy)" Institute for Finance and Economy.

Okada, Ryoichiro [1881] "Hotoku Fukoku Ron" Dai Nihon Hotokusha.

Okada, Ryoichiro [1898] "Tanzan Ronshu Vol. 1" Dai Nihon Hotokusha.

Okada, Ryoichiro [1909] "Tanzan Ronshu Vol. 3" Dai Nippon Hotokusha.

Okada, Ryoichiro [1931] "Kappo Keizairon ", "Sontoku Ninomiya Complete Volume 36", Ryukei Shosha.

Shizuoka Research Institute [1992] "Shizuoka: Culture that creates entrepreneurs" Shizuoka Shimbun.

Smiles, Samuel (translated by Masanao Nakamura) [1895] "Revised Saigoku Risshi Hen (Self-help)" Tokyo Hakubunkan Collection.

Takeuchi, Hiroshi [1996] "Shizuoka Industry Climate" Shizuoka Shimbun.

Tanaka, Tadaharu [1933] "Toyoda Sakichi Biography" Sakichi Toyoda Biography Compilation Office.

Unno, Fukuhisa and Kato, Takashi [1978] "Shokusan Kogyo and the Hotoku Movement," Toyo Keizai Shimposha.

CHAPTER 4

Meizen Kinpara: The Pioneer of Social Business

Meizen Kinpara (1832–1923). (Source: National Diet Library)

M. Takehara, N. Hasegawa, *Sustainable Management of Japanese Entrepreneurs in Pre-War Period from the Perspective of SDGs and ESG*, https://doi.org/10.1007/978-981-15-6507-6_4

Achievement of Meizen Kinpara and related SDGs

Economy	8 DECENT WORK AND ECONOMIC GROWTH 9 INDUSTRY, INNOVATION AND INFRASTRUCTURE	* Banking (Kinpara Bank) * Sawmill industry (Tenryu timber) * Transportation industry (Tenryu Transportation) * Product sales (Tori Gumi)
Society	3 GOOD HEALTH AND WELL-BEING 4 QUALITY EDUCATION 11 SUSTAINABLE CITIES AND COMMUNITIES	* Tenryu River Flood Control Project (Chiga Cooperation) * Promotion of flood control education (Suiri school) * Promotion of Rehabilitation for ex-prisoners (Shizuoka Kanzenkai)
Environment	12 RESPONSIBLE CONSUMPTION AND PRODUCTION 15 LIFE ON LAND	* Promotion of reforestation (Kinpara forest) * Irrigation (the Kinpara Foundation for Forest Conservation and Flood Control) * Establish an economy of recycling * Promoting an idea of forest conservation and flood control
Governance	10 REDUCED INEQUALITIES 17 PARTNERSHIPS FOR THE GOALS	* Practice of management based on philosophy * Practice of private–government partnership

Source: Created by authors

1 Early Days

Meizen Kinpara was born in 1832, in Anma-town, Higashi-ku, Hamamatsu City, Shizuoka Prefecture. His family were landowners who ran both a sake brewery and a pawn shop. In 1848, Meizen's father, a talented man in business and management, was promoted as the local administrator of the Matsudaira family, which was a direct retainer of the Shogun (head of state). Meizen's father was a person who got up before dawn, prepared for work, predicted the weather of the day, and worked hard until late at night. Meizen was described as a person who worked hard and helped others. It seems that his father's way of life influenced his personality. From an early age, Meizen had a keen interest in practicing his knowledge he learned.

In 1849, when Meizen was 18 years old, his mother died at the age of 37. The deceased mother was worried about the future of the Kinpara family, so she left a will about Meizen's stepmother and Meizen's wife. Meizen and his father followed the will. The father married Meizen's mother's cousin, and Meizen married his stepmother's daughter, Tamaki, when he was 24.

In 1855, Meizen inherited the job of the head of village at the same time he married. In 1857, the lord Matsudaira family convened each regional administrator to Edo (currently Tokyo) to discuss measures of financial reconstruction. At this time, Meizen went to Edo for the first time on behalf of his father. Among the representatives gathered in Edo, there were those who went out for drinking every night while working. However, Meizen refused such an invitation, worked hard on the debt problems of his lord, and used his spare time for studying Confucianism (Fig. 4.1).

After solving the debt problem of his lord's family, Meizen was involved in the debt consolidation of Totoumiya. Totoumiya was a trading house which was established in Yokohama by Meizen's father, his four relatives, and fellow landowners. It worked as a wholesaler selling goods collected from all over the country to foreign traders. In the Enshu region (the western part of Shizuoka Prefecture), the production of high-value-added

Fig. 4.1 Meizen Kinpara's birthplace (Hamamatsu City, Shizuoka Prefecture). (Source: Meizen Kinpara Memorial Hall)

crops became mainstream due to the penetration of the commodity economy. A typical product was cotton.

The suburbs of the village where Meizen's birthplace was located had a textile market and it played an important role as a cluster of agricultural products and goods from the Edo period. In addition, Kaketsuka Port, at the mouth of the Tenryu River, was a logistics base connecting Edo and Osaka, and functioned as a product shipping port in the Enshu region. Taking advantage of the land as a key transportation center, Meizen's father tried to sell goods made in Omi and nearby Shinshu areas to foreign trading houses.

Totoumiya's business started off smoothly. However, the shortage of working capital became more serious as the transaction volume expanded. The management of Totoumiya was entrusted to the Kinpara family. Meizen and his father did not go to Yokohama, entrusting their relatives to manage things there. The Kinpara family conflicted with the co-investor over the investment in Totoumiya, and additional investment was postponed. Local managers were pressed for cash flow, so they repeatedly borrowed money and diverted sales money, which eventually put Totoumiya into bankruptcy.

It was customary in the Edo period that a Han (feudal domain) took over the debts of merchants dealing with the Han's products. Co-investors asked for debts to be dealt with by the Han and the Kinpara family. Meizen decided to use all of the Kinpara family money for reimbursement.

Meizen said: "Responsibility for damages arising from our own greed should not be transferred to the Han. We will throw out all our personal property to solve the problem". Most creditors were shippers of cotton and tea in the Enshu region. They accepted Meizen's graceful attitude and commitment, and abandoned their accounts receivables equivalent to 62.5% of total debt. This experience gave Meizen a guideline for his life. Meizen realized that in his life it was not property that he had to rely on, but morality and trust.

2 The Essence as a Social Entrepreneur

2.1 Tenryu River Flood Control Project

Meizen was born in the basin of the Tenryu River, so he witnessed the horror of flooding from his childhood. Between 1850 and 1868, it was recorded that the Tenryu River underwent five major breakdowns. Among the various social projects that Meizen tackled throughout his life, the flood control project for the Tenryu River was particularly important.

Fig. 4.2 Tenryu River near Hamamatsu City, Shizuoka Prefecture. (Source: Wikimedia Commons)

The Tenryu River originates from Lake Suwa in Nagano Prefecture and it is a rapid stream, 213 km in length, that flows into the Pacific Ocean through Nagano, Aichi, and Shizuoka Prefectures. In its upstream area there are 3000-meter class mountains, and all the tributaries that flow into the Tenryu River are steep. In addition, because the geology is brittle and has a rugged terrain, when heavy rain falls in the mountainous area, a large amount of water and sand flows into the Tenryu River. The residents of the basin were afraid of the Tenryu River and called it the "Violent Tenryu" (Fig. 4.2).

In 1868, Meizen submitted his proposal on the Tenryu River Flood Control Project to the new Meiji government. The proposal was to carry out full-scale river improvement work to permanently protect the river basin residents from the flood damage that caused serious suffering for many years. Meizen's enthusiasm moved the key people of the Meiji government such as Tomomi Iwakura and Takayoshi Kido, and they ordered Meizen to work on the Tenryu River flood control works.

Meizen started work on the restoration of destroyed levees by investing his own money, 800 Ryo (Ryo was a currency in the Edo period) and an additional 80,000 Ryo borrowed from shrines, temples, and wealthy families. The work was completed in two months.

For this achievement, Meizen was allowed to have a family name as well as a sword by Emperor Meiji when the emperor was on his trip to Tokyo.[1] Later, Meizen was ordered by the Hamamatsu Han to lead the Tenryu River project as project director.

Meizen was planning to close the east branch river of the Tenryu River as a drastic flood control measure. This was because sediment accumulation in a combined flow area where a branch river joined with a main river was considered to cause a bank collapse when the river levels rose. In that period, it was rumored that people who opposed Meizen's plan to close the east branch river would attack Meizen's house because the east branch river was used as a waterway to Kaketsuka Port. Eventually, Meizen had to give up the plan because he could not obtain an understanding of the residents in the river area.

After that, he came up with a new plan in which a canal leading to Lake Hamana would be excavated, the Tenryu River would be diverted, the meandering Tenryu River would be repaired, and a cobblestone embankment installed.

In 1874, Meizen established Tenryugawa-dori Teibo Kaisha (Tenryu River Embankment Company).

Meizen grasped the essence of the company as a for-profit business and a non-profit business, according to its business purpose. He took a for-profit business as a business that benefited his company as well as others, and a non-profit business was a business that benefited others without seeking its own profit. He called the company promoting non-profit business as Jikei kaisha (Charity company). Meizen stated that the Tenryu River Embankment Company was a charity company.

The following year, he renamed the company Chiga Kyoryoku Sha Company (Chiga Cooperation Company) and the company was operated mainly with capital contributions and subsidies from the Shizuoka prefecture. However, subsidies from the government were reduced due to the Seinan War.[2] In addition, the company's inability to expect dividends due to the nature of the charitable company made the company suffer a shortage of funds from the beginning.

To resolve this situation, Meizen decided to devote all his property and met with Toshimichi Okubo, the minister of Interior, who had great influence within the Meiji government. Meizen talked to Okubo in person and requested that he dispose of the entire property of the Kinpara family and use the proceeds for the riverbank protection project so the government would financially support the lack of funding. Meizen's request was accepted, and the government decided to partially shoulder the construction costs.

In 1878, Shizuoka prefectural governor accepted Meizen's request to donate his family property.

The total amount of assets that Meizen declared was 63,516 yen. Of this amount, 56,016 yen was donated to Chiga Cooperation Company, after deducting 5000 yen for the Kinpara Family's assets and 2500 yen for their living expenses and operating capital. The government promised a subsidy of 23,000 yen for ten years.[3]

As part of his efforts on flood control measures, Meizen established a school to train professionals for water controls. The school had a main course (two years) and a preparatory course (two years). In the main course, engineers for river improvement were trained by conducting on-the-job training at the embankment construction site in the Tonegawa River basin.[4] Meizen and his wife donated their assets and moved to a simple hut on the banks of the Tenryu River, which served as an office and residence called a river barn. In 1878, Meizen was granted an audience with the Emperor Meiji in this river barn when the emperor was making an Imperial tour.

In 1880, the government changed its policy and river improvement costs were to be paid from local taxes. For this reason, the grant to Chiga Cooperation Company was abolished with the 1881 grant as the last grant. The embankment construction came under the direct control of Shizuoka Prefecture, and Chiga Cooperation Company undertook only river improvement. Although the subsidies were terminated, the company's financial base was stabilized and its social reputation enhanced due to Meizen's steady management.

Many residents of the river basin, who tried to keep away from Meizen before, wished to invest in Chiga Cooperation Company, but Meizen declined all of these offers. Chiga Cooperation Company was a non-profit organization (NPO) running public works, stating that the company would conduct social business based on Article 1 of company rules enacted in 1881.

However, as the company was allowed to put the remaining funds from Shizuoka Prefecture into the capital reserve after deducting construction costs, the people who noticed this offered to invest in the hope of receiving dividends. Of course, Meizen did not use this mechanism to line his own pocket, but those whose investments offer were refused criticized Meizen by saying that he used private donations and grants to make his own money.

The residents of the river basin asked the Governor of Shizuoka Prefecture to allow them to invest in the Chiga Cooperation Company, because they could not bear Meizen monopolizing the company's profits. The prefectural governor, who was informed by the Ministry of the Interior, recommended that Meizen accept the investment from the basin residents.

Meizen understood that the purpose and policy of the project would be decided by majority vote. Those who wanted to invest in Chiga Cooperation were those who initially refused to invest. Meizen asserted that they did not properly understand the purpose of the company and he was worried that the company's funds would be diverted for wrong purposes decided by majority vote.

Meizen firmly refused to accept new investment, and in 1885 he decided to dissolve the Chiga Cooperation. Of the ¥170,000 reserve fund owned by the company, 100,000 yen equivalent to the subsidy was returned to Shizuoka Prefecture, and about 70,000 yen that the prefecture did not accept was left in the hands of Meizen. This fund was later spent on afforestation projects.[5]

Meizen held his silence on a series of criticisms. There is no evidence that he attempted to engage with the basin residents. In order for the river organization to achieve its objectives, it may have been necessary for Meizen to engage in dialogue with stakeholders in the basin. If Meizen had understood expectations, opinions, and evaluations of the people in the basin, there is a possibility that the company and the river basin community might have been integrated by reflecting them in the company's activities.

NPOs and social entrepreneurs who are leading social business today value stakeholder engagement. Although Meizen complained about the responses of the river basin residents and Shizuoka Prefecture, it is very doubtful whether the residents fully understood the philosophy and business objectives of Meizen's activities at the time because social communication was limited. So the question remains as to why Meizen avoided dialogue with the local residents.

The main projects carried out by the Chiga Cooperation Company were as follows:

(1) Comprehensive survey of the Tenryu River,
(2) Height survey from Lake Suwa to Kasjima, Futamata-town, Tenryu-ward, Hamamatsu-city
(3) Survey from Futamata Town (Tenryu-ward, Hamamatsu) to the Tenryu River Estuary
(4) Installation of Watermarks in 21 locations.

The river rehabilitation project, handed over to the government, was completed in 1899. The total construction cost reached about 660,000 yen.

2.2 *Reforestation Business*

Meizen used the 70,000 yen which was returned to him with the dissolution of the river embankment company for reforestation projects. He set out the following philosophy when he started a reforestation project.

> "Land management must first manage mountains and rivers ... The mountains of Shinshu, Enshu, and Mikawa regions, which are the water sources of rivers, are lined with bald mountains, with landslides and exposed rocks. Therefore, we need to improve this, protect and recharge the water source, and solidify the base of flood control".

Thus, Meizen devoted the remaining 40 years of his life to reforestation. The reforestation project was conducted as Meizen's private business.

Meizen inspected the Tenryu River basin by himself and determined that the government-owned forest in Tatsuyama-town, Tenryu-ward, Hamamatsu-city, would be a site for reforestation and submitted a proposal to improve the government forest in 1885 to the Ministry of Agriculture and Commerce. It was a large-scale project, planting about 2.9 million cedars and cypress trees for 15 years from 1887 to 1901. There was some objection within the government, but permission was granted with good words of Yajiro Shinagawa, vice-minister of the Ministry of Agriculture and Commerce.

In 1889, the forest in which Meizen conducted the tree planting project (Sejiri forest) was designated as a royal forest (forest owned by the Imperial Family). Meizen purchased privately owned forests adjacent to the Imperial Forest at his own expense and established the Kinpara Forestry Office as a management base. The cost of the reforestation project for the Imperial Forest was approximately 54,000 yen, and including the 36,000 yen for the Kinpara Forest, the total project cost reached 90,000 yen. The total project cost could not be covered with the returned funds when the river cooperation company was dissolved; therefore, additional funding was needed. The funds required for the reforestations were provided by the profits of the finance business and the lumber business described below.[6]

In 1890, Meizen was appointed as advisor of the Bureau of Imperial Property (Goryo-kyoku in Japanese) on the recommendation of Yashiro Shinagawa, Director of the Bureau, who was in charge of the management of the Imperial Forest. Meizen was asked to work on reforestation of the Amagi Imperial Forest in Izu in Shizuoka Prefecture. It is said that Shinagawa's intention was to show the model of a well-preserved forest and to correct the trend at the time when the public interest was not respected, giving priority to private interests. The Ministry of the Imperial Household appreciated Meizen's achievements of preserving the Imperial Forest in Sejiri and gave Meizen a pair of gold cups and a reward of 50,000 yen.

Meizen is said to have stated as follows (Fig. 4.3):

Fig. 4.3 Meizen continued his visit to the forest until the age of 92. (Source: Meizen Kinpara Memorial Hall)

> Investing in reforestation is just like bank deposits, and reforestation is more profitable than bank deposits. However, this deposit cannot be withdrawn for 100 years. Therefore the money to be invested in reforestation should be surplus money. And this surplus money comes from frugal life.

It was Meizen's spirit of hard working and helping others that supported the reforestation project that required substantial financial resources.

2.3 *Hydrophobic Business*

Meizen had a strong interest in dividing the Tenryu River and planned to open an irrigation channel connecting the Tenryu River and Lake Hamanako, located west of Hamamatsu. However, Shizuoka Prefecture opposed that plan which had many technical challenges and required huge construction costs.

In 1903, Meizen proposed to the governor of Shizuoka Prefecture that he would donate his forests and establish the Tenryu River Canal Association, which would undertake the construction of the canal from the Tenryu River. The following year, the Kinpara Canal Foundation was established, funded by 1200 hectares of forest owned by Meizen. The foundation was aimed at diverting the Tenryu River to draw irrigation water into the Mikatahara plateau, promoting agriculture, and supplying inexpensive power to improve industrial development and transportation.

However, the diversion work began only after Meizen died. In 1938, the Kinpara Canal Foundation was renamed the Kinpara Foundation for Forest Conservation and Flood Control, and with the donation from the foundation for all of the local construction costs, the construction of the Hamana drainage improvement project started. The Mikatahara Irrigation Project was completed in 1968, and the Lower Tenryu River Irrigation Project was completed in 1979.

2.4 *Project to Protect Ex-prisoners*

Meizen's desire to protect and nurture ex-prisoners came from his encounter with Ichiro Kawamura from Oita Prefecture. Meizen met with Kawamura through an introduction by Kenzaburo Okamoto, who used to serve as an official in charge of water control in the Department of the Imperial Household.[7] Okamoto met Kawamura in prison when he was imprisoned in Shizuoka Prison as a political prisoner. At the request of Okamoto, Meizen hired Kawamura at Chiga Cooperation Company. Meizen also learned through Okamoto and Kawamura about severe situations inside prisons and plights of ex-prisoners after they were released, so he established a new organization, the Kanzenkai, which aimed at protecting the ex-prisoners. The purpose of Kanzenkai was to help ex-prisoners find a path to social rehabilitation by providing them with protection, education, and placement services.

Activities of Kanzenkai started when the Hamamatsu Kanzenkai was established in Hamamatsu in 1882, and the Shizuoka Kanzenkai was established in Shizuoka in 1883. The Kanzenkai commissioned two persons in each village in Shizuoka Prefecture to serve as guardians to support ex-prisoners. In 1882, in cooperation with Kawamura, who was hired as chief of the Shizuoka Prison, Meizen established the Shizuoka Ex-prisoners Protection Company.

The former detainees transferred their income from work to the company, and the company made a reserve after it deducted some money for their cost of living. When the saved amount reached 55 yen, the entire amount was returned to the inmates, and they took the first step to live independently. Meizen's efforts became the origins of modern thought of rehabilitation and protection for ex-prisoners, and they were expanded by vigorous private sector efforts.

In 1939, a related law was enacted and rehabilitation and protection for ex-prisoners were clearly positioned as a national system.

3 Meizen's Footsteps as Entrepreneur

3.1 Transportation Industry

Meizen's mission was to use the profits from business for public interest. When discussing Meizen, we tend to focus on his social activities, but we should not forget the fact that he was an outstanding entrepreneur (Table 4.1). His reforestation activities spawned for-profit businesses such as transport and sawmills. He thought that in order for the reforestation activities to spread throughout the country, he had to show that forestry could be a viable business. Therefore, Meizen devised a business model based on inexpensive transportation systems and high-value-added sawmill technology.

In 1889, the entire Tokaido Line, a railway connecting Tokyo to Kobe Station in Hyogo Prefecture, was opened. In response, Meizen came up with an idea of a timber transport business by rail and established the Tenryu

Transport Company in 1892. When the Tenryu-River Station was opened in 1898, the company connected the Tenryu-River Station and the west bank of the Tenryu River to improve the efficiency of freight transportation.

Traditionally, wood produced from the upper reaches of the Tenryu River was collected to Kaketsuka-port in rafts and transported to various consumption areas by sea route. The development of rail transportation greatly enhanced the forestry business in the Tenryu River basin.

The Tenryu Transport Company opened branches in Shinbashi, Minami-Senju and Akihabara in Tokyo, handling timber, paper, ore, sundries, and other goods. Later, it was absorbed into Nippon Express under government control during World War II. After the war, it served as a logistics hub linking water transport and railroads. However, when the construction of a dam interrupted timber transportation by raft, it began to transport mainly gravel and oil. The rails developed by the Tenryu Transport Company operated as Nippon Express's Tenryu-River Railway until 1993.

3.2 *Lumber Industry*

Meizen worked to improve the profitability of reforestation activities by increasing the added value of timber produced from the Tenryu River basin. In 1881, the predecessor company of Tenryu Timber Co., Ltd. was founded by an executive of the Chiga Cooperation Company. The company operated a modern, mechanized sawmill powered by steam. However, it had only a few employees who were skilled in machine operations, and demand was stagnant due to the recession; eventually the company was dissolved four years after its establishment.

The company changed its name and restarted as Meizen's private business, but it could not show an indication of performance recovery. After that, the company restarted in 1907 as Tenryu Timber. The company's management was led by Meizen's students. Among them were Shinichi Suzuki, who served as one arm of Meizen and later became chairman of the Kinpara Forestry and Flood Control Foundation, and Matajuro Hirano, founder of the Shizuoka Bank. Meizen was not a shareholder or board member of the company, but he was a de facto founder.

3.3 *Banking*

The Chiga Cooperation Company deposited funds at Maruya Bank established in 1879. However, the bank was forced into bankruptcy in 1884, impacted by a recession as a result of fiscal austerity policies promoted by then Minister of Finance, Masayoshi Matsukata. The founder of the bank, Hayashi Yuteki, took over as president of the bank, and organized a credit management company with the cooperation of creditors and shareholders wishing to save the bank. Meizen played a core role as one of its creditors.

Prior to the enforcement of the commercial law, banks' shareholders had unlimited liability, forcing them to pay more than their stake in response to creditor demands. In 1886, Meizen established a credit management company called Touri Exchange Store in order to protect the receivables held by the former Maruya Bank. The Touri Exchange Store collected loans on behalf of the former Maruya Bank, and spent the collected loans to pay creditors.

In 1899, the Touri Exchange Store was reorganized into a general partnership company, Kinpara Bank, and Meizen became president. In 1917, the bank was reorganized into a joint-stock company, and Meizen's adopted grandson, Misaburo Kinpara, became president. Entering into the Showa era in 1920, when the war became more intense, the government took measures to accelerate the merger of banks in order to establish a wartime economic system. As a result, in 1940, the Kinpara Bank was merged by the Bank of Mitsubishi and closed its history.

Meizen's bank management was based on his philosophy that "money needs to be made in valueless places (urban areas) and needs to be used in valuable places (countryside)". It is clear that the valuable places referred to the Tenryu River flood control project. Virtually, the financial base of social business Meizen promoted was supported by the Kinpara Bank. Furthermore, the Kinpara Bank had as its slogan that "if you abandon selfishness, you can achieve anything".

4 Meizen Kinpara's Management Philosophy

Meizen Kinpara practiced business by spending the profits earned from commercial business for social projects. He maintained his attitude of raising social value throughout his life. His philosophy is expressed in his belief that "(1) Gaining practical interest has higher priority over honor, (2) Value practice, and (3) Place importance on outcomes and do not stick to own interests".

Meizen criticized attitudes of those who said they would start philanthropic activities or donate money after they accumulate wealth. He argued that true charity should be done at any time, regardless of how much we possess, and that the use of surplus wealth for charity while living a luxurious life is a false charity.

Shinichi Suzuki, who served as the president of the Kinpara Forestry and Flood Control Foundation, described Meizen as follows: "While he was leading a frugal life in his private life, in his work, he worked hard for the country's economic development".

Both for-profit businesses and non-profit businesses were created as the result of Meizen's hard work and saving. The strong will expressed in his words "We can't do anything alone, but someone must take the first step" is an indispensable quality for every entrepreneur.

Under his management philosophy, Meizen ultimately aimed at creating public interests while he emphasized the economy. For him, businesses were not for earning profit, but a means of realizing public interest. With his ability in business, he might have been able to succeed as an owner of local conglomerate. However, Meizen ran a profit-making business in order to obtain the funds necessary to solve social issues.

Meizen was not interested in accumulating his own wealth at all, as his action of using his entire property for the Tenryu River flood control project showed. When the business Meizen established started to take off, he gave it to others and started the next business. Many businesses established by Meizen left his hands, changed their shape, and have been succeeded to the present day.

Meizen pointed out the following four points were necessary for successful business:

(1) have a right mindset, (2) do not deceive or disturb others, (3) proceed with honesty, and (4) have good wisdom and excellent technology. Meizen's management philosophy had many elements in common with the Hotoku thought that permeated the Enshu region in Shizuoka Prefecture and had a great influence on the people who wanted to be entrepreneurs.

The characteristics of Meizen as an entrepreneur can be summarized in the following three points: (1) promoting businesses aimed at realizing the public interest, (2) emphasis on financial independence, and (3) moral sentiment controlling profit motives.

For Meizen, profit was only a means to realize moral beliefs. Needless to say, profits are necessary for the sustainable development of companies. However, business with excessive profit motives will cause adverse effects.

Today, we see scandals in many companies. Investigating the root causes of corporate scandals often leads to the lack of morality of managers and the pursuit of personal interest. It can be said that Meizen's point accurately describes the pathology hidden in modern enterprises.

Table 4.1 Social and commercial businesses established by Meizen Kinpara

Type	*Organization*	*Established*	*Business*
Social business	Chiga Cooperation Company	1875	Established as the Tenryu River Embankment Company to tackle Flood Control in the Tenryu River
	Toumi Konosha	1882	Breeding Western breeds of horses and cows
	Kinpara Forestry	1887	Reforestation project at the private forest in the upper Tenryu River basin
	Shizuoka Kanzenkai	1888	Established as a company to protect and educate ex-prisoners
	Hokkaido Kinpara Farm	1896	Reclamation and settlement in Hokkaido
	Kinpara Forest Conservation and Flood Control Foundation	1904	Started as the Kinpara Canal Foundation to work on Irrigation project by diversion of the Tenryu River
Commercial business	Tenryu Wood Co., Ltd.	1881	Lumber business
	Kinpara Bank, Ltd.	1884	Launched as the Tori Exchange Store to promote the banking business
	Nakaya store	1885	Bookbinding and printing, stationery sales. Transferred from Maruya Bank shareholders
	Maruya woodworker	1885	Sales of Western furniture. Transferred from Maruya Bank shareholders
	Izutsuya balm store	1887	Transferred from Kyoto Onoya, later became Izutsu Pomade Co., Ltd.
	Tori gumi	1888	Sales of special products of Hachijojima Island
	Tenryu Transportation Co., Ltd.	1892	Transportation. Later absorbed by Nippon Express

Source: Created by author based on various materials

Notes

1. The Edo period in Japan maintained a hierarchical class system which ranked samurai (warriors) at the top, followed by farmers, artisans, and tradesmen. Among them only the samurai class were allowed to have a surname and carry a sword and ordinary people in other classes were not allowed. However, the Edo Bakufu (Japanese feudal government headed by a shogun) sometimes gave special permission to some tradesmen to use a surname and carry a sword. Meizen Kinpara's case was a such case.
2. Seinan War was the large-scale anti-government rebellion caused by Takamori Saigo and members of his shizoku (families or persons with samurai ancestors) in Kagoshima Prefecture in 1877.
3. It is difficult to accurately convert past monetary values to present values, but various efforts have been made to calculate approximate values using various price indices. One estimate shows the monetary value in the Meiji period (1868–1912) to be approximately 3800 times the current value. Based on this estimate, the total assets of 63,516 yen that Meizen donated is now approximately 241 million yen, which is equivalent to about $2.2 million (1 USD is calculated at 110 yen).
4. The Tonegawa River is one of Japan's largest rivers flowing from north to east in the Kanto region, including the Tokyo metropolitan area, and pouring into the Pacific Ocean.
5. For grasping the monetary value in Meiji era, please see footnote 5.
6. For grasping monetary value in Meiji period, please see footnote 5.
7. An official in the Department of the Imperial Household is called "Goryokake".

References

Kawazoe, Noboru and Yamaoka, Yoshinori edited [1987] "Japanese Entrepreneurs and Social Cultural Business" Toyo Keizai Shimpo sha.

Shizuoka Prefectural Modern History Study Group [1999] "The pioneer of modern Shizuoka", Shizuoka Shimbun.

Suzuki, Seitaro [1963] "Shizuoka Kanzenkai History" Shizuoka Kanzenkai.

Suzuki, Yotaro [1966] History of the Kinpara Foundation for Forest Conservation and Flood Control" the Kinpara Foundation for Forest Conservation and Flood Control.

Suzuki, Yotaro [1979] "Meizen Kinpara: His History and Hometown", Hamamatsu Historical Site Survey Committee.

Suzuki, Yotaro [1981] "Meizen Kinpara Story", Hamamatsu Historical Site Survey Committee.

The Japan Association of Corporate Directors [2008] "Corporate Ethics Learned from the Meiji Era: Exploring CSR at the Origins of Capitalism" Japan Productivity Center Publishing.

Tsuchiya, Takao [1956] "History and Guiding Principles of Meizen Kinpara" the Kinpara Foundation for Forest Conservation and Flood Control.

Tsuchiya, Takao [2002] "History of Japanese Management Philosophy", Reitaku University Press.

CHAPTER 5

William Merrell Vories: Toward a Socio-Economic System for Mutual Support Based on Stewardship

William Merrell Vories (1880~1964). (Source: Public interest incorporated foundations Omi Brotherhood)

Achievement of William Merrell Vories and related SDGs

Economy		* Pharmaceutical business (Menterm)

(*continued*)

M. Takehara, N. Hasegawa, *Sustainable Management of Japanese Entrepreneurs in Pre-War Period from the Perspective of SDGs and ESG*, https://doi.org/10.1007/978-981-15-6507-6_5

(continued)

Society	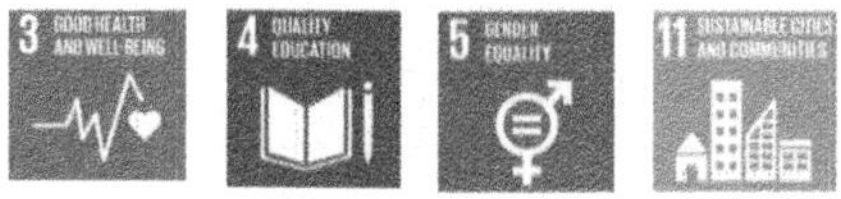	* Christian Mission (Omi Mission) * Medical care (Omi sanatorium) * Education (Omi Brotherhood School) * Architectural design (Vories architecture) * Town planning through architecture
Governance		* Practice of stewardship management * Collaboration with local residents

Source: Created by authors

1 Early Life and Formation of Thought

1.1 *Parents*

William Merrell Vories was born in 1880 in Leavenworth, Kansas, USA. Vories' father, John, graduated from a commercial school in Missouri and then moved to Leavenworth to find employment there. As his mother was a Baptist,[1] John worked at the Presbyterian Church[2] in Leavenworth.

When Merrell's mother, Julia, was a student, she wanted to become a missionary and put her efforts into missionary work in foreign countries. Although her dream didn't come true, she expected her child to become a missionary and fulfill her dream.

In 1914, Vories' parents came to Japan to reside permanently, supporting Vories and the Omi Brotherhood throughout their lives. We can get a glimpse of Vories' personality in his speech for the funeral ceremony of his father John in 1925. Vories said, "I can't imagine a father as ideal as the deceased. He always helped his son's life work and strived to promote it, and he did not care about himself at all" (Ichiyanagi [1970], p. 61).

1.2 *From Childhood to Entrance to University*

In 1888, the Vories family moved to Flagstaff, Arizona. It was Vories' father's decision to consider Vories' health. Moving to Flagstaff greatly benefited Vories' spirit and health. Vories became a paid organist at the Flagstaff School, and also became an organist at the Flagstaff Presbyterian Church.

In 1896, the Vories family moved to Denver, Colorado, and Vories enrolled in the East Denver High School. In 1900, Vories passed the entrance exam of the Massachusetts Institute of Technology (MIT) to become an architect. MIT accepted his first year at the University of Colorado[3] and allowed him to transfer from the second year.

In addition to academic activities, he joined the YMCA (Young Men's Christian Association) and the SVM (Student Volunteer Movement for Foreign Mission).[4]

In 1902, the fourth SVM World Congress was held in Canada, and Vories represented the state of Colorado. During this congress he listened to Mrs. Howard Taylor's lecture on her missionary work in China and this experience changed his life significantly.

Inspired by Mrs. Taylor's speech, Vories began to believe that his wish to be an architect was just pushing his will and ideas against God's order.

At the SVM World Congress, decision cards were distributed to the participants to confirm their will to participate in overseas missionary work. Vories signed his decision card after thinking thoroughly about his religion and future life. He added that he wished to travel to a country where missionaries had never been before and wanted to create a self-sufficient kingdom of God (Ichiyanagi [1970], p. 71). Vories gave up his initial wish to become an architect and changed his college course from his third year, and graduated from the University of Colorado with a bachelor's degree of Philosophy (PhB) in 1904.

1.3 Faith in Puritan and Missionary Mission

Vories considered the missionary mission to be in the practice of Christian life. He said, "Many businesspeople say they cannot work satisfactorily if they are tied to the Christian spirit. I want to try this out in my own life to see if this is true" (Ichiyanagi [1970], p. 72).

Vories' parents embraced the teachings of Calvinism. An important concept for the Calvinists was the view of vocation, and all occupations were regarded as sacred by God. The Calvinists believed that working in God's occupational work was a response to God's will, and that working in the profession would provide salvation (Table 5.1).

Table 5.1 The development of the Calvinist reform movement in Europe

	Region	*Name of Calvinist*
Calvinist Reform Movement (Switzerland)	England	Puritan
	Scotland	Presbyterian
	France	Huguenot
	The Netherlands	Goissen

Source: Created by the author

The Calvinists strongly denied making money, but did not deny gaining wealth by abstinently committing to employment. Rather, the "resulting wealth" of diligent vocational work was considered sacred. The wealth gained by the ascetic efforts of religion and labor in the secular was considered to be a proof of practicing neighborly love.

In his *Ethics of Protestantism and the Spirit of Capitalism*, Max Weber pointed out that the Calvinist philosophy of preaching secular abstinence with emphasis on vocational work created the spirit of capitalism.[5] Protestantism is an active asceticism that strictly regulates living attitudes toward a certain purpose, suppresses laziness and lameness, and organizes actions.

2 Christian Activities at the Shiga Prefectural Commercial School

2.1 Bible Class

In January 1905, Vories departed from the port of San Francisco and arrived at Yokohama in Japan over 19 days by steamship. He moved to Hachiman, Shiga Prefecture[6] (currently Omi Hachiman City, Shiga Prefecture) and became an English teacher at the Shiga Prefectural Commercial School (currently the Shiga Prefectural Hachiman Commercial High School).

Immediately upon arrival, Vories started to hold a Bible class and invited students to join. The Bible class was attended by students, including Etsuzo Yoshida,[7] who was involved in the formation of the Omi Mission,[8] and Yasumi Shimizu, the founder of J. F. Oberlin University.

Vories gave each student a New Testament in English, which was then expensive. Many students rushed to the Bible class to obtain the Testament.

The first Bible class was attended by 45 participants, far exceeding Vories' expectations, and the number of participants increased with each round (Yoshida [1923], pp. 18–19). As the understanding of the Bible grew, interest in Christianity grew, and the number of people who were baptized gradually increased.

2.2 Formation of YMCA and Opposition to Missionary Activities

In 1905, the members of the Bible Class formed the Christian Youth Association of Shiga Prefectural Commercial School (YMCA). The establishment of a YMCA by students at a commercial school was unprecedented in Japan. The YMCA started its activities with 38 members, including Vories, 35 students, and 2 teachers. Within a year after Vories arrived, 19 students were baptized.

The biggest reason why Vories gripped students' heart was that he had no racial prejudice and treated students as equals. However, as more people became interested in Christianity, there were many other people who did not like this situation.

As commercial school students' interest in Christianity increased, so did the Christian rejection movement. Buddhist temples felt threatened by Vories' ability to inspire students. Therefore, they organized the Young Men's Buddhist Association (YMBA), supported by affiliated temples of the Higashi Honganji temple.

With the growing influence of Vories on commercial schools and local communities, forces led by Buddhist temples urged Shiga Prefecture and the principal of the commercial school to dismiss Vories. Under such external pressure, the principal made the following demands on Vories (Kimura [2010], pp. 34–35):

1. If Vories promised that he would not perform any Christian ministry in the future, he could stay and teach at commercial schools.
2. If Vories did not stop Christian ministry, he must leave the school immediately.

For Vories, who had no option to stop religious activities, the principal's demand was virtually a notice of dismissal. Vories expressed his will to continue his missionary work and he was dismissed. What he feared most was that his ministry would fail due to the loss of income and public trust.

One of Vories' student, Etsuzo Yoshida, decided to give up going on to advanced schools and leave his future to Vories. Then Vories started to live with Yoshida.

3 The Establishment of the Omi Mission

3.1 The Night Before the Birth of the Omi Mission

With his initial missionary activities in Omi, Vories realized that his missionary mission was to build a bridge of love between God and neighbors, and that love would conquer everything. When a student at Shiga Prefectural Commercial School was asked why he was baptized, he replied, "He caught me by His love". The unwavering religion of Vories became a strong inspiration and gripped the souls of the students.

Dismissed from a commercial school, Vories devoted himself to Christian missionary work in the Omi area, based on the Yahata Christian Youth Center. Vories supported the activities of nearby churches and wrote a booklet titled *The Omi Mustard Seed*, which was sent to US supporters.

In 1910, Vories returned to the USA via Europe. On this trip, he met Albert Alexander Hyde. Hyde was the founder of Mentholatum and had a deep interest in self-sufficient evangelism in foreign countries. Hyde sympathized with Vories' self-sufficient missionary work and offered him the Mentholatum's distributorship. Thus, Omi Sales Co., Ltd. was established as an import and sales company for this mentholatum.

3.2 What Omi Mission (Omi Christian Mission) Aimed For

The Omi Christian Mission, later called Omi Mission, was launched in 1911.[9] With the establishment of Omi Mission, missionary work evolved from personal activities of members such as Vories and Etsuzo Yoshida to more organized activities.

The Omi Mission Platform was set out as follows (Yoshida [1923], pp. 89):

1. Preach the gospel of Christianity in Shiga Prefecture, regardless of denomination.
2. Do not build a church. Concentrate on missionary work.

3. Both Japanese and foreigners will live together regardless of customs, nations, races, and so on, and achieve unity.
4. Don't go to areas where missionary work is already conducted.
5. Conduct missionary activities in rural and fishing villages.
6. Train leaders.
7. Recognize that alcohol and tobacco are harmful and promote physical education and hygiene. Resolve poverty.
8. Go to a land where no one has come for missionary work.

Vories' belief is shown in the scripture, "Seek for the kingdom of God and his righteousness, and all these things will be given along" (Matthew 6:33). He aimed to build a kingdom of God on the shores of Lake Biwa, starting from Omi Hachiman.

4 The Business Structure of Omi Mission

4.1 *Outline of Business Organization*

Omi Mission's Christian activities developed with Vories General Partnership (founded in 1910) as its core organization. The company was made up of a ministry department that conducted Christian missionary work and an industry department that financed missionary work. For Omi Mission, which advocated self-sufficiency missionary work, economic independence was an important issue.

When Omi Mission was founded, the ministry department and the industry department were integrated. However, in 1920, Vories General Partnership was dissolved, and Omi Sales Co., Ltd. and Vories Architects were newly established.

Table 5.2 shows the organizations and their members right after the dissolution of Vories General Partnership (1921). The business division mainly consisted of newly established Vories Architects and Omi Sales Co., Ltd. The main product of Omi Sales was mentholatum, but its contribution to profitability was not significant as its import and sales were just started.

On the other hand, Vories Architects, an architectural firm with 25 employees (70% of the business division), played a substantial role in supporting Omi Mission's activities (Table 5.2).

Table 5.2 Organization and members of Omi Mission (1921)

Department	*Business (37)*					*Mission (15)*						*Medical (3)*	*Education (3)*	*Total*
	Architectural firm	*Omi Sales*	*Industrial dept.*	*Administration*	*publication*	*PR/ Missionary*	*General mission*	*Hachiman YMCA*	*Railway YMCA*	*Student YMCA*	*Galariya Maru*	*Omni Sanatorium*	*Playground*	
No. of staff	25	6	2	2	2	2	3	2	2	2	4	3	3	58

Source: Created by the author based on Yamagata (2002), p. 217

4.2 *Architectural Design Business*

Omi Mission's early activities were largely supported by its architectural design business. Its business philosophy was to provide buildings that would be comfortable and promote the health of residents.

Vories Architects was said to be involved in over 590 buildings between 1910 and 1945. The architectural design variations Vories Architects offered ranged from large Western buildings to small houses of 66 m^2. Vories' architectural style skillfully blended the early 1900s American and Japanese architectural designs. Its practical and affordable works gained many supporters.

Figure 5.1 shows the number of works by building year, and Fig. 5.2 shows the number of works by architecture type. Vories Architects received orders mainly for churches, schools, and private homes, but also received orders for building banks, insurance companies, and shops from the 1920s.[10]

The architectural design business was based on Christian spirit with the primary aim of fostering the health and well-being of the people who lived there. The work which combined functionality and elegance has fascinated many people to the present day.

4.3 *Mentholatum Business*

In 1913, Vories and Etsuzo Yoshida traveled to the USA on the invitation of Albert Alexander Hyde. Vories came to know Hyde on his temporary return to the USA in 1910. When they met in 1913, Hyde offered Vories the right to sell Mentholatum in Japan[11] and donated a motorboat for evangelism. Hyde was a Calvinist, as was Vories, a man with a strong belief that human value was not determined by his wealth but by his service to God.

Mentholatum's raw materials, menthol and camphor, were mainly produced in Japan. When Hyde founded Mentholatum, he pledged to devote 10% of his earnings to Christian missionary work. Ultimately, he is said to have donated up to 90% (Okumura [2005], p. 99).

Mentholatum was launched in Japan through Omi Sales Co., Ltd. Aggressive marketing activities, such as newspaper advertising, were successful, and in 1923 the company expanded its sales channels to Manchuria and the Korean Peninsula (Fig. 5.3).

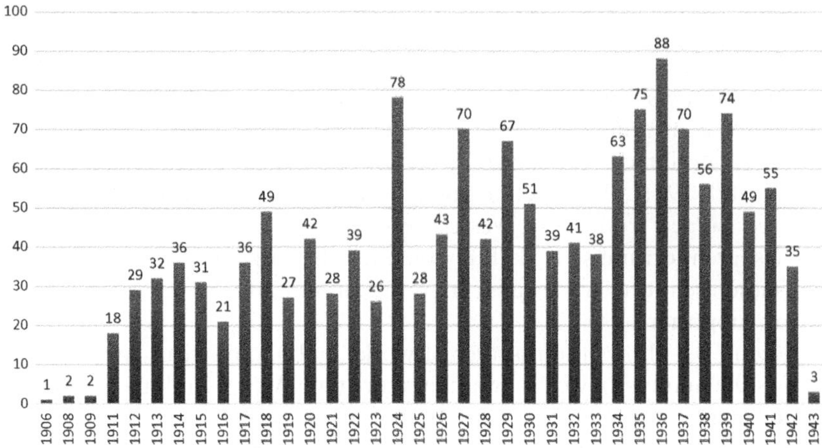

Fig. 5.1 The number of works by construction year (unit: projects). (Source: Created by the author based on Yamagata [2002], p. 235)

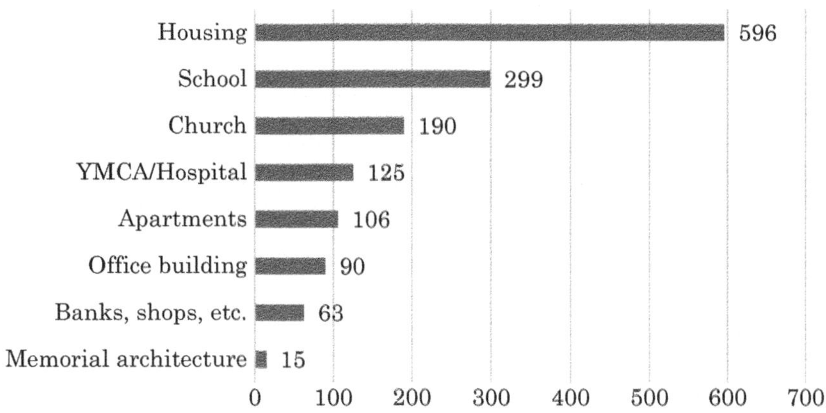

Fig. 5.2 Number of architectural works by type (unit: projects). (Source: Created by the author based on Yamagata [2002], p. 235)

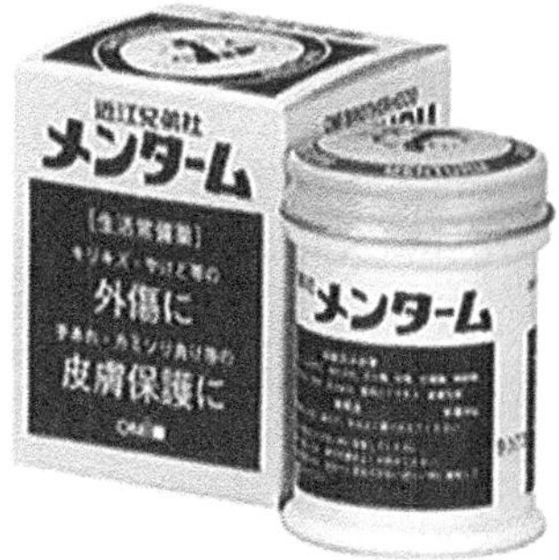

Fig. 5.3 Mentholatum (Menterm). (Source: The Omi Brotherhood Ltd.)

The articles of incorporation of Omi Sales Company stipulated that "the majority of profits were to be donated to the Omi Christian Charity Foundation (Omi Mission)" (Article 2).[12] Judging from the idea that a corporation is operated with the aim of maximizing shareholder returns, the company's operating policy deviated significantly from that of a corporation. However, the founder and investor of the company were limited to the core people of Omi Mission, and they refused external investment for the purpose of dividends; hence, this unique company was born.[13] The reason why their business philosophy was accepted by Japanese society was that it was the fusion of social justice and economic efficiency based on Christian principles.

At the heart of Vories' business philosophy was the Calvinist view of vocation. For Vories, architectural design and the sale of mentholatum were divinely given vocations, and working on those jobs was a secular abstinence. It was an ethical duty for him to build the kingdom of God by dedicating the wealth obtained from Vories Architects and Omi Sales to Omi Mission (Fig. 5.4).

Vories saw business as a social system of dealing with neighbors, a social service activity similar to education, medical care, and evangelism. In other words, for him business was not about maximizing self-interest, but about creating joint interests with stakeholders. The economic ethics practiced by merchants in Omi area (currently Shiga Prefecture where Vories settled in) are "Sampo-Yoshi", which means "good for buyer, good for seller, and good for society". This Omi merchant's philosophy shares some underlying ideas with the creation of common interests among stakeholders Omi Mission pursued.

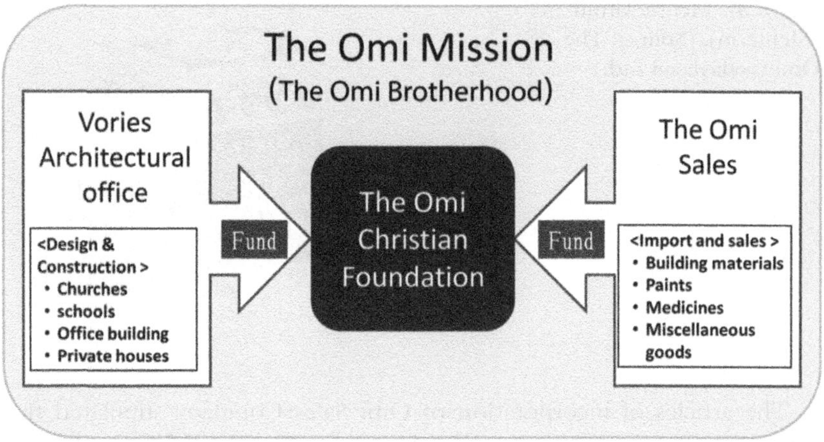

Fig. 5.4 Relationship between Omi Mission and Vories' business activities. (Source: Created by the author)

Vories and his student Etsuzo Yoshida felt the need for an organization name that clearly described the philosophy of Omi Mission. Therefore, it was named Omi Brotherhood, which meant a business organization for realizing Vories' philosophy of "Kingdom of God". It was Christian social activist and social entrepreneur Toyohiko Kagawa who came up with this name.

5 Emergence of Social Business

5.1 Establishment of Omi Sanatorium

Vories was worried that many Japanese youth were losing their lives due to pulmonary tuberculosis. In 1918, he built the Omi sanatorium to treat tuberculosis. The construction was funded by a $5000 donation from American supporter Mary Tooker,[14] while its operation was supported by revenues of Vories Architects.

Omi Sanatorium was requisitioned by the army during World War II, but resumed medical treatment after the war. The sanatorium was renamed Vories Memorial Hospital in 1971 and has continued to this day. The beds for tuberculosis were closed in 2000 after completing their role. At present, Vories Memorial Hospital provides medical care with 168 beds.

5.2 *Education*

In 1919, Vories married Makiko, daughter of Viscount Hitotsuyanagi. The two met because Makiko's older brother, Keizo Hirooka (President of Daido Life Insurance), asked Vories to design his house.

When Makiko started a new life in Omihachiman, she was concerned about the children living in a poor and unsanitary environment. In response, she rebuilt a vacant lot that was a garbage dump and made it a playground. In 1922, as part of Omi Mission education activities, Seiyuen Kindergarten was established. Later, integrating Seiyuen Kindergarten and the Omi Working Women's School, which was founded by Etsuzo Yoshida, the Omi Brotherhood School was established in 1942.

On the other hand, Etsuzo Yoshida also established the Kojo Gakuen School as a place to practice education of female employees working for the Mentholatum factory. At the school, a variety of liberal arts education was provided, including moral training, Japanese language, geography, history, childcare, nursing, natural sciences, cooking, dressmaking, physical education, and music. After the war, when the Omi Brotherhood High School was established, the school was reorganized as a part-time school, and continued until the part-time school was abolished in 1978.

Entrepreneurs who promoted employee education in those days include Tsurukichi Hatano (1858–1918) of Gunze spinning (currently Gunze Limited) and Magosaburo Ohara (1880–1943) of Kurashiki Spinning (currently Kurabo Industries Ltd). Hatano thought that creating an environment in which female workers would voluntarily work was the first step for creating high-quality products, and he actually tried to polish their abilities and personality with great affection.

Magosaburo Ohara set up an education department within the company and, with the approval of the Minister of Education, opened an elementary school in the factory. Ohara took employee education as a social reform through education, not just funding support.

Hatano and Ohara were both Christians who had been baptized and were diligent followers of Hotoku thought. They tackled issues such as improving product quality, earning profits, satisfying customers, fulfilling employees, and building good relations with local community, based on the spirit of Christianity and morality. Their altruistic philosophy has much in common with Vories' philosophy.

6 The Significance of Omi Mission

Modern enterprises are required to tackle a variety of social issues, such as climate change, resource depletion, human rights protection, and rectification of inequalities, as corporate social responsibilities in order to build a sustainable society.

Market economic mechanisms that permeate global societies do not incorporate means to control growth supremacy thinking based on the logic of capital.

In order to correct the values of modern society that is biased toward creating economic value and to propose solutions to the complex problems of the international community, we need a new approach that integrates the creation of social and economic value.

What is required of business management in the twenty-first century is to build a new relationship between business and society with sustainability as a discipline. To achieve sustainability, it is essential to shift the paradigm from a mass-production and mass-consumption society to a recycling-oriented society.

In 2011, Michael Porter advocated "Creating Shared Value". Creating shared value is a management model in which companies provide solutions to social needs and issues as a business, thereby simultaneously increasing social value and economic value (Michael E. Porter, Mark R. Kramer [2011], pp. 8–31).

Vories worked with wearing diverse hats: architect, manager, social entrepreneur, educator, and missionary. All his efforts were aimed at building a socio-economic system based on mutual support, and included the CSV element of simultaneously creating social and economic values.

Vories said that the worst sin in society was egoism and he denied any level of egoism including individuals, families, and nations (Vories [2014], p. 185). He argued that practicing a business based on Christian values required new motivations and organizations different from capitalism and socialism (Vories [2014], p. 143).

Christian values–based business can be regarded as a responsible business activity that simultaneously creates values expected by both external and internal stakeholders. The integrated value of both external stakeholders (e.g. citizens, communities, consumers) and internal stakeholders (e.g. shareholders, management, employees) can be regarded as shared value.

Michael Porter argues that "the fundamental purpose of a company should be redefined not as a mere pursuit of profits but as a creation of shared value" (Michael E. Porter, Mark R. Kramer [2011], p. 11).

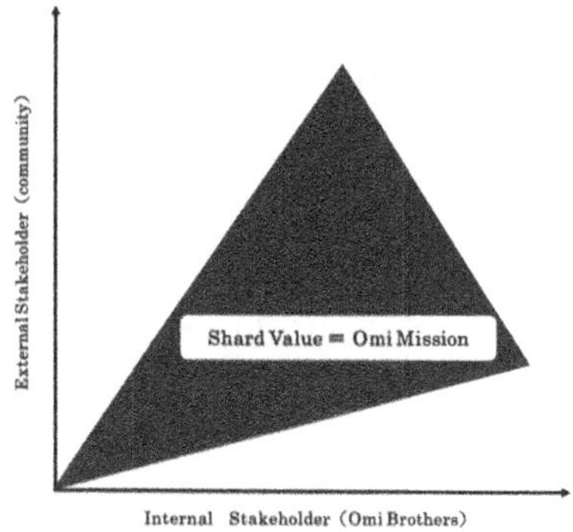

Fig. 5.5 Relationship between shared value and stakeholder value. (Source: Created by author based on Oliver Laasch and Roger N. Conaway [2014], page 98)

Creating shared value is an expression of corporate behavior that gains sympathy from society, and it has many elements in common with businesses based on Christian values set forth by Vories.

Figure 5.5 shows the framework of shared value. Each stakeholder cannot add value alone. Therefore, companies are required to cooperate with external and internal stakeholders to create shared value. This is the responsible management expected by modern society.

Vories describes the relationship between Omi Brotherhood and society in a word of stewardship. He believed that all things of monetary value belonged to God and he was only entrusted as a steward to use them for the kingdom of God. In other words, the more wealth we own, the more we are entrusted by God and the greater our obligation to use it for the public good.

Vories described the world as "country of God", which can be replaced with the word "society". In modern society, there is a view that companies are regarded as public institutions. Responsible management is not just about satisfying internal stakeholders, mainly shareholders, but is also about management that takes into account all stakeholders and aims to realize the optimization of society as a whole. This is a stewardship-based management.

Notes

1. Baptist is a Christian Protestant sect. It began in the UK in the seventeenth century. The Baptist is the largest religion in Protestant United States.
2. Presbyterian Church is a Christian Protestant Calvinist religion. The origin of the name was the adoption of the elder system in church organizations.

3. The University of Colorado was founded in 1874 as a Christian university with Evangelical personal donations.
4. The SVM was established in the University of Colorado in 1895.
5. According to Weber, the spirit of capitalism consists of the following three core components: (1) spirit of pursuing profit forever, (2) ethical feeling that imposes pursuit of profit as duty on oneself, and (3) attitude of leading a reasonable life that, if necessary, abstains, plans, and organizes one's actions to achieve the purpose.
6. Shiga Prefecture is a prefecture of Japan located in the mid-west (called Kansai region) of Japan's main island, Honshu.
7. Yoshizo Etsuzo (1890–1941) was one of Vories' students. He was baptized in 1905, abandoned school, and joined the Omi Mission.
8. The Omi Mission is a Christian missionary group Vories established in 1907.
9. Omi Mission was renamed Omi Brotherhood in 1934 and has continued its activities to this day.
10. Makiko's second brother, Keizo Hirooka, was President of Daido Life Insurance. Hirooka went on an inspection trip to the United States from April to August 1920 with Vories as he planned to construct the Daido Life headquarters building.
11. Mentholatum is currently owned by Rohto Pharmaceutical. Omi Brotherhood manufactures and sells products with similar ingredients under the product name Menterm.
12. The Omi Christian Charitable Foundation was renamed by the Omi Christian Mission in 1918.
13. In addition, it was fortunate for Omi Sales to borrow money equivalent to its capital from Kashima Bank, whose president was Keizo, Vories' wife Makiko's brother.
14. The main building of the Omi Sanatorium was named Anna Denfores Tooker Memorial Hall after her mother.

References

Hasegawa, Naoya [2011] "Japanese Business History Learned from Entrepreneurs" Yuhikaku.

Hasegawa, Naoya [2013] "Casebook on Japanese Entrepreneurs" Yuhikaku.

Hiramatsu, Ryuen [2010] "Merell Vories and Makiko Ichiyanagi: A Bridge crossed with Love" Suiyosha.

Hitotsuyanagi, Merrell [1970] "Autobiography of the Failed" Omi Brotherhood.

Kimura, Akira (2010) "The spirit of the hero who shines at home: Faith and life of the messenger of peace W. Merrel Vories", Seibo Bunko.

Kimura, Akira (2012a) "Everything is in the hands of the Lord-Faith and Freedom of Vories and Makiko", Seibo Bunko.

Kimura, Akira (2012b) "A Woman Who Established the Omi Brotherhood Academy: Makiko Ichiyanagi" Minato-no-hito.

Laasch, Oliver and Conaway, Roger [2014] "Principles of Responsible Management: Global Sustainability, Responsibility, and Ethics, 1st Edition", Cengage Learning.

Nakagawa, Keiichiro and Yui, Tsunehiko [1969] "The Business Philosophy Vol. 1, Management Philosophy: Meiji and Taisho periods" Diamond Inc.

Okumura, Naohiko [2005] "Vories Biography: an American Who Practiced 'Love your neighbor' in Japan" Shinjuku Shobo.

Okumura, Naohiko [2006] "W. Merrell Vories: Establish Kingdom of the Gods in Omi (new edition)" The Board of Publications The United Church of Christ in Japan.

Porter, Michael, Kramer, Mark [2008] "Competitive CSR Strategy", DIAMONDO Harvard Business Review January 2008, Diamond Inc.

Porter, Michael and Kramer, Mark [2011] "Creating Shared Value", DIAMONDO Harvard Business Review June 2011, Diamond.

Tsuchiya Takao [2002] "History of Japanese Management Philosophy", Reitaku University Press.

Vories, William Merrell [2014] "Sow the seeds of the kingdom of God-Christian messages" Shinkyo Shuppansha.

Yamagata, Masaaki [2002] "Vories' Western Pavilion: A Pioneer of Modern Japanese Housing," Tankosha.

Yamagata, Masaaki [2008] "100 Years of Vories Architecture: Creating a Place of Blessing" Sogensha.

Yoshida, Etsuzo [1923] "The Brothers of Omi" Omi Brotherhood.

PART III

Value Creation Through Innovation

CHAPTER 6

Jokichi Takamine: From Bioscience to the Intellectual Property Business

Jokichi Takamine (1854–1922). (Source: Sankyo Co., Ltd., "Sankyo Centennial History", 2000)

Achievement of Jokichi Takamine and related SDGs

Economy	 	* Production of artificial fertilizer * Pharmaceutical business

(*continued*)

M. Takehara, N. Hasegawa, *Sustainable Management of Japanese Entrepreneurs in Pre-War Period from the Perspective of SDGs and ESG*, https://doi.org/10.1007/978-981-15-6507-6_6

(continued)

Society	3 GOOD HEALTH AND WELL-BEING; 11 SUSTAINABLE CITIES AND COMMUNITIES; 16 PEACE, JUSTICE AND STRONG INSTITUTIONS	* Discovery of diastase (digestive enzyme) * Discovery of adrenaline (hemostatic agent) * Promotion of private diplomacy (Japan Society) * Regional development through traditional industries * Development of pharmaceutical manufacturers * Establishment of research institute for basic research
Environment	7 AFFORDABLE AND CLEAN ENERGY	* Creating local industries utilizing hydropower
Governance	10 REDUCED INEQUALITIES; 17 PARTNERSHIPS FOR THE GOALS	* Utilization of patent system * Creation of intellectual property business * Development of global business

Source: Created by authors

1 Early Life

Jokichi Takamine was born in November 1854, in Takaoka, Toyama Prefecture, as the eldest son of a Kaga clan doctor. Takamine's father, Seiichi, learned Dutch studies in Kyoto and medicine and chemistry in Edo (currently Tokyo), and then he was invited by the Kaga clan to become their doctor. Jokichi's mother, Sachiko, was from the Tsuda family, a brewer in Takaoka.

Later, Takamine worked diligently to study sake brewing methods and succeeded in developing a Takamine whiskey brewing method that used koji instead of malt. His achievement was likely made possible due to his home environment. One year after Takamine's birth, his father, Seiichi, was invited to the Kaga clan's Western-style military school (called Sokan Gyokan). The Kaga clan highly recognized Seiichi's knowledge on chemistry, so the Takamine family moved to Kanazawa. Later, in addition to being a doctor, he also served as translator and warship administrator.

In 1862, eight-year-old Takamine entered Meirindo, a training school for Kaga feudal lords. Meirindo educated the children of the feudal clan for three years, focusing on Chinese studies. In 1865, Takamine, who had studied at Meirindo, was selected by the clan and dispatched to Nagasaki for advanced study. In Nagasaki, he stayed at a residence of a Portuguese consular and entered a Western school of missionary, Guido Herman Fridolin Verbeck (the founder of Meiji Gakuin University), where he received a full-fledged English education. However, with the Meiji Restoration, students of the Kaga clan moved from Nagasaki to Kyoto.

Takamine enrolled in a training school run by Konosuke Adachi, a native of the Kaga clan who was teaching Western-style military studies in Kyoto. Takamine, who was interested in chemistry and physics instead of military science, focused on studying English at Adachi's school. The following year, Takamine enrolled in Tekijuku (school) in Osaka, headed by Ogata Koan, but Ogata Koan had already passed away at that time, and the mainstream of Western studies had moved from Dutch to English. As a result, it seems that Takamine did not absorb much from the Teki school.

In 1868, the Osaka Seimi Kyoku (Bureau) was established as a public institution to promote research, education, and industrialization in the field of chemistry in Japan after the Meiji Restoration. The following year, a science school and a medical school attached to the institution were established. In later years, Takamine entered this medical school.

While Takamine was studying at the Tekijuku school in Osaka, the Kaga clan invited Mr. Percival Osborn from Britain to open an English school in Nanao (Nanao City, Ishikawa Prefecture). Then, Takamine himself transferred to the English school, where he studied until March 1870, when Osborne's term expired. After the school closed, Takamine returned to Osaka and enrolled in the aforementioned Medical School within Osaka Seimi Kyoku (Bureau). At the medical school, he learned about chemical experiments and analysis from a German teacher, Dr. Georg Hermann Ritter. From there, Takamine's career as an applied chemist began.

However, Osaka Seimi Kyoku (Bureau) and the attached medical school were closed in 1872. Takamine had to find a new way to continue his studies. Fortunately, in November of the same year, he was accepted as a government-funded salary student of the Ministry of Industry, and in March of the following year he entered the school of engineering (called Kogaku ryo).

The Kogaku ryo (the school of engineering) was a six-year educational institution established to train technical bureaucrats to be able to work for the Ministry of Industry. The school produced a large number of competent and talented graduates in both the government and the private sector. The teaching staff was composed of professors primarily from Glasgow University, UK. Takamine was a student of the inaugural class in the applied chemistry faculty of the school. The Kogaku ryo was renamed the

Kobu Daigakko (the Imperial College of Engineering) in 1877. The school later became the Faculty of Engineering of the University of Tokyo.

The Imperial College of Engineering recruited many foreign professors; they were mainly British. The reason why British accounted for the majority of the professors was the first president of the Imperial College of Engineering, Hirofumi Ito, and other key officials had studied in the UK, and at the time, the UK had the world's highest level of industrial technologies with the Industrial Revolution.

At the Imperial College of Engineering, Henry Dyer from the University of Glasgow was appointed the head of the college, providing a curriculum based on practical experience as well as theory. At that time, the engineering technology of the University of Glasgow was said to be the highest level in the world, so Takamine received a world-class engineering education.

In 1879, 23 of the 32 inaugural-year students enrolled with government scholarships graduated.

Takamine was among six graduates of the Faculty of Applied Science. Takamine graduated at the top of his class and was selected as a government-sponsored student to study in the UK by the Ministry of Industry. In 1880, Takamine moved to the UK to study applied chemistry at Glasgow University and Andersonian University. In Newcastle, he conducted research on the production of artificial fertilizer. This experience became a great asset to him when he established an artificial fertilizer manufacturing company after he returned to Japan.

During his three years of studying in the UK, Takamine gained world-class knowledge and skills as an applied chemist. The knowledge and skills he gained from the Kobu daigakko (The Imperial College of Engineering) and studying in the UK led him to later discover Takadiastase and extract crystals of adrenaline.

2 From Bureaucrats to Entrepreneurs: Establishment of Tokyo Artificial Fertilizer Co.

In 1883, Takamine returned to Japan from the UK and started to work for the Bureau of Industry, Ministry of Agriculture and Commerce. Takamine was interested in Japanese paper production, indigo production, and sake brewing, and promoted domestic procurement of all ingredients. He also devised a method to prevent the spoilage of sake, which was later patented as the "Liquid Preservation Method and Device".[1]

In 1884, the World Exposition was held in New Orleans, the USA, which also served as the Cotton Centennial Festival. Takamine was ordered to be a secretary of the Japanese delegation and traveled to the USA, where he stayed for about a year. During this time, he was engaged to Caroline Hitch, the eldest daughter of the Hitch family. Takamine lived at their house.

Takamine focused on the phosphate rock exhibited at the expo. He brought lime superphosphate and its raw phosphate rock back to Japan to study artificial fertilizer. When Takamine was studying in the UK, he was conducting research on the production of artificial fertilizer. He believed that the development of artificial fertilizers was urgently needed to increase Japan's agricultural productivity.

In September 1885, Takamine returned to Japan from New Orleans and became a staff member of the monopoly patent office (renamed the Patent Office in 1886) while he was concurrently holding the position in the Bureau of Industry, Ministry of Agriculture and Commerce. Takamine was involved in improving the foundation of the Japanese patent policies.

In those times, Takamine began to seriously consider setting up an artificial fertilizer manufacturing company. He knew that man-made fertilizer production was feasible, as he had mastered the method of producing artificial fertilizers when he was studying in the UK, and he had already obtained the phosphate rock used as a raw material for phosphate fertilizers.

Takamine met Eiichi Shibusawa[2] and Takashi Masuda[3] of Mitsui & Co. who were leading players in the industrial community in Japan at that time, emphasizing the need for production of artificial fertilizers for the development of Japanese agriculture. As a result, both Shibusawa and Masuda began to support Takamine's business plan.

In February 1887, a preparatory organization for the establishment of Tokyo Fertilizer Co., Ltd. was started. Eiichi Shibusawa was appointed as president, and Jokichi Takamine was appointed as chief engineer and production manager. In March of the same year, Takamine traveled to Europe and the USA to purchase machines and raw materials for the production of artificial fertilizer. During his trip, he officially married Caroline Hitch in New Orleans.

In December 1887, the Tokyo Fertilizer Co., Ltd. was officially established, and full-scale production of artificial fertilizer began in September of the following year. The company is now the Nissan Chemical Industry Co., Ltd. In March 1888, after working for about five years, Takamine resigned from the Ministry of Agriculture and Commerce, and started to take a path as a researcher and entrepreneur. Eiichi Shibusawa highly valued Takamine's ability as an entrepreneur, saying, "He is originally a scholar, but he also has the talent to handle the business".

3 R&D Activities and Entrepreneurship in the US: Discovery of Takadiastase and Adrenaline

3.1 *Development of the Takamine Brewing Method*

With the establishment of the Tokyo Fertilizer Co., Ltd., Takamine took the first step as an entrepreneur. He opened a private laboratory adjacent to the factory and began researching alcohol fermentation. He first attempted to replace malt with rice koji (rice mold) as the raw material for whiskey production. Rice koji was used for sake brewing. Brewing sake and distilled whiskey had completely different production methods. Takamine noted that alcohol fermentation in the early stages of the manufacturing process is common to both sake and whisky.

In the production of whiskey, malt obtained by germinating barley is used, and saccharifying enzymes such as diastase contained in the malt degrade barley starch to sugar. When yeast is added and fermented, the sugar changes to alcohol.

Although koji (rice mold) used for sake brewing had a lower saccharification ability than malt, it had the advantage that saccharification and alcohol fermentation could be processed in parallel, and it had higher alcohol fermentation ability than yeast. Furthermore, Takamine's method utilized husk as a raw material for fermentation. The husk was disposed of as waste in the traditional whiskey manufacturing process. Takamine's method made it possible to significantly reduce manufacturing costs compared to conventional methods.

Whiskey Trust, which had a 95% share of the US whiskey brewing industry, paid attention to Takamine's production method. The company offered Takamine an experimental facility, and Takamine accepted the offer. However, many people, including Shibusawa, expressed opposition against Takamine's will to resign from the Tokyo Fertilizer Co., Ltd. as the company was just established and Takamine was playing the central role.

Eventually, the mediation efforts of Mitsui & Co.'s Masuda Takashi and others succeeded, so in 1890, Takamine successfully left Tokyo Artificial Fertilizer Company and moved to the USA. The following year, Takamine succeeded in experimenting with a distillation method using koji, and he applied for patents in the USA and the UK.[4]

Whiskey Trust's president, Joseph Greenhut, strongly supported the Takamine method. However, he faced strong opposition from the company's shareholders who felt threatened by the Takamine method. Most of the shareholders were the owners of malt-based brewing companies.

Opponents held a shareholders' meeting and resolved the dissolution of Whiskey Trust, as the ultimate means of preventing the Takamine method. As a result, commercialization of the whiskey manufacturing business using the Takamine method was abandoned.

Losing the way to commercialize the whiskey production with his new method, Takamine established the Takamine Ferment Company in Chicago. The company aimed at utilizing the patent rights that Takamine acquired through his R&D efforts to obtain royalties. Takamine obtained a license of the US patent attorney and applied numerous patents for his research findings.

3.2 Discovery of Takadiastase

With the strong opposition from malt-based brewing companies, the whiskey manufacturing business was abandoned. As a result, Takamine shifted his research focus from brewing to pharmaceutical manufacturing. In the course of his research on whiskey brewing with koji (rice mold), he discovered a rice mold that secreted an enzyme (diastase) that had a much stronger starch digestibility.

Diastase is a digestive enzyme that promotes the breakdown of starch and glycogen into sugars. In 1833, Anselme Payen (1795–1871) and Jean François Persoz (1805–1868) of France first successfully separated diastase from malt.

Until then, it was believed there was only one type of diastase, but the discovery of Takamine revealed the existence of another type of diastase which had higher saccharification ability. In 1894, Takamine succeeded in extracting this enzyme and named it Takadiastase (or Taka-diastase). And he obtained patents for the Takadiastase manufacturing method in the USA and the UK.

While obtaining a patent for Takadiastase, Takamine was also thinking about commercializing it. In 1897, the Detroit-based Park Davis Company

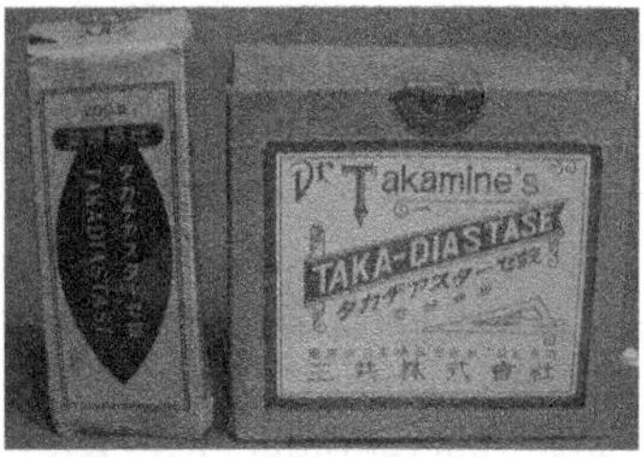

Fig. 6.1 Takadiastase (Taka-diastase). (Source: Daiichi Sankyo Co., Ltd.)

acquired the right to manufacture Takadiastase and market it globally except in Japan, making it a worldwide brand.

Takadiastase was widely used as a component of stomachic drugs because of its digestive promoting effect. In Japan, pharmaceutical companies such as Sankyo Co., Ltd. launched Takadiastase as a gastric drug (Fig. 6.1).

3.3 Extraction of Crystal of Adrenaline

In the 1890s, the Western medical community was focusing on the effects of animal adrenal glands. It was long known that the animal's adrenal gland had an effect of increasing hemostasis and increasing blood pressure. Extracting crystalline substances of adrenal hormone was the largest research theme in medical and pharmaceutical communities. At the time, the leading researchers in this field were Otto von Fürth (1867–1938) in Germany and John Jacob Abel (1857–1938) in the USA, and each of them announced substances with completely different chemical structures. There was no definitive conclusion in the academic community about which claim was correct.

In 1897, the Park Davis Company, which partnered with Takamine to manufacture and sell Takadiastase, commissioned Thomas Bell Aldrich (1861–1938), Abel's assistant, and Takamine to conduct an experiment to extract crystalline substance of adrenal hormone. Takamine's research was conducted at the Takamine Research Laboratory in New York, but had no success for the first two years. Takamine's specialty was in the field of fermentation; he was not necessarily a specialist in crystallization.

In 1899, Keizo Uenaka (1876–1960), who graduated from the Department of Pharmacy, the University of Tokyo medical school, came to the Takamine Research Institute as an assistant. Uenaka greatly contributed to breaking this stalemate. He left an experimental notebook (July 20 to November 15, 1900) detailing the experiment for extracting crystal materials of adrenal hormone.

The crystalline material obtained from his experiments had a completely different chemical structure than that of Fürth or Abel mentioned earlier. Takamine named this crystalline substance adrenaline and filed a patent application in the USA on November 5, 1900. He also filed a patent application in the UK on January 22 of the following year.

The discovery of Uenaka's experimental notes proved that the successful extraction of adrenaline was substantially Uenaka's achievement. Takamine introduced Uenaka as a research collaborator in some English papers and oral presentations in the USA, but when Takamine submitted his PhD dissertation to the University of Tokyo in 1906, he did not mention Uenaka's name. In addition, all of the adrenaline patent applications mentioned above were filed under Takamine's sole name and the presence of Uenaka was completely erased.

Uenaka retired as an auditor of the Sankyo Co., Ltd.[5] as his last job in 1933. He did not publish his notebook while he was alive and never expressed any complaint against Takamine. The extraction of adrenaline crystals was a joint achievement between Takamine and Uenaka. If Takamine intentionally erased Uenaka's name from his research work, it would not have been appropriate.

In Japan, the adrenaline that Takamine and Uenaka successfully crystallized was officially named epinephrine. The same name was adopted in the USA, and the name of adrenaline was used only in Europe. Epinephrine was the name of a substance announced by US chemist Abel as a crystalline substance of adrenaline prior to Takamine.[6]

In 1927, Abel claimed in his reminiscence that Takamine and Uenaka plagiarized his research findings on adrenaline. At this time, Takamine passed away, and Uenaka's experimental notebook was not yet disclosed. With the influence of Abel's reminiscence, the name of adrenaline disappeared in the USA, and epinephrine became a common name.

It is now clear that Abel's claim is completely groundless, given the discovery of Uenaka's experimental notebook. Under the amended Japanese Pharmacy Act announced in 2006, epinephrine was changed to epinephrine adrenaline. Takamine and Uenaka's achievements, which were allegedly suspected, were finally able to regain their honor 107 years after their discovery.

The rights to sell Takadiastase and adrenaline globally were owned by the Park Davis Company with the exception of Japan. The reason for

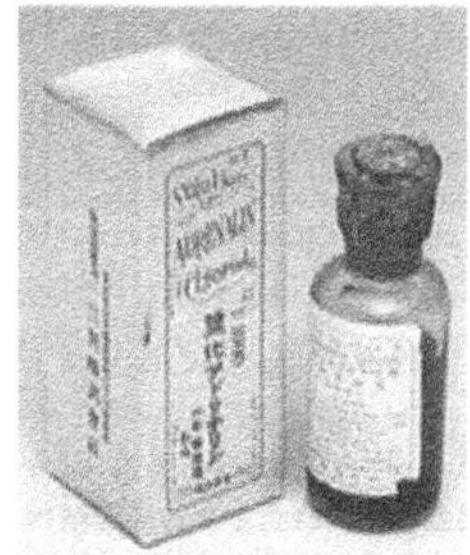

Fig. 6.2 Adrenaline. (Source: Daiichi Sankyo Co., Ltd.)

excluding Japan was Takamine's desire that sales of Takadiastase and adrenaline in Japan were to be conducted by Japanese. In fact, the right to sell in Japan was acquired by Sankyo (currently Daiichi Sankyo Co., Ltd.), which was founded by Matasaku Shiobara and others. Sankyo Shoten was reorganized into a joint-stock company in 1913, and Takamine was appointed as the first president, and Takadiastase and adrenaline were fully manufactured in Japan (Fig. 6.2).

4 Later Life

Takamine established a business model that transformed discoveries and inventions acquired through research activities into intellectual property with the patent system. Also, he actively made policy recommendations about the development of medicine and chemistry and industrial promotion.

One example is the recommendation of the establishment of the National Science Institute in 1913 as a national research institution for fostering scientists and promoting industry. This proposal was supported by many businesspeople, including Eiichi Shibusawa. As a result, RIKEN was founded in 1917 with Shibusawa as the founder's representative. Today, RIKEN is the only natural science research institute in Japan that conducts research in a wide range of fields, including physics, engineering, chemistry, biology, and medicine.

Takamine also proposed the commercialization of aluminum production using casting technology, a traditional local industry in his hometown of Toyama Prefecture. He made this recommendation because Toyama Prefecture had many rapid rivers and therefore was suitable for hydropower generation. At present, Takaoka City, Toyama Prefecture, is a major base of the Japanese aluminum industry.

Takamine also focused on developing Japan-US friendship, because of his success as a chemist and entrepreneur in the USA. At the World Exposition in St. Louis in 1904, when the Russo-Japanese War broke out, he hosted a party and invited US influential figures. The following year, in 1905, he helped the establishment of the Japan Society in New York, making it a base for celebrities' interaction between the USA and Japan. Takamine's efforts to promote friendship between Japan and the USA played an important role in deepening American society's understanding of Japan.

Finally, we would like to look back on Takamine's life from the perspective of an R&D venture. In the first half of Takamine's life, he succeeded in commercializing his research findings as intellectual properties. On the other hand, in the latter half of his life, he struggled to find new technology seeds due to a decline in R&D capabilities because of lack of human resources.

Takamine strongly recognized that fostering scientists and developing science and technology were indispensable for promoting industry. However, Takamine Laboratories, which served as a research and development center in his later life, had no breakthrough achievements since the discovery of adrenaline. This may be due to the shift of Takamine's focus to social activities, but the direct cause of the slump in research results was that he could not attract young capable researchers such as Uenaka.

Takamine died in New York in 1922. He was 67 years old. His body was buried in the Woodlawn Cemetery in New York. His achievements were praised as follows: "In 1896, Dr. Takamine developed a starch-degrading enzyme and was admired as the father of modern biotechnology. In 1900, he separated adrenaline for the first time in the world. In 1912, he donated cherry trees beautifying the banks of Washington, D.C."

Takamine's philosophy was handed over to Matasaku Shiobara who founded the pharmaceutical company Sankyo Company. Shiobara offered the opportunity for commercialization to Japanese scientists who made good discoveries but were not recognized. He also actively promoted the transfer of intellectual property obtained from medical and chemistry research to industry (Table 6.1).

Table 6.1 Trend in profit and capital during the founding period of Sankyo Co., Ltd. (Unit: yen)

Year		*Profit*	*Capital*
1899	1st half	1000	859
	2nd half	1060	1500
1900	1st half	1495	1950
	2nd half	1615	3000
1901	1st half	2111	3000
	2nd half	3918	3000
1902	1st half	5830	3000
	2nd half	4698	15,000
1903	1st half	2191	18,000
	2nd half	3996	30,000
1904	1st half	2789	30,000
	2nd half	3360	30,000
1905	1st half	4106	30,000
	2nd half	11,134	100,000
1906	1st half	10,557	120,000
	2nd half	18,293	300,000
1907	1st half	32,541	300,000
	2nd half	14,555	187,500
1908	1st half	41,727	250,000
	2nd half	51,650	312,500
1909	1st half	42,552	375,000
	2nd half	34,790	500,000
1910	1st half	35,643	500,000
	2nd half	38,580	500,000
1911	1st half	96,583	1,000,000
	2nd half	50,914	1,000,000

Source: Author created based on Sankyo Co., Ltd. (1960), "Sankyo 60 Years History" pages 38

Note: Takadiastase launched (1899) and Adrenaline launched (1902)

5 Conclusion

Jokichi Takamine was a first-generation applied chemist who received state-of-the-art European and American education right after the Meiji Restoration which began in 1868. He was highly skilled in the discovery of Takadiastase and crystallization of adrenaline. In addition, he succeeded as an entrepreneur by commercializing these scientific achievements. Even today, Takamine is highly regarded as the first bio-venture entrepreneur in Japan.

Takamine was an outstanding chemist before becoming an excellent entrepreneur. The most important thing for an R&D-type venture is the innovative discoveries and invention that form the core of the business. In the case of Takamine, discoveries of Takadiastase and adrenaline through R&D became the core competence of his business. Even if one has good entrepreneurial qualities, it is difficult to succeed in an R&D venture business unless he or she can grasp the innovative seeds.

R&D investment plays an important role in increasing corporate value through the creation of innovation. To achieve this, it is important to commercialize the seeds acquired through R&D.

In this regard, Takamine's histories of entrepreneurial activities give us many valuable lessons.

One of the hallmarks of Takamine's entrepreneurial activities was his deep understanding about the importance of intellectual property (knowledge). He was fully aware of the importance of intellectual property in business from his experience of working at the Patent Office. Therefore, by turning his discoveries and inventions into intellectual property, he succeeded in establishing a business model with knowledge as its core competence.

The purpose of Takamine's active use of patents was not to obtain a huge amount of wealth by earning huge royalties, but to secure the funds needed for the next R&D. For Takamine, making money was not a purpose, but merely a means to promote research and development.

Finally, we need to add the difficulties of succession of a R&D-type venture company. Takamine was not blessed with a successor. Successors who are expected to further develop the R&D venture companies must have the qualities of both excellent researchers and entrepreneurs. However, there are very few people who have both research ability and entrepreneurial qualities. Therefore, to date, Takamine has been the role model of R&D venture entrepreneurs.

Notes

1. Takamine's mother's family ran the brewing business.
2. Shibusawa Eiichi (1840–1931) was a leading figure in the development of Japan's modern society. In the late Edo period, Shibusawa served the

Tokugawa shogunate and was acquainted with the socio-economic situation of advanced European countries. After the Meiji Restoration which began in 1868, he worked for the Ministry of Finance and was involved in the establishment of the Daiichi (first) National Bank, and focused on the creation and development of stock companies. He was involved in establishing about 500 enterprises and 600 organizations for social welfare and education.
3. Takashi Masuda (1848–1938) became the first president of Mitsui & Co. when he was 29 years old. He created a new business form called a general trading company. He also launched Chugai Price Shimpo, the predecessor company of the Nihon Keizai Shimbun (Nikkei, Inc.).
4. Takamine obtained patents in the UK in 1887, France and Belgium in 1888, and the United States in 1889.
5. Sankyo Co., Ltd. later became Daiichi Sankyo Co., Ltd., one of the major pharmaceutical companies in Japan.
6. Epinephrine discovered by Abel is a substance with a different molecular structure from adrenaline, and it was found that epinephrine cannot be extracted by Abel's method.

References

Arai, Toshimitsu [1998] "Patents support venture business" Invention Association

Iinuma, Nobuko [1993] "Jokichi Takamine and His Wife" Shin Jinbutsu Orai sha.

Iinuma, Kazumasa, Sugano, Tomio [2000] "The Life of Jokichi Takamine", Asahi Shimbun.

Ishii, Tadashi [2005] "History and modern times of intellectual property: Historical approach to the intersecting area of economy, technology and patents.

Manabe, Shigeki [1999] "A Grand Dream" Kodansha.

Sankyo Co., Ltd. [1960] "Sankyo 60 years history".

Sankyo Co., Ltd. [2000] "Sankyo Centennial History".

Seki, Ken [2003] "Innovation in Modern Japan-Patents and Economic Development" Fuko-sha.

Ueyama, Akihiro [2004] "Portrait of Japan as an Invention-driven nation" Bungei shunju.

Yamashima, Tetsumori [2001] "Jokichi Takamine, a pioneer in science in Japan" Iwanami Shoten.

Yamashita, Aiko [2000] "A Biography of Jokichi Takamine: 100th anniversary publication of adrenaline discovery" Yushodo.

CHAPTER 7

Sakichi Toyoda: No Product, No Invention

Sakichi Toyoda (1867–1930). (Source: National Diet Library)

Achievement of Sakichi Toyoda and related SDGs

Economy	8 DECENT WORK AND ECONOMIC GROWTH	9 INDUSTRY, INNOVATION AND INFRASTRUCTURE	* Automatic loom business * Weaving fabric business * Develop infrastructure for vehicle production

(*continued*)

M. Takehara, N. Hasegawa, *Sustainable Management of Japanese Entrepreneurs in Pre-War Period from the Perspective of SDGs and ESG*, https://doi.org/10.1007/978-981-15-6507-6_7

(continued)

Society		* Improve productivity through development of power loom * Support for working-style reform of workers * Promotion of R&D * Strict quality control * Utilization of patent system * Creation of intellectual property business * Development of global business
Governance	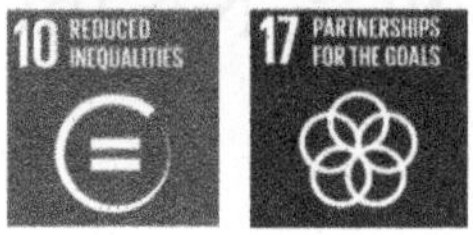	

Source: Created by authors

1 Early Days

It was process innovation through Kaizen—aiming at improving quality and reducing costs—that supported Japan's post-war rapid economic growth. On the other hand, Japanese companies have not been very good at product innovation that creates original technology and products.

In order for the Japanese economy to maintain sustained growth, it is necessary for businesses to promote product innovation.

Sakichi Toyoda, who was a founder of the Toyoda Group, invented the automatic loom for the first time in Japan, being inspired by an engineer who supported the Industrial Revolution in the UK.

In the early Showa period, in elementary school textbook, Toyoda was portrayed as a success story and a hero. In this chapter, we will look back on Toyoda's activities and explore the characteristics of entrepreneurs who succeeded in creating product innovation.

Sakichi Toyoda was born in 1867 in present-day Kosai City, Shizuoka Prefecture, located on the west coast of Lake Hamana (Hamana-ko). The Toyoda family was engaged in agriculture, but their land was not large, and it was difficult for them to make a living from agriculture alone.

For this reason, Sakichi's father, Ikichi Toyoda, became a carpenter seeking a livelihood other than agriculture. Sakichi's father was a craftsman with a sense of responsibility and ethics. He was a devout believer of Nichiren-shu (a school in Buddhism), a traditional Japanese religion, and he believed in Hotoku thought[1] as his life creed. Sakichi Toyoda sincerely worked on technical development throughout his life. It seems the formation of his professional ethics was influenced by his father.

Sakichi Toyoda began helping his father with carpentry at the age of 13, and he rapidly grew to become the right-hand of his father in just two years. Sakichi received regular education until elementary school. He did not receive regular education after graduating from elementary school, but he was very keen on obtaining new knowledge. Therefore, he held an independent study meeting every night with his comrades aged between 18 and late 20s and had a lively exchange of opinions.

It is said that Sakichi Toyoda began to work on the development of automatic looms in earnest after he read and was inspired by a translation of Samuel Smiles' *Self Help* (1870) (the book was titled *Saigoku-risshi-hen* in Japanese).[2] Also, he was encouraged by promulgation of newly established Patent Monopoly Ordinance of 1885.

S. Smiles' *Self Help* was translated into Japanese by Masanao Nakamura as *Saigoku-rishi-hen* and became the best-selling book with one million copies issued throughout the Meiji period. The book explained the importance of the spirit of self-reliance as symbolized by the words "Heaven helps those who help themselves".

Saigoku rishi hen was an enlightenment book that had a great influence on the citizens who were liberated from the feudal status system by the Meiji Restoration.

The book repeatedly stated that people can always succeed if they have ambitions and make continuous efforts. The book explains that the happiness of life comes from diligence and self-learning and maximizing the happiness of the people who make up society, by drawing on the numerous entrepreneurial activities that supported the Industrial Revolution.

On the other hand, the Patent Monopoly Ordinance of 1885 was promulgated as the first patent law in Japan. In the era when the patent system did not exist, Gaun Tatsumune,[3] who invented a pure Japanese-style spinning machine, received an award at the first National Trade Fair held in 1877. Ironically, however, this resulted in domestic traders copying his spinning machine. Moreover, because these imitators advertised that they invented this spinning machine, Gaun was pressed for daily living expenses.

Saigoku rishi hen stated that the patent system protected the rights of inventors and this became the driving force of the Industrial Revolution. Toyoda earnestly read the book and fully understood the significance of the Patent Monopoly Ordinance.

A biography about Toyoda stated the following story:

> Sakichi happened to visit a primary school to help his father's work and heard a class discussing the "Saigoku rishi hen". He borrowed the book from a primary school teacher. Also, he learned about the Patent Monopoly Ordinance from the teacher and was very inspired. These experiences drove him to a series of innovative inventions.

The biography says that Toyoda was especially influenced by James Hargreaves,[4] who developed a multi-spinning machine (spinning jenny) and patented it. Hargreaves too was from a poor carpenter family. This story was introduced in Japanese elementary school language textbooks in the early Showa era, and has been handed down to this day as an episode that inspired Sakichi to invent innovative products.

However, according to Hirakawa (2006), it became clear that the episode that has been told in Toyoda's biography is fiction. The episode first appeared in 1931 in a book, *The Loom Tycoon Toyoda*, written by Matsusaburo Yora. Since then many Toyoda biographies followed its description, so it was taken as a fact.

Even if the episode about Toyoda's encounter with *Saigoku rishi hen* was fiction, it is highly likely that Toyoda read the book. *My Record of Invention*, which Toyoda authored, described that in 1884, Toyoda tried to join the Enshu Futamata Spinning Company, which was established as a spinning mill by the Meiji government for the purpose of promoting industrial development, but he failed. The Enshu Futamata Spinning Company was founded by Ryoichiro Okada, President of Dainippon Hotokusha based in Kakegawa City, Shizuoka Prefecture. It was one of ten spinning companies established throughout the country. Okada explained the significance of entrepreneurial activities by citing the cases of James Watt[5] and Richard Arkwright[6] who were introduced in *Saigoku rishi hen*.

As Sakichi Toyoda was an enthusiastic follower of Hotoku thought, it is possible that he came to know about the *Saigoku risshi hen* through Okada's writings and lectures. Okada developed the philosophy of Hotoku thought originally promoted by Sontoku Ninomiya and emphasized the significance of integrating economy and morality and advocating the idea that the pursuit of economic rationality led to the moral completion of entrepreneurs.

Okada aimed for economic independence in the Enshu region through the cultivation of the spinning and cotton fabric industries. As a result of this influence, many automatic loom manufacturers were established in the Enshu region such as Toyoda Loom Industries established by Sakichi Toyoda and Suzuki Loom industries established by Michio Suzuki (founder of predecessor company of Suzuki Motor Corporation).

Sakichi Toyoda began to develop a power loom while receiving direct and indirect influences from Hotoku Thought and "Saigoku risshi hen". However, as Toyoda was still an amateur at this time, he couldn't develop a power loom overnight. Therefore, for the time being, he focused on improving manual looms to enhance productivity. Thus, Toyoda's more than 40 years' research and development activities began.

2 Development of the Power Loom

In 1890, the third National Industry Fair was held in Tokyo. At the first exposition, the above-mentioned Gala spinning machine invented by Tatsumune Gaun attracted attention and spread nationwide. Toyoda has an anecdote that he visited the exposition hall every day and was suspected by guards. It is considered that Toyoda lacked mechanical engineering expertise and was unable to understand by just looking at the exhibited machines.

After returning home, Toyoda made the first wooden human-powered loom as his first invention (Fig. 7.1). This loom was an improvement over the traditional hand-woven loom, called the "Battan loom", and it gained a reputation for its efficiency that was 40–50% higher than the previous loom. In 1891 Toyoda acquired the first patent for this invention.

Toyoda established a weaving factory in Tokyo to manufacture this wooden human-powered loom. He had to secure funds to develop the power loom. However, the development of the power loom did not proceed as expected, and the management of the weaving factory was stalled. In 1893, Toyoda returned to his hometown. The following year, his eldest son Kiichiro was born. Even after returning to his hometown, Toyoda continued his research in the room all day long, but the development of the power loom was slow. His wife, Tami, was tired of living with research-centric Toyoda and left him, leaving the little Kiichiro.

Fig. 7.1 Wooden human power loom. (Source: Toyota Motor Corporation website)

Despite this situation, in 1895, Toyoda succeeded in developing a yarn knitting machine (reeling machine), his second invention. The yarn knitting machine was a necessity for farmers who made woven fabric as their side business, but conventional products were operated by hand and were difficult to handle. Toyoda made a foot-operated (pedaling) yarn knitting machine and succeeded in improving the efficiency by two or three times. This yarn knitting machine was very well received and achieved great business results.

As Toyoda was able to rebuild his financial base with the success of the yarn knitting machine, he went to Nagoya and began selling this product in earnest. Utilizing the funds he obtained, Toyoda resumed his research on power looms. Toyoda succeeded in developing the wood-iron mixed power loom in 1897, two years later (Fig. 7.2). The invention of the yarn knitting machine became a turning point in the development process of the power loom.

Fig. 7.2 Wood-iron hybrid automatic loom. (Source: Toyota Motor Corporation website)

Becoming financially stable with the success of the yarn knitting machine, Toyoda conducted a field survey of the looms used in regions from Enshu to Aichi Prefecture. Toyoda studied the actual situation of small and medium-sized farmers using looms, listened to their requests, and addressed them in the development of power looms.

After repeated weaving experiments using prototypes, the first Toyoda-style wood-iron mixed power loom was completed around the summer of 1897 in Japan. Toyoda obtained a patent for this product the following year.[7] Toyoda succeeded in producing a power loom as a modern machine seven years after he developed the wooden manpower loom.

Although a power loom was developed by Toyoda, the production of hand looms was the mainstream in the weaving industry at that time, and there was much demand for inexpensive wooden man-powered looms. Although constructions of some large-scale weaving factories were planned, the prospect of its realization was not feasible. And Toyoda himself did not have enough funds to start commercial production of power looms, so he did not have an opportunity to stimulate demand for power looms.

Amid this situation, Tohachi Ishikawa, a middle merchant in Aichi Prefecture, who was a yarn knitting machine customer, suggested that Toyoda establish a weaving company using a Toyoda wooden power loom. Ishikawa carried out a business of bringing yarns to the farmers and having them weave and buy the fabric. Toyoda agreed with Ishikawa's proposal under the condition that Ishikawa pay for the construction cost of the weaving factory and Toyoda provide 60 power looms he developed. Thus, the Otsukawa Cotton Cloth joint-stock company was established in 1897.

Because the cotton fabric produced by the Otsukawa Cotton Fabric was uniform in quality, it attracted the attention of Mitsui & Co., Ltd., the purchaser of the cotton fabric. It was common that the quality of fabric conventional human-powered looms made was not uniform, but the fabric made by Otsukawa Cotton Fabric did not have such unevenness. Mitsui dispatched their staff to Otsukawa Cotton Fabric, and they found out that the secret was the power loom developed by Toyoda.

As Mitsui promoted power looms, Toyoda quickly became known to the public as an inventor of power loom. Demand for power looms from small- and medium-sized craftsmen increased day by day, and the Otsukawa Cotton Fabric Joint Stock Company developed steadily. Toyoda decided to give his shares of interests to Ishikawa and concentrate on manufacturing looms and research and development.

In Japan at that time, the main power source of power looms was hydropower. The Industrial Revolution in the UK was powered by a steam engine using coal as an energy source. In Japan in the early Meiji period, as coal was expensive, hydropower using a turbine was the main energy source. However, hydropower had a fatal flaw as a power source in that it was difficult to secure stable power. The failure of the Enshu Futamata spinning company, which Toyoda once tried to join, was due to its inability to effectively use the hydropower of the Tenryu River.

Then Toyoda newly developed an oil engine–driven loom to solve the power source problems, which prevented the spread of power looms. The development of this oil engine–driven loom became a factor that accelerated the spread of power looms in the Enshu region.

As mentioned earlier, Mitsui & Co. was first interested in Toyoda's power looms. Let's look back on the background of Mitsui's interest in power looms.

At that time, the Meiji government was worried about the processing of "Gun-pyo", a military note issued in Manchuria during the Sino-Japanese War. Gun-pyo was a bill issued by the Japanese military in the battlefield or occupied area to finance the military budget. The bill had a condition that it could be exchanged for Japanese currency if it was brought into a Japanese government agency. However, if all Gun-pyo funds were to be exchanged for Japanese currency, the government would have to be forced to issue a huge amount of currency, resulting in possible negative effects such as inflation.

The Meiji government planned a policy to export large quantities of cotton fabric to Manchuria as a way to collect military bills without exchanging them for Japanese currencies. However, Japan did not have a capacity to mass-produce cotton as it had only man-made looms at that time.

Mitsui & Co. showed their will to cooperate with the policies of the Meiji government, but did not have a specific way to mass-produce cotton. Thus, Mitsui came to know about the power loom developed by Toyoda. Toyoda had been working on his invention with the purpose of contributing to the nation and society. The power loom he invented contributed to saving the nation from a financial crisis.

3 Establishment and Failure of the Toyoda Loom

In 1899, Mitsui & Co., Ltd. established a joint company, Igeta Shokai, for mass production of power looms, and Toyoda became the chief engineer. During this period, Toyoda made an important technological breakthrough for the development of automatic looms. He successfully developed a device that could supply weft yarns while the loom was in operation. It was an important technical element indispensable for the automation of the loom.

However, it is clear that no matter how much technically important an invention is, if the invention does not lead to commercialization and monetization, it has no meaning for a company. Faced with the difficulty of balancing R&D and corporate earnings, Toyoda left Igeta Shokai (Company) and started a weaving business again at Toyoda Shokai.

The business of the Toyoda Company was very smooth, so Toyoda left the management to his second wife Asako and his younger brother Sasuke, and he focused on research and development of automatic loom by investing much of company's earnings.

"Thirty-eight year model" and "Thirty-ninth year model" Toyoda developed during 1905–1906 were mixed wood and iron power looms. These new looms improved so that thick fabrics could be woven, enhancing durability, versatility, and efficiency. Even with these improvements, the price was kept low, so a flood of orders poured into the Toyoda company.

In 1905, there was an event that had a major impact on the development of automatic looms.

A performance comparison test of looms from Japan, the USA, and the UK (two companies) was conducted at the Hyogo Factory of Kanegafuchi Spinning. As a result, the normal loom of Platt, UK, showed the best results.[8] The loom developed by Toyoda was not able to deliver satisfactory performance. The reason why Pratt's loom achieved a good result was that it delivered stable performance even when poor quality cotton yarns were used. This provided an important suggestion for Toyoda's product development.

It was Mitsui & Co., once again, who was the first to set its eyes on the rapid growth of Toyoda Company. In the past, Toyoda was forced to leave the Igeta company that both Toyoda and Mitsui established because of a conflict between the management team from Mitsui and him. Mitsui & Co. proposed to reorganize Toyoda Shokai as a stock company. Toyoda agonized over whether to accept the Mitsui's proposal for about six months because of the bitter experience at the Idate Shokai. He finally accepted the proposal.

In 1906, Toyoda Loom Co., Ltd. (capitalized at one million yen) was established as the first full-scale loom manufacturer in Japan. Toyoda became the chief engineer.

The new company's business was sluggish from its establishment. Toyoda was held responsible for the poor business performance, so the president Taniguchi forced him to resign. Toyoda focused on pre-sales trials aimed at improving product quality, but his plan was opposed by the management team who wanted to sell products as soon as possible to secure profits. Eventually, Toyoda was forced to resign, losing the financial base and the place for research and development he accumulated since his time at Toyoda Shokai.

4 Completion of the G-type Automatic Loom

Toyoda, who was forced to leave the Toyoda Loom Company, visited the USA and the UK. In the USA, he researched Northrop-type automatic looms that was well known in Japan, but Toyoda had an impression that its technical level was not necessarily high compared to the automatic looms he produced.

The automatic loom has a function that can automatically replenish the weft. For the weft replenishment method, there are two methods: a method that replaces a wooden pipe wound with yarns and a method of replacing shuttle. Around 1894, J. Northrop in the USA completed the former method, and in 1926 Toyoda completed the latter method.

During his visit to the USA, Toyoda visited Jokichi Takamine, who discovered Takadiastase and adrenaline. Takamine was well informed about Toyoda's invention and his personality, so he was pleased with Toyoda's visit. Sakichi Toyoda Biography Compilation Committee (1933) introduced the following Takamine's comment:

> Many inventions are often buried unsuccessfully. It is not only a crime of society but also the responsibility of the inventor. (Omitted) The inventor should not leave the invention until it is expected that it will be safe to use in society. But until the prospect of being able to fly enough in the sky, the inventor is responsible for taking care of it. I think this may be the reason for the completion of the invention.

Takamine's remark was in line with Toyoda's belief that the true value of a new invention cannot be launched into the market unless it goes through complete sales testing. The words of Takamine, who established a solid record as a manager of a bio-venture in the USA, helped broken-hearted Toyoda regain himself and his courage. Toyoda, who had been fighting alone, is reported to have visited Takamine several times since then as if he enjoyed the encounter with a person who, for the first time, understood his feelings as an inventor.

In 1912, Toyoda returned to Japan with a new determination and established the Toyota Auto Woven Fabric Factory in Nagoya to obtain R&D funds. In 1914, he established a new factory and entered the spinning industry. At that time, the quality of the cotton yarn was poor and hindered the testing of the automatic loom, so Toyoda ran both a woven fabric business and spinning business to secure high-quality cotton yarn. The management risk associated with entering the spinning industry was high, but the spinning industry was growing rapidly on the wave of the economic boom of the First World War.

In 1918, Toyota Auto Woven Fabric Factory was converted to a stock company and Toyoda Boshoku Corporation was newly established. Later, Toyoda Boshoku developed into the Toyota Motor Corporation.

The cessation of imports of British cotton products in China due to the effects of World War I accelerated Japanese textile companies' entry into China. In 1921, Toyoda established Toyoda Boshoku Sho (a kind of subsidiary) in Shanghai and moved to China. Toyoda instructed Kiichiro, his eldest son who just graduated from a university, to continue research and development on the automatic loom.

Kiichiro developed a loom equipped with a newly developed automatic shuttle changing device on a Toyoda's ordinary loom, and conducted a test operation with these 200 new automatic looms at the Kariya test plant newly established in 1923. This new automatic loom was named the "G-type automatic loom", and the first machine was completed in November 1925 (Fig. 7.3).

Kiichiro was instructed by his father, Sakichi Toyoda, to mass-produce the "G-type automatic loom" and planned to build a new factory. In constructing the new factory, a new company for automatic loom manufacturing named Toyoda Automatic Loom Manufacturing was established in Kariya in November 1926. The method adopted by Kiichiro in the development of the "G-type automatic loom", which was gradually increasing production capacity while mastering production technology, was also utilized in their automobile business.

With conventional ordinary looms, the number of looms that one worker could operate was four or five, but the "G-type automatic loom" enabled one worker to operate 50 looms. In 1929, late-night work of

Fig. 7.3 G-type automatic loom. (Source: The Toyota memorial Museum of Industry and Technology)

women and young people was banned based on a resolution of the International Labor Conference, so the demand for automatic looms in order to secure productivity increased sharply. It can be said that the innovation Sachi and Kiichiro realized was a solution to social issues at the time. In addition to the Japanese market, Toyoda-type automatic looms were exported to countries including China, India, the USA, Canada, and Mexico

Pratt, a leading loom manufacturer in the UK, highly praised the performance of the Toyoda-type automatic loom. Platt applied for the transfer of the patent right of the "G-type automatic loom", and in December 1929, the Toyota-Platt agreement was signed. The patent transfer agreement between Pratt and Toyoda was for a patent on a shuttle-type automatic loom developed by Toyoda.

Under this agreement, Pratt paid Toyoda £100,000. This money was used to fund Kiichiro's research into the automobile business and laid the foundation for today's Toyota Motor Corporation.

After the completion of the automatic loom, Toyoda was based in Shanghai and worked on the research of the circular loom[9] that he had tried before. He was also interested in social contribution activities and made a donation of 1,000,000 yen to the Imperial Invention Association to encourage the invention of a storage battery. The qualifications for applying for this research grant were limited to Japanese. This reflects Sakichi's desire to improve the Japanese capabilities of technical development.

After 1927, he suffered a cerebral hemorrhage and was unable to research as he wished. He died of an illness in October 1930 without seeing the completion of the circular loom he was working on. The spirit of Sakichi Toyoda was handed over to his son, Kiichiro's, automobile business (Table 7.1).

Table 7.1 Major Innovations by Sakichi Toyoda and Kiichiro Toyoda

Name	*Year*	*Description*
Toyota wooden human-powered loom	1890	First loom Sakichi invented. The previous loom required both hands to weave, but the model Sakichi improved enabled one-hand operation with the shuttle running to either side. This improved productivity by 40–50%.
Yarn knitting machine (Reeling machine)	1894	The conventional hand-operated loom was improved to a foot-operated type. Work productivity increased by a factor of two to three. This success enabled Toyoda to cover the cost to develop the power loom.
Wood-iron-mixed power loom	1896	The first power loom in Japan developed by Sakichi Toyoda. A single person could operate three to four units. Productivity increased 20-fold. The quality of the fabric was very high and the loom became very popular.
38-year loom	1905	The 38-year loom was equipped with a device that would stop the operation when weft or warp was cut, preventing problems such as weaving of damaged fabric.
Circular loom	1906	An ideal loom which contained a revolving shuttle. Sakichi worked hard for its commercial application, but died without seeing the finished products of the circular loom.
L-shaped iron-powered loom	1909	In order to create a robust and efficient loom that would address the large-scale industrialization of the weaving industry, Toyoda transformed a wood-steel-mixed power loom into a complete steel-made power loom.
N-type wide-powered loom	1914	To address a growing demand for cotton fabric from overseas, the N-type wide-powered loom was created by improving a conventional wide loom with adding new functionalities such as a warp-cutting stop device. This loom became the basis for the G-type automatic loom.

Source: Created by the author based on various materials

5 Conclusion

Sakichi Toyoda acquired his knowledge and skills in mechanical engineering on his own and succeeded in creating and commercializing epoch-making innovations that were recognized by advanced countries in the machine industry such as Europe and the USA. He is highly regarded as the pioneer of R&D-type venture entrepreneurship in Japan.

Importantly, Sakichi Toyoda was a good engineer before becoming an entrepreneur. What is most important for R&D venture companies is a core innovative technology for their business. No matter how good their entrepreneurial qualities are, it is difficult to create a research-and-development-type venture company unless they grasp the core innovative technology by themselves.

Needless to say, R&D investment creates innovation and this contributes to increasing corporate value. As the external environment surrounding companies changes, companies are required to accurately grasp the potential needs of society and return to society as innovation.

In order to revitalize the economy, it is important to commercialize the seeds acquired through R&D, but R&D in Japanese companies has not been necessarily linked to commercialization and therefore has become a major bottleneck in the Japanese economy. From this point of view, it can be said that there are many points that modern companies need to learn from Toyoda's way of life as an entrepreneur.

Also, one of Toyoda's unique characteristics as an entrepreneur was his high awareness of patent rights (knowledge). In light of the promulgation of the Patent Ordinance, Toyoda actively acquired patents for the results of his technological innovation.

Toyoda's active use of patents was not to gain huge wealth by commercializing the acquired patents, but to secure sufficient funds for his next R&D projects.

Today, for some venture entrepreneurs, their purpose is to make money, but for Toyoda making money was not a purpose, but just a means of research and development. Toyoda did not own the patents he acquired, but instead had his company own them. From such attitudes, we can guess his philosophy as an entrepreneur.

Succession of the business of an R&D-type venture company is very difficult. This is because entrepreneurs themselves must have excellent R&D capabilities. In the case of Toyoda, he was blessed with Kiichiro, a successor who was a better engineer than his father. Kiichiro acquired his own technological seeds through his efforts on the development of an automobile that his father Sakichi never worked on and made the cornerstone of today's Toyota Group. Human resources that have the skills of both researchers/technologists and entrepreneurs are extremely rare, and that is why Sakichi Toyoda is regarded as the ideal and desired figure for R&D- type venture entrepreneurs to date.

Notes

1. Hotoku thought is a philosophy that Sontoku Ninomiya advocated and propagated. Ninomiya appealed for the integration of economy and morals, and argued that if one contributed to society, rather than seeking private interests, the return would eventually return to him. Ninomiya especially emphasized "Suijo" (concession), "Kinben" (hard work), "Shisei" (sincerity), and "Bundo" (computational general equilibrium).
2. Samuel Smiles (1812–1904) was a Scottish doctor and writer. *Self-Help*, which was published in Japan as *Saigoku rishi hen*, had a significant impact on the formation of the philosophy of young people during the Meiji era.
3. Gaun Tatsumune (1842–1900) was an inventor who invented the Gaun-type spinning machine in the early Meiji era. He won the first prize at the first National Industrial Expo held in 1877 in Japan. However, as his invention was released before the patent protection ordnance was enacted, his products were driven out by imitations.
4. James Hargreaves (1720–1778) was a British carpenter and inventor. In 1764, he invented a Jenny spinning machine by dramatically increasing the yarn production efficiency.
5. James Watt (1736–1819) was a mechanical engineer from Scotland. The Industrial Revolution in the UK advanced with his steam engine improvements.
6. Richard Arclight (1732–1792) was a British inventor. He developed a hydraulic spinning machine powered by a water in 1771.
7. Patent No. 3173 (August 1898).
8. The automatic loom operates continuously replenishing weft unless the warp is broken. A loom without this function is called a normal loom.
9. Toyoda invented the "circular loom" in 1906 and obtained a patent the following year. Since the circular loom inserts the weft yarn by the circular motion of the shuttle, it reduced energy loss and noise generation.

References

Arai, Toshimitsu [1998] "Patents support venture business" Invention Association.

Hirakawa, Y. [2006] "Heaven helps those who help themselves: Masanao Nakamura and Saigoku risshi hen", Nagoya University Publishing.

Hosokawa, Mikio [2002] "Key to Toyota's Growth-Human Relations in the Foundation Period" Kindai Bungeisha.

Ishii, Tadashi [2005] "History and current circumstances of intellectual property: Historical approach to the area where economy, technology and patents intersect" Invention Association.

KajiNishi, Mitsuhaya [1987] "Sakichi Toyoda", Yoshikawa Hirobun kan.
Kamiyama, Akihiro [2004] "Portrait of Invention-driven Nation Japan" Bungei Shunju.
Kan, ken [2003] "Innovation in Modern Japan-Patents and Economic Development" Fukosha.
Mainichi Shimbun [1971] "Sakichi Toyoda: The Secret of Toyota Group Growth".
Sakichi Toyoda Biography Compilation Office [1933] "Toyoda Sakichi Biography".
Shizuoka Pref. Kosai-city Board of Education and Kosai-city [1990] "Sakichi Toyoda, a great man born in Kosai".
Toyota Motor Corporation [1958] "Toyota Motor 20 Years History".
Wada, Kazuo and Yui, Tsunehiko [2002] Kiichiro Toyoda, Nagoya University Press.

CHAPTER 8

Michio Suzuki: Customer-Oriented Business Strategy Utilizing Knowledge

Michio Suzuki (1887–1982). (Source: Suzuki Motor Corporation [2002] "History Photo Book 'with Suzuki'")

Achievement of Michio Suzuki and related SDGs

Economy	 	* Automatic loom business * Motorcycle/Light vehicle development

(*continued*)

M. Takehara, N. Hasegawa, *Sustainable Management of Japanese Entrepreneurs in Pre-War Period from the Perspective of SDGs and ESG*, https://doi.org/10.1007/978-981-15-6507-6_8

(continued)

Society	1 NO POVERTY 12 RESPONSIBLE CONSUMPTION AND PRODUCTION	* Improve productivity through power loom development * Local industry support * Drive R & D * Strict quality control
Governance	10 REDUCED INEQUALITIES 17 PARTNERSHIPS FOR THE GOALS	* Utilization of patent system * Creation of intellectual property business * Differentiation strategy

Source: Created by authors

1 Early Days

The Enshu region, centered in Hamamatsu City, Shizuoka Prefecture, is a multi-industry city with three pillars of textiles, musical instruments, and motorcycles and automobiles. From the Meiji era to the early Showa era, textiles was the main industry and so was the transport equipment, mainly motorcycles after the war. Also, the region is known for producing many entrepreneurs.

The Enshu region is the birthplace of Honda, Suzuki, and Yamaha Motor, the three major motorcycle manufacturers in Japan. The motorcycle industry in the Enshu region began in 1946 when Soichiro Honda started to sell an engine-equipped bicycle. The engine-equipped bicycle was equipped with an engine for a former army wireless generator. Meanwhile, an automatic loom maker, Suzuki Looms (now Suzuki Motor Corporation), manufactured motorcycle motors in 1952, and started producing finished motorcycles the following year. Nippon Gakki Co., Ltd. (currently Yamaha Corporation) started to develop motorcycles in 1953 as the last entrant.

Suzuki promptly withdrew from the loom manufacturing business, which it had been leading the industry, and completely changed its business domain to a motorcycle and light car manufacturer. It was Suzuki's founder, Michio Suzuki, who led this seemingly reckless new business.

The outstanding feature of Suzuki as an entrepreneur is that he maximized the dynamic synergy of his business activities by making use of the knowledge generated from the current core business for future new businesses. This chapter looks back and tracks some of Suzuki's entrepreneurial activities, especially how he used the dynamic synergy to launch a new business.

Michio Suzuki was born in Hamamatsu, Shizuoka Prefecture, in 1887. Suzuki wanted to become a carpenter when he graduated from Hokawa Village Jinjo Elementary School in 1898. In 1901, he signed a seven-year apprenticeship contract with Kotaro Imamura, a carpenter's master, and began his training as a carpenter.

However, carpentry fell sharply in the aftermath of the Russo-Japanese War in 1904. Suzuki's master, Imamura, had no choice but to make foot-operated wooden looms. Thus, Suzuki unintentionally had the opportunity to acquire basic knowledge of weaving. This coincidence that Suzuki entered into the apprenticeship of Imamura was a major trigger for him to develop automatic looms.

Sakichi Toyoda (the founder of Toyota Motor Corporation), a leading manufacturer of automatic looms in Japan, was also from the Enshu region (currently Kosai City, Shizuoka Prefecture). Toyoda utilized his skill and experience as a carpenter to manufacture wooden looms and laid the foundation for the automobile manufacturing business through the success of automatic looms he developed with unique technology. There are many common points in the traces of entrepreneur activities between Toyoda and Suzuki.

Due to the influence of Sakichi Toyoda, automatic looms emerged in the Enshu region relatively earlier than other regions. The introduction of automatic looms, which began around 1900, became decisive due to the economic boom from the Russo-Japanese War, and many loom makers, including Sakichi Toyoda and Michio Suzuki, expanded their businesses. The number of automatic looms increased from 991 in 1907 to 8119 in 1914. With the increase in automatic looms, textile output increased 2.63 times in seven years from 1907 to 1914.

2 Success as an Automatic Loom Manufacturer

2.1 Establishment of Suzuki Looms

In 1909, Suzuki became independent and established a privately run Suzuki Looms factory and produced a wood-iron-mixed foot-operated loom every three to four days. Suzuki's loom was more productive than conventional loom, so it gained a good reputation and eventually many orders. It is needless to say that product development capabilities have a significant effect on competition between companies. The only way for a late comer, such as Suzuki Looms, to survive was to create innovative products. The one-shuttle-foot loom, which was mainstream loom at the time, was suitable for weaving white fabric cotton, but it was unable to weave striped patterns. Through diligent dialogues with weavers, Suzuki realized there was a strong need for a loom that could perform striped weaving

Just one month after he started to work on the development, he was able to complete a two-shuttle foot-operated loom that could weave horizontal stripes using dyed yarn. The emergence of this innovative weaving loom had a major impact on loom manufacturers. For the first time, Suzuki obtained a utility model for the technology incorporated in this loom product.[1] This technology became the core technology for the production of multiple shuttle looms, and was subsequently used in various ways. The market for the two-shuttle foot-operated loom expanded not only to the Enshu region but also to textile production areas such as Owari, Ashikaga, Ome, Harima (Hyogo), Toyama, and Niigata.

2.2 *Establishment of the Suzuki Brand*

In 1920, Suzuki Looms Works was reorganized into Suzuki Looms Corporation. Excluding Toyoda Loom, which moved to Aichi Prefecture, there were only two companies in the Enshu region, namely Enshu Loom (now Enshu Co., Ltd.) and Suzuki Looms.

It was the innovative automatic loom created by Michio Suzuki that supported the rapid growth of Suzuki Looms. Many loom manufacturers, such as Toyoda Automatic Loom and Enshu Loom, produced loom for white fabrics. To differentiate from them, Suzuki began to specialize in producing striped looms using dyed yarn. Until Suzuki Looms developed a four-shuttle automatic loom, there were no looms capable of weaving a vertical and horizontal stripe pattern. Suzuki's differentiation strategy of focusing on a striped loom with few competitors was successful, and the Suzuki Looms was able to maintain a stable growth.

The stock market crash of October 1929 in New York triggered the Great Depression. As the economic environment worsened, Michio Suzuki succeeded in developing an innovative product called Sarong Loom (Fig. 8.1).[2] Sarong was a waistband-style garment favored by Muslims in Southeast Asia. The UK, the Netherlands, and India were the main producers.

An attractive point of Sarong looms was that they significantly reduced manufacturing costs.

Fig. 8.1 Sarong loom (1929). (Source: Author took this photo in 2004)

Taking men's handkerchiefs as an example, Sarong Loom succeeded in reducing the cost of replacing card equipment by about 90% compared to conventional loom. Sarong exports greatly benefited the cotton fabric industry in the Enshu region, and Michio Suzuki was steadily building a brand as a top manufacturer of striped looms.

It was small- and medium-sized weavers with less than 20 looms that supported Sarong weaving in the Enshu region. Though they did not have enough financial resources, they were the first to purchase Sarong looms. They could purchase Sarong looms by using monthly installment (loan) sales.

Although the installment payment system was unusual at that time, Suzuki introduced it due to his strong desire to repay small- and medium-sized industrialists who supported his company.

Michio Suzuki always focused on customer-centric product development. He strongly believed the following idea: "Business is not just about making good products, it doesn't work if they don't sell well".[3] Therefore, it was natural for him to seriously listen to any requests from loom users and repair a broken loom by staying up all night. When Suzuki repaired a loom, he often redesigned the loom. In this way, Suzuki gained trust from small- and medium-sized local looms users as a reliable person. The Suzuki brand was built through grass-roots exchanges with customers.

3 Entering the Motorcycle Business

Suzuki Looms entered the motorcycle business. The motorcycle business had two major significances for Suzuki Looms. Firstly, Suzuki entered the motorcycle business last, but eventually secured a market position as one of the three major manufacturers together with Honda Motor and Yamaha Motor. When Suzuki entered the motorcycle business, the Honda Motor

Co. already had a decisive competitive advantage in the market. Secondly, the entry into the motorcycle business paved the way for automobile development.

3.1 *Hardship from the Management Crisis*

When Honda Motor Co., Ltd. started full-scale motorcycle production in the 1950s, Suzuki Looms suffered a severe business slump due to the impact of labor disputes. Although this difficult situation was barely overcome by the financial support from Toyoda Automatic Loom and a special procurement boom created by the Korean War, the future of the automatic loom was gloomy.

In 1951, based on the idea of Managing Director Shunzo Suzuki, Michio Suzuki's son-in-law, Suzuki Looms' development department started to make a motorcycle motor prototype. This led Suzuki to enter into the motorcycle business. Many of the members of the development team were involved in test-making an automobile prototype which was interrupted by the war, and they had experience in prototyping motorcycle engines.

The development team received an order to commercialize the product within six months. They developed a two-cycle, 36 cc, 0.7 horsepower "Power Free" in April 1952 (Fig. 8.2). Shunzo Suzuki felt that in order for a follower company like Suzuki to survive, it was necessary to incorporate original functionalities in the products that were not found in the preceding companies' products.

He gave the following homework to the development team of "Power Free":

1. Install the motor at the center of the vehicle to enhance stability.
2. Drive using the bicycle chain as it is.
3. Make the pedals easy to use.
4. Attach a free device to the pedal.

Fig. 8.2 Power Free (1952). (Source: Suzuki Motor Corporation 2002)

In response to these demands, the development team adopted a chain drive system, enabling free switching from stepping to engine and from engine to stepping. In addition, they succeeded in incorporating added value through unique features such as easy starting, easy operation, and high durability.

In July 1952, the Road Traffic Law was amended to require no test permission for motorized bicycles (up to 60 cc for two cycles and 90 cc for four cycles). Following this amendment of the law, a new "60 cc Diamond Free" was developed. The 60 cc Diamond Free became a successful product with monthly sales of more than 6000 units despite its high price of 38,000 yen per unit. Its high-power (2 horsepower) and two-speed shifting functionality were highly evaluated.

3.2 Development of the Completed Motorcycle

When Suzuki Looms began mass production of the Diamond Free, Honda Motor Co., Ltd. had steadily solidified its foundation as a leading finished motorcycle manufacturer. Being confident in the success of the Diamond Free, Shunzo Suzuki ordered the development of a finished motorcycle. In December 1953, the four-cycle 90 cc "Koreda CO type" was completed. About five years after Honda Motors, Suzuki Looms also became a motorcycle manufacturer.

Let's look back on the trends in the motorcycle industry at the time. Nippon Musical Instruments Manufacturing (currently Yamaha), which had been planning to enter the motorcycle business, announced the first finished motorcycle in October 1954 (Yamaha 125) and entered the motorcycle business. Nippon Musical Instruments Manufacturing, with its sophisticated craftsmanship and streamlined production system cultivated through the production of musical instruments and the production of propellers in the military factory era, was a major threat to competitors. This year marked the commemorative year that Honda Motor Co., Ltd., Suzuki Looms, and Nippon Musical Instrument Manufacturing entered the motorcycle business, as well as the year when the weak manufacturers began to be withdrawn from the market.

In September 1954, Japan's driver's license system was revised, and motorized bicycles were categorized into two types: the first type was 50 cc or less and the second type was 51 cc or more to 125 cc. In addition, up to the second class, the practical test was exempted, and people could ride only with a permit. It was expected that this revision of law would create potential demand, which had been hindered by obtaining a license until then; therefore, motorcycle manufacturers focused on developing highly practical new 125 cc class vehicles. Suzuki Looms expanded the engine of the "Koreda CO" from 90 cc to 125 cc, while starting to develop a new two-cycle engine (125 cc).

Suzuki Looms pointed out two reasons for choosing a two-cycle engine: (1) better output and performance than four-cycle engines; (2) simpler structure and easier handling. It was difficult for Suzuki to catch up with Honda Motor in the field of four-cycle engines, and Suzuki's financial base was weak, so the production costs had to be kept low. Therefore, it was a logical strategy that Suzuki focused on a two-cycle engine. The development of the two-cycle engines proceeded under two major concepts: noise reduction and enhancement of durability. The newly developed "Koreda ST 125 cc" became a hit product with a total production volume of 100,000 (Fig. 8.3).

For a follower company to be recognized in the market, it needs to increase the attractiveness of its products. Shunzo Suzuki used motorcycle racing as a place to emphasize Suzuki's product performances. Fortunately, Suzuki's motorcycle delivered good results in the race, so Suzuki successfully enhanced its brand value as a motorcycle manufacturer. As a result, many companies wanted to become Suzuki's distributors and Suzuki's sales network expanded nationwide.

Needless to say, Suzuki's success in the motorcycle business was attributed to the technical knowledge accumulated through the production of automatic looms. Technologies such as castings, machining, and parts processing were directly diverted to motorcycle production. For engineers who had experiences in research in automobile engine and motorcycle engine prototyping, it was not so difficult to develop original products based on products of leading companies. The reason why Suzuki Looms and Nippon Gakki, which were not necessarily innovative compared to Honda Motor, succeeded in the motorcycle business was because their overall ability as a company was excellent (Table 8.1).

Fig. 8.3 Koreda ST5 Type (1958). (Source: Tomizuka 2001)

Table 8.1 Motorcycle production in Japan by major manufacturers

Company	*Vehicle*	*1950*	*1951*	*1952*	*1953*	*1954*	*1955*	*1956*	*1957*	*1958*	*1959*	*1960*
Honda	Two-wheeled motor vehicle					120	1243	1719	2557	2840	3771	4848
	Light two-wheeled motor vehicle	924	3282	14,188	30,344	29,419	20,632	28,442	36,939	58,484	68,726	85,293
	Motorized bicycle						20,293	30,275	45,475	49,886	80,639	108,511
	Total	924	3282	14,188	30,344	29,539	42,168	60,436	84,971	111,210	153,136	198,652
Yamaha	Two-wheeled motor vehicle								270	298	284	639
	Light two-wheeled motor vehicle						576	6698	9665	12,770	31,425	25,444
	Motorized bicycle						2452	4389	8804	18,033	39,198	39,532
	Total	0	0	0	0	0	3028	11,087	18,739	31,101	70,907	65,615
Suzuki	Light two-wheeled motor vehicle							3059	4481	5907	7050	11,683
	Motorized bicycle						12,518	17,554	28,482	34,085	45,118	46,201
	Total	0	0	0	0	0	12,518	20,613	32,963	39,992	52,168	57,884
Marusho Motor Co., Ltd.	Two-wheeled motor vehicle					217	153	5			227	326
	Light two-wheeled motor vehicle		496	2443	6435	4274	4580	6381	6117	3826	7406	5724
	Motorized bicycle						3358	3546	2161	4329	3608	5263
	Total	0	496	2443	6435	4491	8091	9932	8278	8155	11,241	11,313
Kitagawa Motor Co., Ltd.	Light two-wheeled motor vehicle			4458	4692	3155	1848	769	377			
	Motorized bicycle						1844	570	41			
	Total	0	0	4458	4692	3155	3692	1339	418	0	0	0

Source: Small car newspaper company (1958) "The history of the small car industry making rapid progress" Pages 16–21

4 Progress to a Mini Car Manufacturer

4.1 Conflict Over the Automobile Manufacturing Business

In 1937, the production of Sarong looms peaked. Michio Suzuki was already looking for an alternative product to automatic looms. He found a new business domain to replace automatic looms with his entry into the motorcycle business. His success was largely driven by the presence of technical knowledge accumulated through pre-war automotive development.

Michio Suzuki's real intention was to enter the automotive business early, but he was faced with strong opposition from the management team, including his successor Shunzo Suzuki. Michio Suzuki decided to focus on the motorcycle business for the time being, giving higher priority to business restructuring, while leaving room for entry into the automotive business.

The unexpected success of the motorcycle business reignited a fierce debate within the Suzuki company over entry into the automotive business. The confrontation between the promotion group (Michio Suzuki) and the opposition group (Shunzo Suzuki) sharpened, and this shook the company.

In April 1953, Michio Suzuki finally decided to develop a small car and formed a development team led by Saburo Suzuki, Director of Manufacturing. Saburo Suzuki had an experience of working as a leader in automotive development in pre-war period. With the success of motorcycle business, the company could afford to invest in new businesses; therefore, it started to develop small cars. However, some board members and banks continued their strong opposition. As a result, actual development work did not start until January 1954.

The small car development was under the direct control of Michio Suzuki. The development team consisted of a total of five staff members, including Saburo Suzuki and others. Many of the team members were occupied by young engineers from Hamamatsu Technical College (currently Faculty of Engineering of Shizuoka University). However, they had no experience building cars, so they started their work by learning the basic mechanisms of a car while disassembling domestic Datsun and US-made Pontiac.

After approval of the general shareholders meeting, Michio Suzuki changed the company's name to Suzuki Motor Corporation in June 1954. Motorcycle manufacturers such as Yamaha Motor, Nippon Expressway Engine, and Tokyo Motor clearly indicated in the company names that they were engine manufacturers. In the case of Suzuki, the word "automobile" was added to the company name even before the prototype was completed. This reflects Michio Suzuki's extraordinary commitment to the automotive business.

Under Michio Suzuki's strong leadership, the small car development advanced at an unusual speed.

The technical knowledge accumulated during prewar automotive development also contributed significantly. The development team purchased the Volkswagen Beetle, Lloyd LP400, Citroen 2 CV, and Renault 4 CV for further research. And, taking into account driving performance, maintainability, and the company's technical level, the company started to produce a prototype vehicle with a front engine/front drive (FF) system and a two-cycle engine, based on a German-made Lloyd LP400.

According to the regulations based on the Road Transport Vehicle Act enacted in 1951, four cycles were 360 cc and two cycles were 240 cc. Suzuki's engine development was also conducted in accordance with this standard. However, the Road Transport Vehicle Law was partially revised in April 1955, and all tricycles and mini cars were unified to 360 cc regardless of engine type.[4] In light of this revision, the development team completed a new 360 cc with a two-cycle engine.

4.2 *Completion of Suzuki Suzulight*

In October 1954, the development team completed two prototypes. Michio Suzuki rode a prototype car and performed a long-distance test drive to Tokyo. He successfully drove through Hakone, the hardest part of the route, and headed for Tokyo. Upon arriving in Tokyo, Suzuki visited Jiro Yanase, founder of Yanase Co., Ltd. which was operating car dealerships, and asked for his evaluation of the prototype. Yanase praised the prototype and encouraged Suzuki to mass-produce it.

In April 1955, the third prototype was completed. Based on this prototype, Suzuki obtained government type approval of motor vehicles for three models: a sedan, a light van, and a pickup. The new products were named "Suzulight". It was 18 years after Suzuki started to develop automobiles.

Although Suzuki took the first steps as a finished car manufacturer, its production capacity was only about four or five vehicles per month. The company set an immediate production target for 30 vehicles. The selling price was set at 420,000 yen for a sedan, 390,000 yen for a light van, and 370,000 yen for a pickup. However, due to the inadequate production system and sales network, the effects of mass production could not be achieved, and the deficit in the automotive business continued to grow. But fortunately, the motorcycle business continued its strong earnings, so it enabled the continuation of the automobile business.

The characteristics of Suzulight, which laid the foundation for mini cars, can be summarized in the following six points.

1. Commercialized a two-cycle automobile engine that was considered for small motorcycles.
2. Innovative operability with FF system, rack, and pinion steering system.
3. People could drive with a license for mini car.
4. There was no need for periodic inspection and maintenance costs were low.[5]
5. A 360 cc air-cooled two-cycle two-cylinder engine had high acceleration, and the FF system enabled stable driving and indoor habitability.
6. The product had a variety of sedans, light vans, and pickups, which could meet various customer needs.

In the process of developing a car without compromise, Michio Suzuki emphasized practicality and durability of the product. High levels of technologies were implemented in the Suzulight to make it a solid and practical car. Suzuki wanted his car to be useful for people's lives. His emphasis on practicality and durability in product development was consistent since the days he was making looms, and this was clearly reflected in the product concepts of motorcycles and mini cars.

One thing that should not be overlooked in Suzuki's automobile development is the existence of its partner companies. Many of those partner companies had business with Suzuki even before the war, and the slump in Suzuki's loom business was also a serious problem for them. Suzuki's success of motorcycles and mini cars opened new avenues for those partner companies. At the time of 1955, there were 50 partner companies, and their technical knowledge also helped Suzuki open up new business domains.

4.3 Leading Mini Vehicle Company

Even though Suzuki succeeded in the development of Suzulight, the next big challenge was its mass production. Controversy between pro-mass production and opponents intensified again. Pro-mass production, including Michio Suzuki, argued that the motorcycle business's earnings should be invested in the car business, while cautious groups were still skeptical of the car business itself. The opposition thought that mass production was premature due to domestic demand for automobiles and the company's weak financial base (Fig. 8.4).

As the mass production of Suzulight was postponed, the company's business base stabilized due to the boom in the motorcycle business. In 1957, Michio handed over the position of president to his son-in-law, Shunzo Suzuki (he was then senior managing officer). After resigning from the president, Michio Suzuki did not assume the post of chairman, and completely withdrew from the forefront of management. The new president, who showed a cautious attitude to the automotive business, maintained a strategy centered on the motorcycle business, and the mass production of Suzulight was virtually shelved.

Fig. 8.4 Sunlight (1955). (Source: Ozeki 1977)

Here, let's look back on the trends in the automobile industry at that time. In 1955, when the Suzulight was launched, the Ministry of International Trade and Industry (MITI) announced the National Car (People's Car) concept. This concept gave bright hope to Suzuki Motor which was aiming for mass production of mini vehicles. Michio Suzuki frequently visited the Automobile Division in MITI, asking for opinions on whether to focus on cars or trucks.[6]

The National Car concept was not announced after a formal ministry decision. Nine members of the Automobile Manufacturers Association (Toyota, Nissan, Isuzu, Hino, Mitsubishi-Nihon, Shin Mitsubishi, Minsei Diesel, Fuji Seimitsu, Ota) expressed opposition to the standards set out in the National Vehicle Initiative. The product standards set forth in the National Vehicle Initiative were closest to those for mini vehicles, which spurred mini vehicle development.

The Subaru 360, launched by Fuji Heavy Industries in 1958, was a mini car developed with the National Car concept in mind. The Subaru 360 succeeded in creating demand for private cars as the first mass-produced mini car in Japan. In 1961, the production volume of Subaru 360 reached 21,800 units, taking the No. 1 position in mini vehicles market. On the other hand, the production volume of Suzulight in 1961 was 13,283 units, only about 50% of Subaru 360.

In 1959, Suzuki's automobile plant was destroyed by the Isewan Typhoon (Typhoon Vera), which caused serious damage to Japan. Shunzo Suzuki was pursuing a motorcycle-oriented business strategy, but after the rebuilding of the automobile factory, he decided to mass-produce the Suzulight.

It is easy to imagine that his decision to change Suzuki's business strategy drastically was impacted by the National Car concept and the success of Subaru 360. At the time of its launch, Suzulight had a lineup of three models. However, during mass production, Suzuki focused on the light van as it was exempted by commodity tax and could be used for both passenger and cargo. As a result, the production process was streamlined and exhibited a mass production effect. Suzuki's actual first step toward a mini car manufacturer began at this time (Table 8.2).

Table 8.2 Suzuki Motor's production volume trends

Year	*Motorcycle division*				*Motorcycle total*	*Automobile division*			*Automobile total*
	Below 50cc	*Below 125cc*	*Below 250cc*	*More than 250cc*		*Passenger car*	*Commercial car*	*800cc*	
1952	9993	0	0	0	9993	0	0	0	0
1953	37,251	5	0	0	37,256	0	0	0	0
1954	25,699	6336	0	0	32,035	3	0	0	3
1955	11,279	11,267	0	0	22,546	28	0	0	28
1956	14,129	15,783	2525	0	32,437	228	0	0	228
1957	18,150	19,754	3933	0	41,837	399	0	0	399
1958	41,802	27,216	4535	0	73,553	480	0	0	480
1959	22,173	41,586	3147	0	66,906	480	677	0	1157
1960	93,602	36,730	15,857	0	146,189	0	5824	0	5824
1961	108,456	43,680	6604	0	158,740	0	13,283	0	13,283
1962	84,224	77,300	4055	0	165,579	0	33,792	0	33,792
1963	126,388	140,002	4595	0	270,985	1551	38,295	0	39,846
1964	182,447	191,514	6377	0	380,338	1792	39,087	27	40,906
1965	122,474	188,925	22,965	0	334,364	1370	40,210	457	42,037
1966	191,825	211,243	44,404	0	447,472	2147	64,704	1316	68,167
1967	203,151	174,869	23,584	937	402,541	26,052	89,577	563	116,192
1968	173,775	176,421	5932	10,482	366,610	93,133	96,878	279	190,290
1969	222,243	151,450	18,177	8747	400,617	121,654	116,403	108	238,165

Source: Created by the author based on 512 pages of Suzuki Motor Industries (1970), "50 Year History"

5 Conclusion

Starting with the Suzulight in 1955, the mini car industry produced the Subaru 360 (1958), Mazda R360 Coupe (1960), Mazda Carroll 360 (1962), Mitsubishi Minica (1962), Daihatsu Fellow (1966), and Honda N360 (1967). Stimulated by the National Car concept, various manufacturers successively entered into the mini car market. Suzuki Motor Co., Ltd. gradually survived fierce competition and gained the top share in the domestic mini car market in 1974. To date, Suzuki maintains its position as a leading mini car company.

Michio Suzuki had the following three entrepreneurial characteristics.

The first is excellent self-innovation ability. Suzuki did not stick to his own success experiences, and constantly challenged new fields. The self-innovation of top management fostered a self-sustaining organization that produced continuous innovation, which achieved spiral growth.

The second point is the use of knowledge. In taking on new business, Suzuki Motor made full use of knowledge it gained as an organization. Suzuki accumulated deep manufacturing technologies. The diversion of technical knowledge was actively explored within company, and this led to new businesses.

The third point is the creation of shared value. Shared value means creating social value by responding to social needs while creating economic value. By addressing the social needs of the mass production of mini cars that emerged from the advent of motorization in Japan, Suzuki also realized the creation of economic value as a company. In other words, Suzuki succeeded in linking corporate success with social development through their business activities.

Notes

1. Utility Model No. 26199 (December 18, 1912).
2. Patent No. 88338 (September 15, 1930).
3. Suzuki Motor Corporation [1960], p. 163.
4. Japan Light Motor Vehicle and Motorcycle Association [1979], p. 220.
5. For small cars, the tax was 16,000 yen and the annual insurance premium was 2410 yen.
6. Koiso [1980], p. 37.

References

Hamamatsu Chamber of Commerce [1971] "The history of the development of Machinery and Metal Industry in Enshu region".

Hasegawa, Naoya [2005] "Michio Suzuki, A Man Who Created Suzuki" Mie University Press

Hisano, Amano [1993] "Hamamatsu Motorcycle Story" Kyodo Publishing Company.

Inagawa, Seiichi [1992] "My Youth 17" "Shizuoka Shimbun April 25, 1992 Article".

Japan Light Motor Vehicle and Motorcycle Association [1979] "Thirty Years of Small and Mini Vehicles".

Koiso, Katsunao [1980] "Record of the birth of a mini car", Japan Light Motor Vehicle and Motorcycle Association.

Koseki, Kazuo [1993] The Story of Japanese Motorcycles, Miki Shobo.

Koseki, Kazuo [1997] "Suzuki Story 1955–1997" Miki Shobo.

Ozaki, Masahisa [1966] "History of Japanese Automobiles" Jikensha.

Shiramizu, Yutaka [1964] "Ideal Warrior Michio Suzuki" Industrial Research Institute.

Suzuki Motor Corporation [1960] "40 Year History".

Suzuki Motor Corporation [1970] "50 Year History".

Suzuki Motor Corporation [1990] "70 Year History".

Suzuki Motor Corporation [2002] "History Photo Book 'with Suzuki'".

The Small Automobile Newspaper [1958] "The History of the Small Automobile Industry".

Tomizuka, Kiyoshi [2001] "History of Japanese Motorcycles" Miki Shobo.

Wada, Hiroshi [1963] "The path was built" Chubu Keizai Shimbun.

CHAPTER 9

Shojiro Ishibashi: Pioneer of Automobile Tire Manufacturing in Japan

Shojiro Ishibashi (1889–1976) (Source: https://www.bridgestone.com/corporate/history/)

Achievement of Shojiro Ishibashi and related SDGs

Economy	 	* Transformation of business domain * Innovation in marketing methods * Development of domestic tires

(*continued*)

M. Takehara, N. Hasegawa, *Sustainable Management of Japanese Entrepreneurs in Pre-War Period from the Perspective of SDGs and ESG*, https://doi.org/10.1007/978-981-15-6507-6_9

(continued)

Society	3 GOOD HEALTH AND WELL-BEING; 4 QUALITY EDUCATION; 12 RESPONSIBLE CONSUMPTION AND PRODUCTION	* Improve employees' working conditions * Support for educational institutions * Operate museum * Drive R&D * Strict quality control
Governance	10 REDUCED INEQUALITIES; 17 PARTNERSHIPS FOR THE GOALS	* Management based on appropriate profit * Progress from family business * Alliance with foreign companies

Source: Created by authors

1 Early Days

Shojiro Ishibashi, Bridgestone Corporation's founder, was born in 1889 as the second son of Shimaya, who ran a tailoring shop in Kurume, Fukuoka Prefecture. When he was young, he was a sickly and unobtrusive child. In 1902, he entered Kurume Commercial School as the youngest student. At that time, there were only about 30 commercial schools nationwide and it was extremely difficult to be accepted (Ishibashi Shojiro Biography Publication Committee [1978], p. 17).

When he was attending Kurume Commercial School, Shojiro met Koujiro Ishii, who later became the chairman of the House of Representatives, and Shigejiro Sakamoto, who later received the Order of Culture award from the government as a successful Western painter. Shojiro deepened his knowledge of painting through exchanges with Sakamoto, and paintings he collected are renowned worldwide as the Ishibashi Collection. Also, Shojiro came to have a deep relation with politicians Ichiro Hatoyama and Shigeru Yoshida, both of whom became prime ministers after World War II.

As a next step after graduation from the Kurume Commercial school, Shojiro hoped to go to the Kobe Higher Commercial School, but he could not get his father's permission. While watching his classmates go on to study, Shojiro felt bitterly disappointed. However, Shojiro was quick at changing his thinking.

He decided to take over the family business and renewed his determination as "I want to create a business that develops nationwide and benefits society" (ibid., p. 29).

2 From Family Business to Full-Scale Business

2.1 *Transformation of Business Domain*

Shimaya had an inefficient business of producing various products after receiving orders. The first step in the management reform that Shojiro implemented was the restructuring of the business domain.

Shojiro abolished order-made production of many varieties and concentrated his business on manufacturing and selling tabi (Japanese split-toed socks). In addition, he hired unpaid apprentices as paid employees to increase their motivation. Shojiro broke away from the cottage industry and pursued business innovation to establish a business that introduced modern management.

In 1908, as the first step in mechanization, the company constructed a new factory, invested in equipment such as oil engines and power sewing machines, and hired 30 new workers. As a result, Shimaya's production began to increase rapidly (Table 9.1).

Before shifting to specialized tabi manufacturing, tabi production capacity was 280 pairs per day. However, after becoming a specialized tabi manufacturer, the number increased to 700 pairs per day (Bridgestone [1982], p. 10).

After that, Shojiro pursued his management reforms, focusing on (1) setting appropriate profits and (2) establishing brands. These two points were the core of Shojiro's management vision.

Shojiro set the appropriate profit at 10% of sales, and decided on manufacturing costs and selling prices based on the appropriate profit. A price determination method widely used in companies is the cost addition method. In this method, a price is determined by adding a certain margin to direct and indirect costs. This method is expected to be stable from a corporate perspective. However, in a market where competition between companies is fierce, this method would be risky because customers may not accept the price calculated by the cost addition method (Fig. 9.1).

Table 9.1 Shimaya tabi sales

Year	*Tabi Sales (unit)*
1906	90,000
1907	134,000
1908	148,000
1909	232,000

Source: Ishibashi [1978], p. 32

Fig. 9.1 Shimaya Tabi (Japanese split-toed socks) factory. (Source: Bridgestone 1978)

In those days, Kurume was crowded with competitors. Tsuchiya tabi (the predecessor of Moonstar Co., Ltd.), founded by Unpei Kurata, a pioneer tabi maker, had a large presence, and Fukusuke Tabi, a leading manufacturer of machine-stitched tabi based in the Kansai area, also entered the market.

Shojiro gained customer support by drastically reducing both costs and prices and at the same time succeeded in balancing the difficult task of securing appropriate profits.

Shojiro developed a new branding strategy centered on trust and originality. Due to the nature of tabi (split-toed socks), in the summer when sales decreased, working capital was in short supply, and there was a great need for a bank loan. Shojiro's Shimaya, which was a late entrant, had poor creditworthiness and had difficulty obtaining financing. Therefore, Shojiro succeeded in building a brand of trust by strictly observing the repayment date of the debt. His close relationship with financial institutions greatly helped his company to advance business innovation (Ishibashi Shojiro Biography Publication Committee [1978], p. 34).

Shojiro devised creative advertising to build a corporate brand. In 1912, he rode a car for the first time in Tokyo. From that experience, he came up with an idea of advertising tabi using a car. He purchased a very expensive foreign-made open car, decorated it with fancy signs and banners, and toured the entire Kyushu area, advertising tabi. The power of this advertising car was enormous. Shojiro's bold advertising campaign was a huge success (Fig. 9.2).

Although Shojiro conducted an innovative advertising campaign based on novel ideas that attracted the public's attention, he had a negative opinion of advertising that merely appealed to consumers to buy products. With the belief that the products themselves were the best advertisements, once the company's name was better known, he avoided spending too much on advertising, opting to spend on improving quality and lowering prices instead.

Fig. 9.2 Advertising by car (1912). (Source: Bridgestone 1978)

2.2 Product Development and Marketing Strategy

In 1914, Shojiro launched a new product that overturned conventional wisdom in the industry. It was "20-sen Asahi tabi" sold at a low set price.[1] At that time, tabi were priced according to type and size. In Shimaya, the production system was modernized and mechanized so mass production of high-quality products was possible.

Shojiro improved complex distribution processes and focused on customer-oriented product development. Shojiro's strategy, which consistently expanded from manufacturing to sales, seems to have some underlying ideas with strategy of today's UNIQLO which is gaining customer support by providing high-quality classic casual clothing in low prices.[2]

The responses from competitors for Ishibashi's flat-price tabi were extremely cold. Rivals entered flat-price tabi two years after the launch of Asahi Tabi. However, Ishibashi's strategy was a great success. Before the launch of Asahi Tabi, Shimaya's sales was 600,000 pairs a year, but by 1918, it had grown to three million pairs a year (Bridgestone [1982], p. 13). Asahi Tabi grabbed the customer's heart in terms of both quality and price, and swept the market.

In 1918, Shojiro established Nippon Tabi Co., Ltd. (hereinafter referred to as Nippon Tabi) with a capital of one million yen and switched from a small family business to a more organized, larger business. In 1921, Nippon Tabi started to develop an advanced form of tabi called jika tabi. Jika tabi was made of durable cloth and a rubber plate was pasted on the sole so that it could be worn outdoors (Fig. 9.3). At that time, ordinary workers used straw shoes (straw sandals). Shoes were not durable, and when workers put them on with bare feet, they were often injured by fragments or nails, so tabi was a necessity for workers.

The price of the straw shoes was 5 sen (0.05 yen) per pair, and when added to the tabi fee, 1.50 yen per month (about 18 yen per year) had to

Fig. 9.3 Jika tabi. (Source: Bridgestone website)

be spent on footwear. The average wage of workers at that time was around 1 yen per day, so the cost of footwear was not light.

Tabi with rubber soles was not product of Nippon tabi. It was produced in the Kinki region around 1902. However, it was not widely spread because the rubber sole was easily peeled off.

After trial and error, Nippon Tabi technically overcame this shortcoming, and succeeded in commercializing Asahi jika tabi (split-toed heavy cloth shoes with rubber soles). The name "jika tabi" was an original trademark of Japanese Tabi, but it has become a common name.

At that time, the price of one pair of jika tabi was 1.50 yen. The useful life of a jika tabi was about half a year, so the annual cost of footwear using jika tabi was 3 yen. Compared to 18 yen per year for using the straw shoes, the cost was reduced to one sixth. Consumers were very pleased with the emergence of jika tabi which was both economical and safe. In January 1923, the production of jika tabi was 1000 pairs per day, but in December in the same year, it increased dramatically to 10,000 pairs per day (Bridgestone [1982], p. 17).

Nippon Tabi, which solidified its base with strong sales of jika tabi, started to produce rubber shoes in October 1923. With the spread of Western clothes, the mainstream of footwear was about to shift from clogs and sandals to shoes. Focusing on these changes, Nippon Tabi anticipated increased demand for inexpensive rubber shoes. Nippon Tabi's anticipation turned out to be right; orders for rubber shoes surged from abroad, and the export of Japanese rubber shoes even caused international trade friction.

Let's look back on the competition between companies in the age of tabi makers.

In the first phase, homogenization (imitation/improvement) activities took place. The first mover was "Tsuchiya tabi", a local maker in Kurume. Shojiro's company, Shimaya, which was a follower, tried to homogenize the first mover by thoroughly imitating the innovative business of Tsuchiya tabi.

In the second phase, actions for differentiation were taken. The keyword here was price destruction. The first mover in the second phase was "Shimaya (Shojiro's Nippon Tabi)", and its followers were "Tsuchiya tabi" and other major manufacturers such as Fukusuke.

Shimaya made a bold differentiation with the "20 sen priced Asahi Tabi". Tsuchiya tabi and other major manufacturers underestimated this and allowed Shimaya to run ahead of other rivals. Shimaya succeeded in gaining trust from consumers and retailers, and made a leap to become a top manufacturer in the industry.

In the third phase, companies in the tabi industry returned to the homogenization competition again. The key word here was product innovation. The first mover in the third phase was Nippon Tabi again, and its followers were Tsuchiya tabi and other major manufacturers. Nippon Tabi became the top manufacturer in the second phase by developing a revolutionary product, jika tabi.

However, poor counterfeit goods spread all over Japan, and lawsuits for patent infringement were filed frequently. Nippon Tabi allowed companies following the settlement to manufacture and sell jika tabi under the condition of royalty payments. As a result, many tabi manufacturers accelerated activities to imitate and improve jika tabi products of Nippon tabi.

3 Challenge to Made in Japan Tires

3.1 *Establishment of Bridgestone Tire Co., Ltd.*

Shojiro Ishibashi based his business management on the expansion of retained earnings and the development of new businesses using the funds. What made this possible was the "30% leap forward" campaign which began in 1923 to aim at increasing production by 30% every year (Bridgestone [1982], p. 17). In addition, the company maintained its policy of securing 10% of sales as appropriate profit, so if the company could increase production by 30% every year, internal reserves would expand exponentially.

In a rapidly changing socio-economic environment, companies need to create new businesses based on their strengths (core technologies) in order to survive. Nippon Tabi linearly developed a new business such as jika tabi and shoe boots based on their technologies of tabi manufacturing and rubber processing.

Ishibashi's next goal was to produce car tires that had not yet been domestically manufactured in Japan. This decision is often regarded as a challenge in a different field. From the perspective that the company was a footwear manufacturer, it would be evaluated as a challenge in a different field. However, if the company's core technology was regarded as rubber processing technology, the production of automotive tires can be said to be a natural expansion of business utilizing the core technology.

In its development process, Nippon Tabi evolved its core technology into rubber processing technology. In other words, new technologies were added to the core technologies, and the two complemented each other to achieve growth. In addition, as seen in the export of rubber shoes, Ishibashi's business philosophy of contributing to the country through the development of industry and the spirit of challenge brought him toward the domestic production of automobile tires (Fig. 9.4).

By the time Ishibashi decided to enter the tire business, it was about the time that the main products of the rubber industry in the USA and Europe would shift to automotive tires. Ishibashi loved cars after he bought them for advertising his tabi products. The number of vehicles owned in Japan increased dramatically from 512 in 1912 to 40,070 passenger cars and 12,097 trucks in 1926 (ibid., p. 102).

Only 595 domestic cars were produced in Japan from 1912 to 1926, and automobile tires were dominated by imported goods.

Dunlop Far East Co., Ltd., founded in 1913 by Dunlop, UK, began producing tires in Japan and controlled the domestic market.

On the other hand, Yokohama Electric Wire Manufacturing Co., Ltd. (the predecessor of Furukawa Electric Co., Ltd.) and Goodrich

Fig. 9.4 Production of tire prototype. (Source: Bridgestone 1978)

Corporation of the USA jointly invested to establish Yokohama Rubber Manufacturing Co., Ltd. (the predecessor of the Yokohama Rubber Co., Ltd.) and began its production of tires in 1921.

The business of Yokohama Rubber Manufacturing was interrupted by the Great Kanto Earthquake in 1923, but its Yokohama factory was rebuilt, and production of domestic tires started in 1930.

When Ishibashi announced his plan to enter into the tire business, strong opposition was raised from inside and outside of the company. However, Professor Takeo Kimijima of Kyushu University and Takuma Dan, president of Mitsui Godo Company, who knew Ishibashi through the tabi business, supported Ishibashi's plan. After examining the technical and cost challenges, Kimijima, a rubber research expert, suggested that tire manufacturing was possible.

In 1929, Ishibashi ordered a tire manufacturing machine with a production capacity of 300 tires a day, and he set up a tire factory in a corner of the Kurume factory of Nippon Tabi. The following year, Shojiro Ishibashi became the president of Nippon Tabi to replace his brother Tokujiro and declared his plan to enter into the automobile tire business. In April 1930, after various technical issues were overcome, a prototype of an automobile tire was completed. The biggest challenge was ensuring quality. Since there were no tire specialists in Nippon Tabi, they tried to improve the quality by scouting Japanese engineers from Dunlop Far East Co., Ltd.

In 1931, Bridgestone Tire Co., Ltd. was established, and Shojiro Ishibashi became its president.[3] The new company was established with a capital of one million yen, jointly funded by Shojiro and his brother Tokujiro. The investment ratio was 66% for Shojiro and 34% for Tokujiro. At that time, imported cars accounted for most of passenger cars and trucks in Japan, and the brand power of foreign products was overwhelming. Car tires were in a similar situation. In addition to reducing the quality gap with imported tires, the company was also required to eliminate the image of tires manufactured by a tabi maker.

Ishibashi thought that in order for Bridgestone, a follower, to compete with first movers such as Dunlop and Yokohama Rubber, it was imperative for Bridgestone to gain customer trust for its products. Therefore, he introduced a new system which would respond to customers' complaints. It was a customer service that unconditionally replaced tires when customers made a complaint about a tire they purchased. Many customers abused the system and the losses were not small, but Ishibashi endured.

In 1932, Bridgestone Tire products were recognized as excellent domestic products by the Ministry of Commerce and Industry. Starting as being recognized as a qualifying product by Ford Japan, Japan General Motors and Chrysler successively adopted Bridgestone tires as genuine tires. The entry of Bridgestone tires created price competition, forcing foreign manufacturers, which used to dominate the domestic market, to cut prices. As a result, the price of tires dropped sharply, bringing great benefits to consumers.

3.2 *Bridgestone Management During the War*

In 1937, Bridgestone Tire moved its headquarters from Kurume to Tokyo. At that time, Bridgestone Tire had a problem of securing natural rubber, the raw material for manufacturing tires. In the midst of the wartime block economy, natural rubber production in Southeast Asia was dominated by Britain and the Netherlands. Ishibashi planned to develop synthetic rubber instead of natural rubber and use it as a raw material for automobile tires. In 1938, rubber distribution control regulations were promulgated and securing natural rubber was even more difficult. In 1941, Bridgestone Tire successfully commercialized synthetic rubber and named it BS Rubber.

In 1939, production quotas and distribution controls for tires and tubes for private vehicles were enforced. In response, Bridgestone Tire (shares 27–28%), Dunlop (shares 42%), and Yokohama Rubber (shares 32–33%) agreed to evenly divide the market share by 1/3. Also, agreements on sales territories were concluded (ibid., p. 158).

Under this agreement, Bridgestone Tire's area of business was determined as from Kyushu to part of Kansai (around Osaka, Kyoto, and Kobe). In 1942, the name of the company was changed from Bridgestone Tire to Nippon Tires as the military pointed out that the company name Bridgestone was not appropriate as it was described in English, the language of enemy countries.

In 1944, Nippon Tires was designated as a munitions company. In addition to automobile tires, Nippon Tire also produced aircraft tires, anti-vibration rubber, and solid tires for tanks and bulletproof tanks. The army and navy fought a fierce battle for these products.

4 Regeneration of Bridgestone and Technological Innovation

Immediately after the end of the war, Ishibashi came to realize that car tire production was a social mission as it was vitally important for the country to improve the means of transportation to speed up post-war reconstruction. At the Kurume plant, which survived the war, car tire production resumed just two months after the end of the war.

In 1951, Ishibashi changed the company name from "Nippon Tire" to "Bridgestone Tire" again. In the same year, Bridgestone Tire entered into a production and technical alliance with Goodyear, the world's top tire manufacturer. During World War II, Ishibashi was entrusted with the management of Goodyear's Java plant, which was requisitioned by the Japanese army, but after the war, he returned it to Goodyear intact. This deepened the bond between the two companies.

The details of the alliance with Goodyear were as follows (Bridgestone [1982], pp. 156–157).

1. Goodyear would provide technical guidance to Bridgestone Tire, while Bridgestone Tire would pay technical guidance fees.
2. Bridgestone Tire would provide Goodyear with a portion of their production capacity and produce Goodyear brand products, and Goodyear pays production costs.

In the final stages of the partnership negotiations, Goodyear requested that it would take a 25% equity stake in Bridgestone. During this period, many Japanese companies were willing to accept foreign capital, but Ishibashi refused this request. He wanted to protect the management independence of Bridgestone. Eventually, the partnership was formed, as Goodyear withdrew its request for equity participation. This partnership enabled Ishibashi to absorb the latest tire manufacturing technology using rayon cords.

The cord constitutes the skeleton of the tire, and has the role of maintaining the internal air pressure from the load and impact that the tire receives. When tire cords were developed in the 1920s, Egyptian cotton was used. After that, rayon was used in 1937, nylon in 1942, and polyester in 1962, to improve strength and product life (Hayashi [2009], p. 157).

Tires Bridgestone produced at that time were cotton cord tires, but this product was already discontinued in the USA. Ishibashi was clearly aware

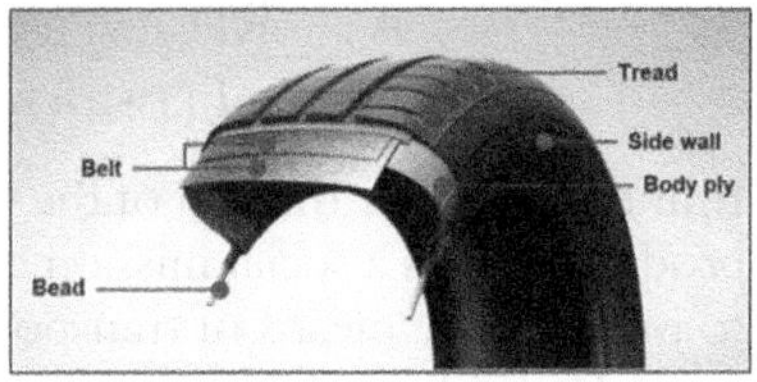

Fig. 9.5 The structure of tires. (Source: Bridgestone website)

Table 9.2 Trend in purchases of tire cord yarn (Unit: *t*)

Year	*Nylon*	*Rayon*	*Nylon ratio (%)*
1958	49	4410	1.1
1959	403	6735	5.6
1960	1210	6644	15.4
1961	3507	5424	39.3
1962	4811	5753	45.5

Source: Bridgestone Corporation [1983], p. 219

of the technical gap and recognized that innovation and improving production efficiency were urgent issues for Bridgestone to address (Fig. 9.5).

After World War II, the Japanese tire industry recovered its production level, supported by special demand from the Korean War. However, after the end of the Korean War, the domestic economy became deflationary and the tire industry suffered a sharp decline in demand. Under these circumstances, Bridgestone started a five-year plan to modernize production facilities in 1951, and Ishibashi ordered the development of rayon tires. Rayon tires were superior in cost and durability, so their commercialization was a necessity for Bridgestone to survive in a stagnant market.

The production of rayon tires in full scale began in September 1951. In May of the following year, 80% of Bridgestone tires were replaced with rayon tires. When the rayon tires were on track, Ishibashi ordered the development of tires that use nylon cords instead of rayon. In 1956, prototypes of nylon tires for trucks and buses were completed, and mass production was decided based on the results of test sales (Table 9.2).

However, a big challenge was the procurement of raw nylon yarn. Nylon yarn production for tire manufacturers was dominated by DuPont. Ishibashi conducted joint research with Toyo Rayon Co., Ltd. to avoid dependence on foreign companies in terms of cost and stable supply, and eventually achieved domestic procurement of nylon raw yarn (Bridgestone [1982], pp. 215–216).

Nylon tires had many advantages such as (1) heavy load resistance, (2) shock resistance, (3) fatigue resistance, (4) temperature rise resistance, (5) water resistance, and (6) improved fuel efficiency by reducing weight. Therefore, it quickly attracted many customers. Bridgestone's technological innovation and modernization of production facilities were successful, and in 1953 its sales exceeded ten billion yen, jumping to the top in the industry.

5 Outcomes of Business Diversification

5.1 *Challenges and Setbacks in Automotive Development*

Ishibashi, who became the manager of the leading tire manufacturer, next planned to move into the automobile manufacturing business. In 1949, Ishibashi invested in Tokyo Electric Vehicle Co., Ltd..

Tokyo Electric Vehicle was founded by employees of Tachikawa Aircraft, which once produced fighter aircraft during the war. They also worked on the development of electric vehicles.

However, as fuel efficiency was improved, the advantage of electric vehicles was lost.

Therefore, the company decided to switch to gasoline-powered vehicles, and commissioned the production of engines to Fuji Precision Industries, which was descended from Nakajima Aircraft. Ishibashi purchased the shares of Fuji Precision Industries held by the Industrial Bank of Japan, aiming for integrated production of engines and bodies. He led management himself as chairman (ibid., pp. 356–357).

In 1949, Tokyo Electric Motor Company changed its name to Tama Motor. In 1951, Tama Motor completed a truck equipped with a gasoline engine developed by Fuji Precision Industries. The following year, the first gasoline passenger car, named Prince, was launched and gained popularity (Fig. 9.6). That year, Tama Motors changed its name to Prince Motor Corporation. In 1953, in line with Ishibashi's intentions, Prince Motor Corporation and Fuji Precision Industries merged. As a result, an integrated automobile production system was realized.

Fig. 9.6 Prince Sedan AISH (1952). (Source: Japan Society of Automotive Technology)

The cars produced by Prince Motors were renowned for their innovative style and advanced technology. However, Prince Motors had no mass-market compact car in its product lineup, which was at the core of motorization in Japan. In addition, the company's corporate culture of seeking technical breakthroughs without being conscious about the development costs had a negative impact on Prince Motors' business performance.

Under these circumstances, the Ministry of International Trade and Industry (MITI), which wanted to strengthen the base of domestic automakers in preparation for liberalization of imported cars, urged the merger of Prince Motor and Nissan Motor (ibid., p. 358).

In 1965, Ishibashi accepted the merger of Prince Motor Company and Nissan. Apart from Ishibashi's personal thoughts, his judgment as an entrepreneur, based on his deep insight into the domestic and international economic situation, seemed to have made him to decide to withdraw from the automobile manufacturing business.

5.2 *Withdrawal from Motorcycle Business*

After the war, Ishibashi started production of bicycles at the Asahi Plant (Tosu City, Saga Prefecture).

In 1949, Ishibashi spun off its Asahi Plant as Bridgestone Bicycle Co., Ltd., but there was a large technical gap in bicycle manufacturing capability from leading manufacturers such as Yamaguchi Bicycle, Miyata Kogyo, and Maruishi Bicycle. In addition, recession due to the Dodge Line policy[4] deteriorated the company's business performance.

In 1952, Bridgestone Bicycle released the motor-driven bicycle "Bamby". The engine was developed by Fuji Precision Industries, which Ishibashi acquired for automobile manufacturing. The Bamby grew rapidly, improving its quality and gaining 52% market share in 1952. But

Fig. 9.7 Moped (motorcycles with pedals) BS Champion Type I. (Source: Oseki 1993)

then, with the advent of the motorcycle age, small motorcycles fell into a slump (Bridgestone [1982], p. 195). Bridgestone Bicycle, which had no experience in full-scale motorcycle production, sought a way via mopeds (motorcycles with pedals). However, with the spread of motorcycles, mopeds were already obsolete. In addition, the company's sales remained sluggish due to a lack of brand power and technical gaps with leading manufacturers (Fig. 9.7).

At that time, the motorcycle market in Japan was oligopolized by Honda Motor Co., Ltd., Suzuki Motor Co., Ltd., and Yamaha Motor Co., Ltd., and their combined share increased from 67.8% (1960) to 92.3% (1966) (Small Car Newspaper [1958], pp. 16–21). In contrast, the Bridgestone's share only increased slightly from 2.1% to 3.4%. With the oligopolistic status of the top three companies completed in the motorcycle market, Bridgestone lost its meaning in continuing its motorcycle business. In 1966, Ishibashi decided to withdraw from the motorcycle business.

6 Out from Family Business and Modernization of Management

In October 1961, Bridgestone went public on the Tokyo and Osaka Stock Exchanges. Though a bank encouraged Ishibashi to list Bridgestone's shares, he was reluctant about listing. However, the rapidly expanding business created strong financing needs. In addition, Bridgestone became a large company and was required to take responsibility as a public institution. Therefore, Ishibashi decided to go public in response to changes in the environment surrounding the company.

Prior to Bridgestone's listing, Ishibashi gave Bridgestone shares at a lower price to qualified employees (approximately 9% of all employees). This not only served as securing stable shareholders, but also aimed at fostering a sense of unity between employees and the company (Bridgestone [1982], pp. 282–283).

In 1963, when he was 74 years old, Ishibashi transferred the position as president to his son Mikiichiro, and he became chairman. He continued to exert strong leadership until 1973 when he retired due to illness.

7 Conclusion

The Japanese automobile tire industry has been steadily growing since the 1960s with the progress of motorization and the growth of the Japanese economy. Even after the bursting of the bubble economy in the early 1990s, the industry has captured global demand in the USA, Europe, and emerging markets, and their business performances have been generally strong.

In 2005, Bridgestone surpassed Michelin in sales-based market share and became the world's number one tire manufacturer. Until now, it has maintained the leading position in the industry. The major tire manufacturers' market shares in FY2016 were Bridgestone (14.6%), Michelin (14.0%), and Goodyear (9.0%).

The characteristics of Shojiro Ishibashi as an entrepreneur can be summarized in the following three points. The first is excellent self-innovation ability. He solidified his business base with the success of the tabi business, but he didn't stick to his successful experience. Instead, he constantly challenged new fields. Top management's self-innovation fostered a self-reliant organization that produced continuous innovation and achieved spiral growth.

The second point is the effective use of knowledge. In taking on the challenge of developing automotive tires, Bridgestone made the most of its knowledge of rubber processing technology. With the leadership of Ishibashi and his support, this diversion of technical knowledge was actively explored in Bridgestone and led to new businesses.

The third point is outside-in thinking. Outside-in thinking is an indispensable ability to create innovations that respond to social needs. Ishibashi captured the social needs of the domestic production of automobile tires and succeeded in capturing it as a business opportunity. It can be said that he practiced management that anticipated creating shared value (CSV) proposed by M. Porter in 2011.

Notes

1. In the early Meiji period, sen was used as the secondary currency unit. One yen was 100 sen, so 20 sen was one fifth of 1 yen.
2. UNIQLO is a casual wear brand operated by Fast Retailing Co., Ltd in Japan. The official name is UNIQUE CLOTHING WAREHOUSE. UNIQLO has gained the support of customers around the world as a brand of high quality and reasonable price for all ages and genders.
3. The company name, Bridgestone, was taken from the name of Ishibashi. Ishibashi said, "The direct translation of my surname Ishibashi became 'Stone Bridge' [*Ishi* means stone and *Bashi* means bridge]. However, Stone Bridge didn't sound good, so I decided on 'Bridgestone' by reversing the word order."
4. The Dodge Line was a fiscal and monetary tightening policy implemented by the Allies in February 1949 for the independence and stability of the Japanese economy. Inflation subsided due to this policy, but deflation progressed, and unemployment and bankruptcy increased.

References

Bridgestone [1982] "Bridgestone 50 Years History".
Bridgestone [2008] "Bridgestone 75 Years History".
Bridgestone Tire Trade Union Federation [1971] "25 years progress".
Hayashi, Yokai [2009] "Bridgestone Shojiro Ishibashi Biography" Gendai Shokan.
Ishibashi, Shojiro [1963] "My Progress", Private Publishing.
Ishibashi, Shojiro [1970] "My reminiscence" Private Publishing.
Ishibashi, Shojiro [1971] "Kumo wa Harukani", Yomiuri Shimbun.
Ishibashi, Shojiro [1980] "Watashi no rirekisho" (my résumé), business person 2" Nihon Keizai Shimbun.
Ishibashi, Shojiro [1989] "Reminiscence of my life" Private Publishing.
Japan Automobile Tire Association [2007] "Knowledge of Tires".
Kimoto, Reiji [2004] "Light and Shadow of Bridgestone", Kimoto Shoten.
Kojima, Naoki [1986] "Founder Shojiro Ishibashi" Shincho Bunko.
Koseki, Kazuo [1993] The Story of Japanese Motorcycles, Miki Shobo.
Shojiro Ishibashi Biography Publication Committee [1978] "Shojiro Ishibashi" Bridgestone.
Tsukihoshi Rubber [1967] "Tsukihoshi Rubber 90 Years History".

PART IV

Management that Enhanced Human Capital

CHAPTER 10

Magosaburo Ohara: The Pioneer of CSR Who Challenged the Realization of Labor Idealism

Magosaburo Ohara (1880–1943). (Source: Kurabo Industries)

Achievement of Magosaburo Ohara and related SDGs

Economy	 	* Expansion of yarn production business * Creation of artificial silk (rayon) business

(*continued*)

M. Takehara, N. Hasegawa, *Sustainable Management of Japanese Entrepreneurs in Pre-War Period from the Perspective of SDGs and ESG*, https://doi.org/10.1007/978-981-15-6507-6_10

(continued)

Society	1 NO POVERTY; 3 GOOD HEALTH AND WELL-BEING; 4 QUALITY EDUCATION; 5 GENDER EQUALITY; 11 SUSTAINABLE CITIES AND COMMUNITIES; 12 RESPONSIBLE CONSUMPTION AND PRODUCTION	* Improve employees' working conditions * Invest in employees' health * Scientific research on labor issues * Scientific research on poverty problem * Operate museum * Drive R&D * Quality improvement through human resource management
Governance	10 REDUCED INEQUALITIES; 16 PEACE, JUSTICE AND STRONG INSTITUTIONS; 17 PARTNERSHIPS FOR THE GOALS	* Expansion and balanced management * Renewal of personnel system * Labor management based on humanitarianism

Source: Created by authors

1 Early Life

1.1 A Series of Setbacks and Awakening

Magosaburo Ohara was born in 1880 as the third son of Koshiro Ohara, the first president of Kurabo Industries in Kurashiki City, Okayama Prefecture. Magosaburo's grandfather was a prominent millionaire in the region, a landowner who ran various businesses such as kimono fabric, cotton wholesaler, rice wholesaler, and financial institution. Magosaburo's father Koshiro was an adopted son-in-law in the Ohara family.

As both the first and the second sons passed away early in the Ohara family, Magosaburo became an heir who was raised carefully. After graduating from Koto shogakko (higher elementary schools), he entered Shizutani School which the Okayama-han (feudal clan) had established and he began dormitory life. However, he left the school within two years and entered the Tokyo Vocational College (the school later became Waseda University) in 1897. As he was not interested in studying, he became absorbed in idle amusements with his friends. However, Magosaburo was very interested in the mining pollution incident at the Ashio copper mine, which was a big social problem in those days, and he actually visited the Ashio copper mine with his friends.

As a result of continuing a life of debauchery, he accumulated a 15,000-yen debt. In those days, the starting monthly salary for a high civil servant, after passing an entrance examination, was about 50 yen. Being the son of a landowner, Magosaburo's sense of the value of money was very distant from ordinary citizens.

Koshiro was very worried about his son's lifestyle, so he ordered Kunisaburo, his son-in-law, to solve the debt problem. As Kunisaburo was much talked about as a bright person, Koshiro highly evaluated his talent and asked him with all eagerness to become an adopted son-in-law in the Ohara family. However, while he was busying with solving Magosaburo's debt problem, Kunisaburo died suddenly at the age of 31. Magosaburo was very shocked to face the fact that his life of debauchery eventually killed his brother-in-law and this incident drastically changed his life.

When Magosaburo was living confined to home in his hometown of Kurashiki, he received a book from a friend in Tokyo. The book was titled *Hotokuki*, written by Sontoku Ninomiya. In those days, much literature related to Hotoku (moral requital) was published and had a significant influence on entrepreneurs such as Sakichi Toyoda (founder of Toyota Motor) and Tsurukichi Hatano (president of Gunze Silk). Ohara made up his mind to proceed with the future of his life by practicing the thought of Hotoku, which was based on Kinken-rikko (which means to work diligently, live a frugal life, and continue your efforts).

1.2 Participation in Social Activities

An encounter with Juji Ishii was a major turning point for Ohara. Ishii was born in Miyazaki in 1865 and he studied at the Koshu Medical School in Okayama Prefecture with the aim of becoming a doctor. He was baptized while attending the medical school and devoted his life to orphan relief. After returning home, Ohara, who had lost sight of his life goals, happened to watch the orphans' performances at the invitation of his friend. He was impressed by the philosophy and activities of Ishii, host of the concert. Then he started to participate in a Bible study meeting with the recommendation of Ishii, and this experience made him grow mentally. Magosaburo's diary at that time had the following description: "I was granted the property not for me but for society. Utilizing the property granted to me, I will work according to the will of God. I was born for God and society and my property was made for God and for society".[1] From this description, we can see the emergence of his awareness of a commitment to social work.

Recognizing his social mission, Ohara concentrated his efforts on social education projects such as (1) the establishment of the Kurashiki Educational Society, (2) development of educational activities, (3) assistance to Okayama Orphanage, and (4) Kurashiki Sunday Lectures.

He established the Kurashiki Educational Society to reform elementary and secondary education. The activities developed into the establishment of the Kurabo Industries Crafts Education Department, the establishment of the Private Kurashiki Commercial School, and the establishment of the Kurashiki Scholarship Foundation. He positioned these educational activities as not just financial support but a social reform.

In 1901, responding to Ishii's request, he took on the role as a financial officer of the Okayama Orphanage. Ishii was aiming for an economically independent orphanage; however, due to a rapid increase of orphans, funds for activities continued to be extremely short. Realizing that financial independence from business revenue was impossible, Ishii came up with a plan to set up an endowment fund from supporting members. When the amount of capital raised for 100 yen per unit reached 200,000 yen, it became the endowment fund, and, thereafter, the operating profit of the endowment fund would be appropriated for operating expenses. His remark "I and Okayama Orphanage are all in one body"[2] implies that Ohara believed the orphan relief project as his lifetime mission.

The Kurashiki Sunday Lectures were inspired by an article of Aizan Yamaji, who was the leading writer of the *Shinano Mainichi* newspaper. Ishii read this article and encouraged Ohara to hold lectures on Sundays in Kurashiki and distribute the minutes of lectures to the general public in order to cultivate religious morality in society.

In 1902, the first lecture was held, and the reputation increased with each round of lectures. All of the operating expenses were borne by Ohara, and in total 76 lectures were given until 1925. The speakers invited to the lectures were leading intellects of the days in Japan, such as Shigenobu Okuma,[3] Meizen Kinpara,[4] Soho Tokutomi,[5] and Inazo Nitobe.[6]

2 The Essence of Magosaburo Ohara's Management

2.1 Organizational Reform of Kurabo Industries

In 1904, Magosaburo Ohara, at 24 years of age, became the seventh head of the Ohara family. The following year, he was formally baptized and joined the Okayama Christian Church. Although there is no official record of how he joined Kurabo Industries, it is believed that he joined the company in about 1906.

Ohara was studying about the social reformer Robert Owen (UK) and the welfare policy of the Krupp Company in Germany. In 1906, a typhoid fever occurred in the girls' dormitory of Kurabo Industries, and the company's response was criticized. Magosaburo's father, Koshiro, decided to retire in order to settle the situation and handed over both positions of the president of Kurabo Industries and the president of Kurashiki Bank to Magosaburo. Assuming the position of president of two companies, Ohara immediately worked on management reforms. The key points of his reforms were (1) renewal of the personnel system, (2) establishment of labor management based on humanitarianism, and (3) aggressive expansion strategy. For human resource development, Ohara actively recruited graduates of educational institutions, and among the graduates who were recruited were those from the Ohara Scholarship.

A review of the labor system began with the reform of the "hanba" (shop) system.[7] In order to reduce costs, the spinning companies used outside contractors to perform a food-related operation called "hanba", a kind of outsourcing. Hanba (shop) dealers, who were selling daily commodities and meals, were misusing the company's inability to control, making a lot of money by reducing the quality of meals and even collecting introduction fees for female workers. Ohara could not overlook this situation, so he abolished the "hanba" system. The hanba dealers fiercely resisted; however, he carried out his original policy without compromise.

Next, he worked on improving employees' housing. The female workers at the spinning mill were forced to live in a poor environment. Kurabo Industries was no exception, and it housed many female workers in a large room dormitory. The factory had a 12-hour work shift throughout the night, and it was a harsh situation where female workers with an early shift and a late shift lived in the same room. In addition, many of them suffered from pulmonary tuberculosis and respiratory diseases from an unsanitary living environment. At Kurabo Industries, about 1000 female workers were forced to live in dormitories.

Ohara decided to build a one-story decentralized dormitory; however, shareholders opposed the construction of a welfare facility that would not make a profit. He tried to gain understanding from the opponents by reducing the bonuses for directors and by distributing most of the net profit for shareholder dividend (30% dividend).

Fig. 10.1 Decentralized dormitories. (Source: Kurabo Industries)

In 1912, 76 new dormitories with sewing rooms, cafeterias and schools were completed (Fig. 10.1). At the end of 1914, ancillary facilities such as clinics and baths were also completed. Ohara talked to the female workers as follows:[8]

Since last year, we have rebuilt the dormitory to prevent you from becoming sick. We also set up a goods distribution center so that you do not have to waste money. We also founded a school so that you can read letters and sew as decent women ... This company policy is based on humanitarianism, and as long as you were born as a human being, we will help you to be a good person ... Our company wants to make you feel comfortable, illness free, and avoid wasting money, so you can send money to your parents and save a lot of money. I want you to spend a happy life by studying and working hard.

Ohara took such measures more than ten years before the famous publication of Wakizo Hosoi's (1925) "Factory Women's Sad History" which depicted the miserable situation of female workers at spinning mills.

The factory law was enacted in 1911, raising social interest in workers' rights. In the spinning industry, which had a greater interest in increasing production capacity than female employees' welfare benefits, Ohara's various initiatives were ahead of the expectations of companies to work on Sustainable Development Goals (SDGs) in the modern era (especially, Goal 9, Decent work).

2.2 *Conversion to Aggressive Management*

The spinning industry in Japan grew rapidly from the middle of the Meiji period (1868–1912) to the Taisho period (1912–1926). However, excessive capital investment caused a disaster, resulting in an excessive supply, which forced a shortening of operations and a merger of companies. The scale of equipment per spinning company increased from 17,215 spindles (1900) to 63,823 spindles (1911).[9] In 1901, Sanji Muto, the president of Kanegahuchi Spinning, announced the "Spinning Industry Joint Theory" and emphasized the necessity of a merger of spinning companies and the economic effects.

In 1906, Kurabo Industries was offered a merger with another company. Ohara, as the president, refused the offer and maintained independent management. In 1908, as the major companies in the industry, Mie Spinning (the company later became Toyobo) had a production scale of 179,604 spindles, Kanebo Spinning had 179,168 spindles, and Settsu Spinning had 125,832 spindles; however, Kurabo Industries produced only 29,584 spindles. Ohara was aware that companies with less than 30,000 spindles could not survive, and the only option to secure 30,000 spindles was to build a new factory or acquire another company. As a result of a series of mergers, the realignment of the spinning industry proceeded rapidly and there remained only three companies in Okayama Prefecture with a scale of more than 10,000 spindles, including Kurabo Industries. Ohara succeeded in acquiring Kibi Spinning, a subsidiary of Mitsui & Company, and named it the Tamashima Factory of Kurabo Industries, and with this acquisition, the production scale of Kurabo Industries expanded to 58,920 spindles.

Subsequently, Kurabo Industries newly established the Masu Plant (1915) and the Takamatsu Plant (1920), and through mergers and acquisitions, acquired five factories: Sakaide and Matsuyama (1918), Hayashima (1921), Okayama Kitakata (1922), and Hirakata (1924). The production capacity of Kurabo Industries expanded from 30,000 spindles (1906) to 231,348 spindles (1924), becoming the sixth largest scale in the industry.

In addition to the dramatic expansion of production capacity, due to the establishment of the Masu Plant, the business performance of Kurashiki Industries grew steadily thanks to favorable economic conditions after World War I. During this period, Ohara worked to strengthen the financial position and paid a high shareholder dividend from the second half of 1917 to the first half of 1920 (Table 10.1).

Table 10.1 Development of Kurabo Industries

Year	*1888*		*1905*		*1924*	
Capital (Yen)	100,000		400,000		12,350,000	
Capital-to-assets ratio (%)	1889/ Second half	83	Second half	78.2	Second half	73.1
Annual net profit (Yen)	1890/ Full year	20,444	Full year	150,019	Full year	2,537,369
Dividend payout ratio (%)	1889/ Second half	16.5	First half Second half	35 30	First half Second half	20 20
Spinning machine (spindle)	4472		29,584		231,348	
National spinning machine (spindle)	129,376		1,472,253		5,125,696	
The ratio to whole country (%)	3.5		2.0		4.5	

Source: Kurabo Industries (1988), p. 105. Author revised

2.3 Development of Rayon—Establishment of Kurashiki Silk Fabric (Kuraray)

Thread prices plummeted due to the post-war recession that began in 1920, and the spinning industry, which expanded its production capacity, was extremely sluggish; therefore, efforts were made to prevent the decline in yarn prices by adjusting production at the industry level. Production adjustments caused criticism from society and were forced to be fully lifted in just two years. As a consequence, spinning companies were forced to seek their own survival strategies. The major spinning companies worked on relocating production to the mainland of China, integrating spinning and cotton weaving, increasing the added value of products, and diversifying their businesses, such as developing artificial silk. Suffering from the recession, the cost of the welfare measures promoted by Ohara put a strain on the management of Kurabo Industries.

Major companies such as Kanebo Spinning and Toyobo Spinning promoted business diversification centering on silk spinning, wool, and artificial silk. At that time, attention was focused on rayon (artificial silk), which had a major impact on raw silk exports. In Japan, rayon development was handled by the trading company Suzuki & Co. in the late Meiji era. In

1918, Teikoku Silk (the company later became Teijin, a major textile company) was established as a full-fledged business company.

In 1925, Ohara established the Kurabo Industries Kyoto Chemical Research Laboratory and invited engineers from the Kyoto Imperial University to begin research and development of rayon. The following year, Kurashiki Silk Weaving Co., Ltd. (the Japanese name was Kurashiki Kenshoku Co., and the company later became Kuraray Co., Ltd.) was established, and the production of rayon yarn began two years later. In 1964, the company created Clarino, an innovative artificial leather, used in various fields such as shoes, bags, sporting goods, jackets, and sofas.

2.4 *Banking*

With the rapid growth of Kurabo Industries, the company needed to respond to the strong financial demand, and Ohara served as the head of Kurashiki Bank, entrusted by his father Koshiro. Many financial institutions in Okayama Prefecture were small in size and had a problem with creditworthiness. In preparation for a reactionary recession after World War I, the government encouraged a merger of financial institutions with a policy of one bank in a prefecture. Ohara agreed with the government policy and took leadership of promoting the merger of banks in Okayama Prefecture.

In 1919, six banks, including Kurashiki Bank, merged to form Dai-ichi Godo (Joint) Bank, and Ohara took over as head of the new bank. After that, Dai-ichi Godo Bank acquired weak financial institutions in the prefecture one after another. However, the austerity policy implemented by the Japanese government at that time, and also lifting the ban on the export of gold, led to the deterioration of the economy, and the business of Kurabo Industries continued to deteriorate. The deterioration of Kurashiki Industries' business resulted in the deterioration of assets of Dai-ichi Godo Bank. Ohara requested a relief loan from the Nippon Kogyo Bank (Industrial Bank of Japan). The financial authorities in return strongly urged a merger with Sanyo Bank, whose financial condition had also deteriorated.

In 1930, Chugoku Bank was established through the merger of Dai-ichi Godo Bank and Sanyo Bank, and Ohara took over as head. Magosaburo Ohara, who survived the crisis by obtaining a relief loan from the Industrial Bank of Japan, carried out rationalization of Kurabo Industries and the Chugoku Bank.

2.5 *Electric Power Business*

Magosaburo's involvement with electric power business began with Kurashiki Dento (electric light) Company (established in 1909). Through the management of this company, he was convinced that key industrial energy would change from steam to electricity. At the extraordinary shareholders' meeting in 1912, Ohara proposed a new plan for the independent power plant of Kurabo Industries (2000 kw). In 1915, the Kurashiki Power Station in Kurabo Industries started to transmit electricity and supplied surplus power to Kurashiki Electric Light Power. He also had a plan for large-scale hydropower generation in the northern mountainous area in anticipation of expanding the power for the demand in the southern part of Okayama Prefecture, where industrialization was progressing.

In order to prepare an environment for integrating power companies in Okayama Prefecture, Ohara merged small- and medium-sized electric companies and developed them into the company Chugoku Godo Electric. Next, he transferred his shares of Chugoku Godo Electric to Sanyo Chuo Hydroelectric Company and planned to merge the two companies. In 1941, the two companies merged to become the Sanyo Distribution, and the new company developed into Chugoku Electric Power, which was established after the war.

3 Challenges to Social Issues

3.1 *Succession of Orphan Relief Business*

Through his regret of a life of debauchery in his youth, his encounter with Hotoku thought, and also Christianity, Magosaburo Ohara acquired puritan beliefs. In particular, meeting with Juji Ishii was an influential turning point in his life.

The Okayama Orphanage had a branch in Osaka, and it was implementing an orphan relief project. In 1914, Ohara became the director of the Okayama Orphanage to take over the activities of Ishii, who had died without fulfilling his life's ambition. Ishii had been aiming to run the orphanage as economically independent; however, it was difficult for the orphanage to break away from its dependence on donations, and with the outbreak of World War I, the operation of the Osaka Branch fell into an extremely difficult situation. In 1917, Ohara made the Osaka Branch independent and established the Ishii Memorial Aizome Foundation with his own assets.

Ohara became aware of the importance of preventing poverty rather than providing relief, as Ishii's poverty relief activities did not always succeed, and he gained a deeper understanding of the social background that created orphans. With a strong awareness of the need to study poverty as a social issue, he was determined to establish an institution which would scientifically study labor issues and poverty relief projects.

3.2 The Ohara Institute for Social Research

Magosaburo Ohara established a poverty relief research laboratory within the newly established Ishii Memorial Aizome Foundation and he began scientific research on poverty relief activities at his private expense. This laboratory later developed into the Ohara Institute for Social Research. A year after this laboratory was established, the so-called "rice riot" broke out in Toyama Prefecture and quickly spread throughout the country.

In regard to the widening economic disparity and intensifying conflicts among classes, Ohara strongly recognized the need to study social issues. He visited intellects, such as Soho Tokutomi and Kaoru Kawakami,[10] to ask for their cooperation. The existence of the Takashi Hara cabinet, established in response to the rice riot, was also a tailwind for him. In 1919, the Ohara Institute for Social Research was established, and research on labor and social issues based on a social scientific perspective started. The institute became close to the personnel research group of Kurabo Industries. In 1937, upon its relocation to Tokyo, the institute transitioned to independent management, and after World War II, the institute was transferred to Hosei University, and continues its research activities as the Hosei University Ohara Institute for Social Research (Fig. 10.2).

3.3 The Institute for Science of Labour

The Ohara Institute for Social Research was conducting research on occupational health as well as social issues. Ohara invited researchers to the Kurabo Industries Masu Factory and disclosed the labor conditions of female workers. In those days, every request for a site visit to a spinning mill had been rejected, and as a result the labor situation of female workers

Fig. 10.2 The Ohara Institute for Social Research, Hosei University. (Source: Hosei University)

was not well known. Researchers are said to have been impressed by the words of Ohara, "Would you please come to our factory and investigate so that our female workers will be able to work more pleasantly and lead a happier life?"[11]

In 1920, the field of social hygiene became independent from the Ohara Institute for Social Research, and the Kurashiki Institute for Science of Labour was established within Kurabo Industries. The institute conducted unique research on topics such as the relationship between temperature/humidity in the factory and production efficiency/health management, and also the calorie requirements and menus for workers. The institute is still conducting research as the Ohara Memorial Institute for Science of Labour.

3.4 *Kurabo Central Hospital*

During 18 years from 1906 to 1924, the spinning equipment of Kurabo Industries increased approximately eight times (231,348 spindles), and the number of employees also increased rapidly. The medical care of employees was carried out at a medical office established within the company's factories; however, its capacity was approaching its limits. In 1918, with the operation of newly built Masu Second Factory, Ohara decided to build a hospital to improve employees' health management. He led the construction project under the policy of: (1) it would be designed to provide the best medical treatment, (2) build a hospital with a pleasant atmosphere, (3) treat patients equally, and (4) build an ideal hospital and the best in Asia.

In 1923, Kurabo Central Hospital (renamed Kurashiki Central Hospital in 1927) was opened with the principle of egalitarianism and treatment as the first policy. The fee for hospitalization was fixed at 2.50 yen, and the employees of Kurabo Industries and their families were subsidized by the company so that their actual cost was less than 20% of the prescribed fee. The hospital wards were expanded after the opening and there were 220 beds in 1926. Some shareholders expressed their dissatisfaction with the huge investment in a hospital which was non-profitable. Magosaburo Ohara remarked as follows and dismissed the voices of criticism:[12]

> When I explained the concept of establishing a central hospital, I used the term "socialization of a profitable company", and this may have caused misunderstanding. However, I have never planned any business plan without careful calculation. (Omitted) It may seem to you that Kurabo Industries incurs losses year after year by establishing the Central Hospital, but in reality, the establishment of the hospital will be beneficial to Kurashiki's economy. And, I'm convinced that these effects will bring great benefits to Kurabo even if they don't appear on the numbers.[13]

3.5 *The Ohara Museum of Art*

The Ohara Museum of Art began with Magosaburo Ohara's encounter with a Western-style painter, Torajiro Kojima, from Okayama Prefecture. Kojima gained the acquaintance of Ohara as a scholar at the Ohara Scholarship Society.

The friendship between the two continued until Kojima's death. Empress Shoken, the empress of the Meiji emperor, very much liked one of Kojima's works titled "Guard of Love" which Kojima painted at the Okayama Orphanage, so it was purchased by the Ministry of the Imperial Household.

Kojima studied in Europe with the help of Ohara, and he came up with the idea of collecting Western paintings as references for painting and teaching materials for young painters. Ohara provided private property to support Kojima's idea. Paintings Kojima collected, such as Monet's "Water lilies" and El Greco's "Annunciation", became the foundation of the Ohara Museum of Art. In 1927, Kojima planned the construction of a museum and Ohara agreed to the plan, but it was forced to be canceled due to the recession. Two years later, Kojima passed away at the age of 47.

Ohara lamented Kojima's death and began to construct the museum. The construction of the museum, requiring huge amounts of investment in the middle of the recession, was criticized; however, he carried out his will. The Ohara Museum of Art opened in 1930 for the purpose of showing Kojima's own works and also the paintings collected by him. At the time of its opening, there was little interest in Western art, and there were few visitors. Ohara argued that the museum was his most unsuccessful work; however, the Ohara Museum of Art continued to exist, and became a public foundation in 2011.

4 Magosaburo Ohara's Management Philosophy: Labor Idealism

Magosaburo Ohara developed modern manufacturing and financial businesses based on the wealth of financial resources he inherited from his ancestors and became an entrepreneur representing the Meiji and Taisho eras (1868–1926). However, he was also deeply interested in social and labor issues, and developed various activities to solve those problems. His thoughts and efforts anticipated society's expectation for companies to work on social issues, as described in SDGs in modern era.

In Japan, wealthy entrepreneurs were considered to have a feudal and conservative character. However, Ohara, who had a management philosophy similar to creating shared value (CSV) as advocated by Michael Porter, can be said to have been unique in his era. As an entrepreneur, who achieved both solving social problems and corporate management, other than Magosaburo Ohara, Osamu Muto of Kanegahuchi Spinning was also conducting pioneering activities. Muto, based on humanitarianism and paternalism, improved the working environment to save female workers from a miserable situation, eventually rebuilding Kanegahuchi Spinning, which was once on the verge of bankruptcy, into one of the largest companies in Japan. Muto and Ohara were both Christians and had much in common with their management philosophy.

Ohara acknowledged Muto's management philosophy based on humanitarianism but argued that humanitarian philosophy alone could not solve social problems. He thought that the essence of the problem should be identified by a scientific method, and then a concrete solution should be taken. The place of searching for the truth was the Ohara Institute for Social Research, and Ohara practiced labor idealism with the expression “principle of personality”. His labor idealism, the foundation of his management philosophy, was to create people’s happiness.

Hyoue Ohuchi, former president of Hosei University, once belonged to the Ohara Institute for Social Research, and he stated:

> Ohara was the biggest entrepreneur in the Kansai region west of Osaka through the Taisho and Showa eras. There were more entrepreneurs than Ohara in making money. However, Ohara was an entrepreneur who produced much better results than Mitsui, Mitsubishi, and any other businesspersons, in that he used the wealth he created to carry out public works. None of the Japanese entrepreneurs were as successful as he was with setting high goals in spending money.[14]

Magosaburo Ohara’s philosophy had both idealism and realism, and his characteristics as an entrepreneur can be summarized in four points: (1) management based on equality and humanitarianism, (2) business activities based on the realization of public interests, (3) emphasis on economic independence, and (4) moral sense that controls the notion of profit.

After becoming the president of Kurabo Industries, Ohara introduced a number of innovative policies in organizational management and production systems. With his management ability, that anticipated the trend of the times, Kurabo Industries grew to become one of the leading spinning companies in Japan. He also actively engaged in research and development, such as the development of rayon, with an eye on the future.

However, the greatness of Magosaburo Ohara as an entrepreneur was that he decided to use the profits for the development of human capital and dedicated himself to such a realization. His awareness of responsibility for both employees and the community and practicing those responsibilities as an entrepreneur can be compared to the practice of the SDGs required of companies today.

Needless to say, profits are necessary for the sustained growth of companies; however, management aimed solely at gaining profits is harmful. In modern society, scandals of well-known companies are unending, and the root cause of corporate scandals is considered to be the lack of ethics and the pursuit of greed. In addition, short-termism in pursuit of immediate profits is accelerating the trend.

In 2010, the International Organization for Standardization (ISO) issued an international standard on social responsibility (SR) (ISO 26000). ISO 26000 lists seven core issues of social responsibility: (1) organizational governance, (2) human rights, (3) labor practices, (4) the environment, (5) fair business practices, (6) consumer issues, and (7) community involvement and development.

The management Ohara practiced is in many ways consistent with the social responsibility required by ISO 26000. In order for the socio-economic mechanism to function smoothly, society may need to have an entrepreneur such as Magosaburo Ohara who had an altruistic morality not controlled by selfishness. His efforts seem to require us to re-examine the relationship between business and society (Table 10.2).

Table 10.2 Magosaburo Ohara–related business

Type	*Business/Activities*	*Established*	*Description*
Public activities	Ohara Scholarship Program	1899	Scholarship program providing student loans
	Kurashiki Sunday Lecture	1902	Promoted social education. 76 lectures conducted (ended in 1925)
	Ohara Agricultural Research Institute	1914	Established as Ohara Agricultural Promotion Association
	Okayama Orphanage	1887	Magosaburo became director of Okayama Orphanage in 1914
	Ishii Memorial Aizzome-en	1917	Became independent from Osaka Orphanage Okayama Branch, providing education and relief for the poor
	Ohara Institute for Social Research	1919	Research on social issues and knowledge dissemination. Succeeded to Hosei University Ohara Institute for Social Research
Private business	Kurashiki Labor Science Laboratories	1921	Medical and psychological research on industrial organizations. Succeeded to Labor Science Laboratories
	Kurabo Central Hospital	1923	A regional medical institution for employees and citizens. Succeeded to Kurashiki Central Hospital
	Ohara Museum of Art	1930	An exhibition of Torajiro Kojima and Western paintings
	Kurashiki Spinning Co., Ltd.	1888	Magosaburo became president in 1906
	Kurashiki Silk Co., Ltd.	1926	Manufacture of artificial silk (rayon). This company later became Kuraray Co., Ltd.
	Chugoku Bank	1930	Magosaburo searved as president of Kurashiki Bank in 1906 and president of First Joint Bank in 1919
	Chugoku Joint Electric	1926	Kurashiki Electric (1909), Chugoku Hydroelectric (1922)

Source: Created by author based on various materials

Notes

1. Magosaburo Ohara Biography Publication Committee (1983), page 42.
2. Magosaburo Ohara Biography Publication Committee (1983), page 49.
3. Shigenobu Okuma was the eighth Japanese prime minister and founder of Waseda University
4. Meizen Kimpara (1832–1923) was an entrepreneur during the Meiji period. He contributed to the development of modern Japan through the flood control project in Tenryu River, reclamation of Hokkaido, and reforestation projects.
5. Soho Tokutomi (1863–1957) was a journalist, thinker, and historian who was active during the Meiji to the post-war Showa era.
6. Inazo Nitobe (1862–1933) was educator and thinker. He studied agricultural economics and agriculture.
7. "Hanba system" is one of the labor management systems carried out in mines and construction projects during the Meiji period. In this pre-modern system, workers were housed in a barn called hanba, and they were made to work under strict surveillance, and their wages were cut.
8. Kurabo Industries Centennial History [1988], pp. 75–77.
9. A spindle is a spinning tool that winds yarn.
10. Kaoru Kawakami (1879–1946) was a Japanese economist. He studied Marxian economics at Kyoto Imperial University, but later he resigned and practiced communism.
11. Magosaburo Ohara Biography Publication Committee (1983), page 163.
12. Magosaburo Ohara Biography Publication Committee (1983), page 161.
13. Magosaburo Ohara Biography Publication Committee (1983), page 161.
14. Ouchi (1963), page 227–228.

References

Japan Directors' Association [2008] "Corporate Ethics Learned from Meiji: Exploring CSR from the Origin of Capitalism" Japan Productivity Center Publication.

Kaneda, Reiko [2003] "Pioneers Who Challenged Practicing Welfare: Kosuke Tsuruoka and Magosaburo Ohara" Fujiwara Shoten.

Kaneda, Reiko [2009] "Magosaburo Ohara's Social and Cultural Contribution" Seibundo.

Kawazoe, Noboru and Yamaoka, Yoshinori [1987] "Japanese Entrepreneur and Social, Cultural activities" Toyo Keizai Shinposha.

Kurabo Industries Ltd. (1988) "100-year History of Kurabo Industries".

Magosaburo Ohara Biography Publications Committee [1983] "Magosaburo Ohara Biography".

Otsuki, Katsusuke [2004] "Ohara Magosaburo's Management Development and Social Contribution" Japan Library Center.

Tsuchiya, Takao [2002] "History of Japanese Management Philosophy" ReiTaku University Press.

CHAPTER 11

Tsurukichi Hatano: Creating Value Through Effective Human Resource Management

Tsurukichi Hatano (1858–1920) (Source: Ayabe City Tourism Association)

Achievement of Tsurukichi Hatano and related SDGs

Economy			* Expansion of yarn production business * World-class product development

(*continued*)

M. Takehara, N. Hasegawa, *Sustainable Management of Japanese Entrepreneurs in Pre-War Period from the Perspective of SDGs and ESG*, https://doi.org/10.1007/978-981-15-6507-6_11

(continued)

Society	1 NO POVERTY; 3 GOOD HEALTH AND WELL-BEING; 4 QUALITY EDUCATION; 5 GENDER EQUALITY; 11 SUSTAINABLE CITIES AND COMMUNITIES	* Improve employees' working conditions * Invest in employees' health * Provide organized employee education * Collaboration with local communities * Drive R&D * Quality improvement through human resource management
Governance	10 REDUCED INEQUALITIES; 16 PEACE, JUSTICE AND STRONG INSTITUTIONS; 17 PARTNERSHIPS FOR THE GOALS	* Shareholders for regional development * Renewal of personnel system * Labor management based on love for humanity

Source: Created by authors

1 Early Days

Gunze Silk Manufacturing Co., Ltd. was established in Ayabe City, located in the northern part of Kyoto Prefecture. Ayabe, a mountainous area with a population of about 40,000, was not a good location for fostering new industries. However, in such a severe environment, Tsurukichi Hatano built the foundation for the development of Gunze Silk. Hatano managed Gunze Silk aiming at enriching the lives of his company employees and the people of the local community both physically and mentally and led Gunze Silk to become one of Japan's leading silk manufacturers.[1]

In 1858, Tsurukichi was born, the second son of the Umuro family. According to the taxpayer ranking in 1887, the Umuro family was 11th place in Kyoto Prefecture and 1st place in the Ayabe and Fukuchiyama area. At the age of seven, Tsurukichi was adopted by the Hatano family. The adoption was based on the premise that he would marry Hana, the only daughter of the Hatano family.

When Tsurukichi was adopted, the Hatano family's luck was in decline and also his wealthy parents were hit by financial crisis and went bankrupt. The life environment surrounding Tsurukichi changed completely due to the bankruptcy of his parents and the decline of his adoptive family. For these reasons, he led a depressed time in his younger days. His adoptive mother and adoptive grandmother passed away one after another, and only the 15-year-old Tsurukichi and the 13-year-old Hana were left behind in the Hatano family. Tsurukichi did not have a regular job, and the two survived by selling the land of the Hatano family.

When Tsurukichi Hatano became 17 years old, he moved to Kyoto alone. Giving him an opportunity to study in Kyoto was a condition of his adoption into the Hatano family. Later, he returned to Ayabe and married Hana; however, he returned to Kyoto, leaving his new wife in his hometown.

Tsurukichi's life in Kyoto lasted for seven years. He not only exhausted all of his family's property, but also accumulated a huge debt of 1000 yen. Later, when he joined Christianity, he said he was like the "Prodigal Son" who appeared in the writings of Luke in the New Testament.

In Kyoto, Tsurukichi wrote an educational book called *Keimou-Houteishiki* (literally, "the Enlightenment Equation") and opened a private school called "Suri-Tankyu-Juku" (literally, School for Mathematical Exploration). However, he failed to succeed in this field of study and as a result experienced uneasy days. At the same time, he made a youthful mistake of becoming infected with syphilis. Being at a loss, he decided to return to his hometown of Ayabe.

Tsurukichi's wife, Hana, was a kind-hearted woman, and while he lived in Kyoto, he often asked Hana to pay his living expenses. She did not complain about anything and continued to send him the money she earned by selling her family's land.

Tsurukichi, who returned home in disappointment in 1881, became a substitute teacher at an elementary school through the introduction of an acquaintance. Although he did not have a formal teacher's license, he maintained a good reputation among the students, and his teacher's life lasted for more than four years. These four years were an important time for Tsurukichi. Through his students, he was able to learn more about the farmers and their situations. Knowing how the poor lived, he began to think about the problems the community faced.

By starting a new life as an elementary school teacher, Tsurukichi Hatano's way of life gradually changed. Because of his previous selfish behavior, when he returned home, local people often looked at him coldly. However, as he changed his way of life, the local people gradually began to trust him. Later, Hatano became deeply involved with the local people through the silk industry.

2 The Road to Entrepreneur

2.1 *Encounter with the Silk Industry*

In Ayabe in the Meiji period (1868–1912), sericulture was widespread as a farmer's secondary business. During the end of the Edo period, the Ayabe-han(domain) was advised by Nobuhiro Sato, a renowned farmer who worked on agriculture and rural reform, to switch its agriculture to the cultivation of commercial crops. Ayabe accepted Sato's recommendation and promptly encouraged their farmers to cultivate commercial crops. After attempts to produce cotton, tea, tobacco, and so on, they found sericulture (cocoons) to be the most suitable for the land of Ayabe. Thus, the sericulture industry developed as a local industry.

The sericulture farmers in those days did not have the idea of cooperating with each other. Consequently, wholesalers took advantage of the farmers who lacked a sense of solidarity with each other and knew little of cocoon price. The wholesalers skillfully persuaded the farmers to reduce the price of cocoons. Even so, the sericulture farmers did not work together to improve the quality of cocoons; they simply contented themselves with their status quo.

Tsurukichi Hatano saw with his own eyes the farmers who produced cocoons using traditional methods without showing any interest in cocoon distribution systems and selling prices. He looked at the problems of each individual sericulture farmer as structural problems of the local community. He was fully aware that the lack of cooperation between farmers resulted in a negative impact on the quality of the silk production industry in the Ayabe region.

In 1875, at the national exhibition of products held in Tokyo, the cocoons and raw silk exhibited by Ayabe famers were evaluated as the worst quality products. The following year, Hatano was appointed as the head of the Silk Industry Association in his region (Ikaruga-gun) and started to work on community reform through sericulture business.

2.2 *Activities as the Head of the Silk Industry Association*

An encounter with Kazusuke Umehara, who was operating a silk thread business in Ayabe, opened the path for Hatano as the head of the Silk Industry Association. When the Ikaruga-gun Silk Industry Association was established, Umehara recommended Hatano to become the head.

Since the Silk Industry Association handled raw silk, a valuable export item, Umehara thought Hatano would be appropriate for the position as he could speak English.

In later years, Umehara said, "I was so fortunate to meet a tremendous talent". This tremendous talent was Hatano. Umehara's words indicate that the recommendation for Hatano to become the head of the silk industry association led to the establishment of the company Gunze Silk and also the benefit of local people. The encounter with Umehara opened a new way for Hatano as an entrepreneur.

Looking back on Hatano's activities as the head of the silk industry association, the biggest mission for him was to improve the quality of the cocoons which had been criticized as the worst quality. To achieve this mission, he thought two elements were important: technological innovation and human resource development.

He dispatched people to Gunma Prefecture, an advanced area of sericulture, to investigate production methods and advanced technologies. Through this investigation, Hatano learned that Gunma's silk thread quality was supported by advanced technology and Christianity. It is needless to say that the introduction of advanced technology is important for quality improvement; however, how did Christianity relate to quality improvement?

In those days in Japan, the silk industry was prosperous in Gunma Prefecture and a large number of foreign residents, who were involved in the raw silk export business, lived there. As a result, Christianity had taken root in Gunma from early times, and many of Gunma's leading silk thread traders were Christians who practiced their faith in business management. For example, at that time, it was common that female workers at a silk production factory were called "Joko" (literally, factory girls); however, at a factory whose manager became Christian, they were called "craft women". There was a note of contempt in the name "Joko" in Japanese. However, entrepreneurs influenced by Christianity valued the personality of female workers by calling them "Kojo" (craft women). In other words, Christian altruism and humanitarianism created a management philosophy whereby cherishing workers led to the companies' prosperity. This management view had a great influence on Tsurukichi Hatano's life.

Why do companies need to value human resources in order to improve the quality of their products? In Japan, quality improvement campaigns centering on quality control (QC) circles were actively conducted during the period of high economic growth. This was because, even if advanced technologies were introduced, products' quality improvement could not be realized without employees' awareness and capabilities. The reason behind the success of the QC movement in Japan was the existence of highly motivated workers. The voluntary actions of employees with high morals and motivation were the driving force for quality improvement. It can be said that it was the companies' commitment to cherish their employees and education that cultivated high professional ethics which enabled those quality improvements.

Hatano began his reform with changing the mindset of cocoon farmers who were reluctant to work voluntarily. He thought that the best way to improve the quality of cocoons was to improve the farmers' mindset first and then to acquire advanced technology.

3 Birth of the Gunze Silk

3.1 From Association to Company

Working on expanding the common interests of the local community as the head of the Silk Industry Association, Hatano came to think that the association needed to be incorporated to further develop local industry.

However, the people in the area were hesitant, and did not understand his vision.

At such a time, Hatano had the chance to listen to a speech of Masana Maeda, the President of the Japan Business Association (Fig 11.1), and he was very impressed. Maeda was a person who served as the Vice Minister of Agriculture and Commerce, and he had the idea that nurturing traditional industries would lead to development of a country with competitive industry and a strong military.

Maeda insisted on the following proposal: "Just as the government sets 'Koku-ze' (national policy), each prefecture should set 'Fuken-ze' (prefecture policy), each county should set 'Gun-ze' (county policy), and each town and village should set 'Cho-son-ze' (town and village policy).[2] And then, integrating these policies together, we should encourage domestic production and promote trade."

Hatano sympathized with Maeda's philosophy of nurturing industry by setting the county policy (named in Japanese "Gunze"). The term Gunze later became the company name of Gunze Silk. The company name included the meaning of bringing together the power of local people and aiming for the development of local communities (Fig 11.2).

Fig. 11.1 Masana Maeda. (Source: Soda, Osamu 1987, "Maeda, Masana" Yoshikawa Kobunkan)

Fig. 11.2 Gunze Silk head office. (Source: Gunze Limited, Website https://www.gunze.co.jp/engligh/)

In 1890, the general meeting for establishing the company Gunze Silk was held, and Hatano's brother, Kaemon Hamuro, became the president. Hatano himself took office as a director and had the executive power of managing the company. The new company started with capital of 98,000 yen, 20 regular employees, and 200 workers.

We can find a characteristic of Gunze Silk in its shareholder composition. A large number of Gunze Silk's shareholders had just one share, and they accounted for approximately 37% (279 people) of all shareholders at the time of its establishment (Fig. 11.3). Those shareholders with just one share were sericulture farmers, and this unique shareholder composition reflected Hatano's strategic intention. Shareholders had the right to receive dividends as the owners of the company. In other words, the profits of Gunze Silk were returned to the local sericulture farmers in the form of stock dividends. Hatano aimed at making the profits of Gunze Silk a common benefit for the local community and enriching people's lives. In order

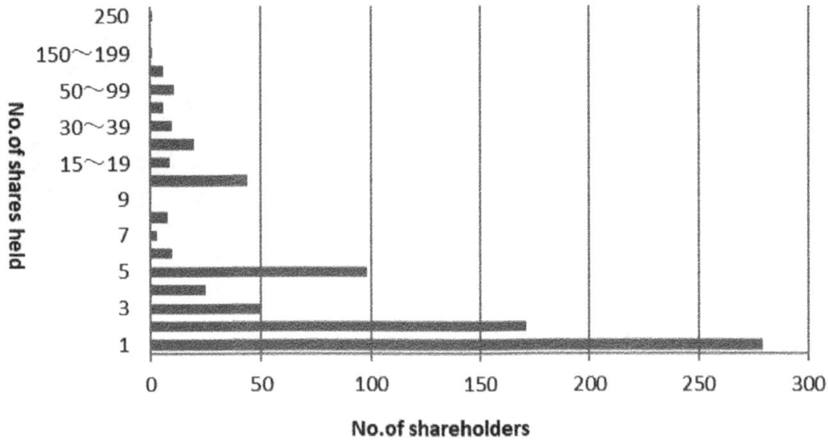

Fig. 11.3 Distribution of shareholders in Gunze Silk (from the 4th business report). (Source: Hiroshi Shikata 1997, "Yuza-no-utsuwa" page 128, the Ayabe Civic Newspaper [Author revised])

to realize such a philosophy, he intentionally made such a shareholder composition, and he clearly denied the idea that only the wealthy would monopolize profits.

Looking at the financial performance of Gunze Silk, the company recorded a deficit of 6200 yen in the first year. However, from the second year, the company achieved a single-year profit, and in the third year it paid a 10% dividend. In the fourth year, the company recorded a profit of 24,000 yen and paid a 40% dividend. From this year, Gunze Silk started business with Mitsui & Co., a major trading company. Gunze Silk continued to perform well, and it developed into the second largest silk manufacturer in Japan, following Katakura Yarn during the pre-war period.

3.2 *Efforts to Improve Quality*

Tsurukichi Hatano took strong actions to fundamentally reform the trading method of cocoons in order to improve quality, a long-standing issue. Until then, a common trading method was sample trading. The sericulture farmers picked up cocoons of excellent quality from the cocoons they produced and provided them as a sample. Then, the wholesalers appraised the sample and determined the grades and prices, a kind of auction method. In sample trading, the wholesaler collated the delivered products with the sample and purchased only the cocoons which passed the test.

However, the problem of sample trading was that there was a big disparity in the quality of the sample and cocoons actually delivered. The rate of delivered products which successfully passed the test was only 10–20%, and the rest of cocoons were all wasted as defective products. Moreover, it took a tremendous amount of time to check the delivered cocoons one by one with the sample.

Even if the farmers produced bad cocoons, if they deceived buyers, they could sell those bad cocoons at the price of the sample. As these bad practices were common, farmers did not make efforts to improve the quality of the cocoons.

Hatano thought that sample trading hindered the improvement of cocoon quality, and he introduced a new trading method, "Seiryo-trading" (literally, "right amount trading").

In this right amount trading, sericulture associations in each village and wholesalers signed a contract in advance, and cocoons produced by sericulture farmers belonging to the sericulture association in each village were delivered collectively.

The price was determined after cocoons were processed into yarns and their quality was evaluated by a scientific method. Hatano introduced the rational method of determining the price of the cocoons after assessing their qualities.

The introduction of this method enabled the setting of cocoon prices to be based on their qualities, not by bargaining or market conditions. In addition, it had the effect of informing the public about the quality of the products of Gunze Silk.

In right amount trading, a contract was made on a village basis. Therefore, individual sericulture farmers were required to make efforts to produce high-quality cocoons. When poor quality cocoons were mixed, they made bad yarns that broke immediately. Thus, sericulture farmers came to have a strong sense of responsibility for quality improvement. The introduction of this right amount trading improved the quality of cocoons dramatically.

3.3 A School for Factories

Gunze Silk also concentrated resources on the education of their employees, and it was said to be a school for a factory. Hatano thought that the key to the quality improvement of cocoon products was both the

Fig. 11.4 Inside Gunze Silk Factory. (Source: Gunze Limited Website, https://www.gunze.co.jp)

reformation of sericulture farmers' mindset and also the moral improvement of female workers at the factory (they were called craftswomen in Gunze Silk). In other words, he was aiming at improving the quality of Gunze's products at both stages of production of raw material and final products.

Hatano is said to have made the following comments to female workers working for Gunze Silk: "If your heart is pure, you can make a glossy yarn. If your heart is honest, you can make homogeneous yarn. If your mind is gentle, you can make a jointless yarn. If you are always careful, you can make a yarn that is unbreakable. If you have nothing to be ashamed of, you can make a strong yarn." Thus, he thought that the improvement of morals and motivations of female workers were indispensable for the quality improvement of products (Fig 11.4).

Hatano thought that creating an environment in which female workers were willing to work was the first step in producing quality products. Instead of treating female workers as consumables, he tried to polish their abilities and personalities with great affection. He opened a night school for female workers from the following year of the foundation of the company. The contents of the lectures were concentrated on general education that women in those days needed to acquire, such as morality, reading, arithmetic, and sewing. In 1908, he established an education department and Gunze Women's Society within the company to further improve employee education. Furthermore, in 1913, a teaching course was set up in the education department, and graduates of the teaching course were dispatched to each factory as teachers. Gunze Silk was said to be "a factory if we look it from the front, but it is actually a school".

At that time, besides Gunze Silk, there were only two other companies, Kurashiki Spinning and Kanebo Spinning, which invested in employee education. The textile industry in those days overworked female workers with low wages and long working hours, and the health of many female workers was harmed due to poor working environments. It seems that female workers realized that working for Tsurukichi Hatano led to their happiness. Thus, the high motivation and morals of female workers at Gunze Silk became the driving force for producing high-quality products.

4 Creating Corporate Value Through Mission-oriented Management

4.1 Tsurukichi Hatano's View of Religion and Management Philosophy

Hatano loved the local people and his employees and focused on realizing moral innovation through education. We can see the influence of both Christianity and also the thought of "Hotoku" (moral requital) as the background of his management philosophy.

When Tsurukichi Hatano returned to Ayabe from Kyoto, he met a person named Keizo Tanaka, who was the first Christian in Ayabe. Hatano learned two things from Tanaka. One was knowledge about sericulture methods. There were two types of sericulture methods: "tensan" method and "kasan" method. The former is a method of keeping silkworms outdoors (wild silkworm), and the latter is a method to raise silkworms indoors (domesticated silkworm). Tanaka insisted on the efficiency of the tensan method, but Hatano was convinced of the superiority of the kasan method from the viewpoint of safety and quality improvement.

Secondly, he met Christianity through Tanaka. Hatano had learned that there were companies in Gunma Prefecture which treated female workers decently, and the reason was that many executives of those companies became Christian. Through Tanaka, Hatano began to accept the teachings of Christianity.

Another element that formed Hatano's management view is Hotoku thought. Hotoku thought, which was advocated by Sontoku Ninomiya at the end of the Edo period, was a management philosophy that aimed at uniting morality and economy, based on the diligence of individuals. Hatano's management philosophy and business spirit were born from the fusion of Christian altruism and the professional ethics of Hotoku thought.

Adding local cocoon farmers to the shareholders of Gunze Silk was a manifestation of Hatano's management philosophy that Gunze Silk was a common property of the local community. This management philosophy was born from the recognition of cherishing collaboration with all stakeholders surrounding the company. Gunze's efforts can be said to be ahead of SDG 17, "Achieving goals through partnerships".

There is an anecdote that shows Tsurukichi Hatano's character. One day, Zenjiro Yasuda, the founder of Yasuda Zaibatsu, one of the major financial conglomerates in those days in Japan, visited Hatano (Fig. 11.5). At that time, the main bank of Gunze Silk was Hyakusanju Bank (the 130th Bank); however, the bank went bankrupt during the Russo-Japanese War (1904–1905). It was Yasuda Bank (this bank later became the current Mizuho Bank, one of three Japanese "Mega Banks") led by Zenjiro Yasuda which took over the business of the 130th Bank. Yasuda went to Ayabe to meet and evaluate Hatano, the manager of Gunze Silk, because the 130th Bank had provided a large loan to Gunze Silk. When Yasuda visited the company, Hatano devoted himself to weeding in a poor cotton kimono. Not knowing the man was Hatano, Yasuda asked him for the president. After a while, the man who was weeding appeared again in front of Yasuda, saying he was the president of Gunze. Looking at Hatano, Yasuda said to him, "I understand your company and your spirit well. You don't have to worry about financing. I, Yasuda support you." and he went home. Probably, Yasuda immediately understood the qualities of Hatano as an entrepreneur and the company's management philosophy from his appearance.

Fig. 11.5 Zenjiro Yasuda. (Source: Portraits of Modern Japanese Historical Figures, National Diet Library, https://www.ndl.go.jp/portrait/e/)

4.2 *Quality Recognized by the World*

In 1900, at the World Exposition held in Paris, the products of Gunze Silk won a gold award. This was the moment that Hatano's many years of efforts bore fruit and it was one of the prime times in his life.

The following year, Hatano became the president of Gunze Silk. He succeeded in raising a product once criticized as "the poorest quality product" to world-class quality in just 25 years after he became the head of the Silk Trade Association.

A major US trading company, Skinner, found that there was a particularly good quality of raw silk imported from Japan. That product was made by Gunze Silk, and Skinner asked Gunze for the right to sell their products. In those days, the biggest demand in the USA was for fine thread used in women's stockings. Chemical fibers, such as nylon were not yet developed, so silk thread was used for stockings. Fine thread was used for stockings and handkerchiefs, but the quality of the fine thread produced by Gunze was much better in quality.

In Japan's domestic silk market, Gunze Silk was second in the industry after Katakura Yarn. However, in the category of export to overseas, Gunze exceeded Katakura Yarn. Successful development of the highest quality products can be attributed to Hatano's management philosophy that fully utilized human capital and social capital.

5 Conclusion

On February 23, 1918, Tsurukichi Hatano fell down with a cerebral hemorrhage during a lecture at a local veterans association and passed away. He was 60 years old. After Hatano's death, his wife Hana was also baptized as a Christian and lived a simple life until she passed away at the age of 96 in 1957.

Hatano's life was dedicated to realizing the happiness of both his employees and people in the community. He boldly challenged management issues that included mutually contradictory elements such as quality improvement, profit making, customer satisfaction, employees' fulfillments, and integration with local communities. As Hatano denied pursuing his self-interest and continued his altruistic spirits, he could solve these challenges and nurture Gunze Silk into a large company. By making clear his mission as a manager, he continued his efforts to gain support from a wide range of Gunze's stakeholders, including shareholders, customers, employees, and local communities. He founded Gunze Silk based on the traditional silk industry, while also aiming at revitalizing the local community. By adding sericulture farmers as shareholders, he tried to generate a sense of unity between Gunze and the local community. He also enhanced employee motivation and morals by enriching employee education. As a result, he and his company succeeded in producing products that achieved internationally recognized quality. The foreign currency earned from the business of traditional industries, such as Gunze Silk, became the foundation for the growth of Japan's modern industry.

It was Hatano's mission-oriented management, based on the spirit of altruism, that supported the growth of Gunze Silk. His management philosophy that companies exist for their stakeholders succeeded in raising the morals and motivation of local people and employees and producing high-quality products with competitive advantage.

Hatano led Gunze Silk to a value-creating company by integrating the company's direction and the local community's sense of values and knowledge. Finally, we should not forget his wife Hana, who continued to support Hatano with altruistic spirit throughout her life.

Notes

1. Gunze Silk is currently Gunze Limited. Fiscal year 2019's annual sales are 150 billion yen and net profits are 4 billion yen.
2. Municipalities in Japan are divided into prefectures, cities, towns, and villages.

References

Abe, Takeshi and Nakamura, Naofumi edited [2010] "History of Japanese Management Vol.2 Industrial Revolution and Corporate Management" Minerva Publishing.

Gerschenkron, Alexander [2005] (translated by Hideki Edokoro, Mine, Yoichi, Amemiya, Akihiko, Suzuki, Yoshikazu) "Economic History of the Late Industrialized Country: Catch-up type Industrialization" Minerva Publishing.

Gunze Limited [1997] "Gunze 100 Year History".

Murashima, Nagisa [1940] "Tsurukichi Hatano" Gunze Limited.

Nakamura, Takahide [1973] "Constructors of Japanese Economy" Nikkei Inc.

Shikata, Hiroshi [1997] "Yuza-no-utsuwa" Ayabe Civic Newspaper.

PART V

Creating Social Solutions

CHAPTER 12

Kenkichi Kagami: Founder of Insurance Business in Japan

Kenkichi Kagami (1869–1939). (Source: https://www.ndl.go.jp/portrait/datas/458.html)

Achievement of Kenkichi Kagami and related SDGs

Economy	 	* Establishment of non-life insurance system * Building a reinsurance network

(*continued*)

M. Takehara, N. Hasegawa, *Sustainable Management of Japanese Entrepreneurs in Pre-War Period from the Perspective of SDGs and ESG*, https://doi.org/10.1007/978-981-15-6507-6_12

(continued)

Society	 	* Stabilize society through risk management * Reduce risk in corporate management * Research on non-life insurance system * Enhancement of underwriting ability * Establish institution for employees education
Governance	  	* Improve transparency by renewal of accounting methods * Management based on trust * Alliance with foreign insurance companies

Source: Created by authors

1 Birth of Non-life Insurance—Marine Insurance Born from Merchants' Wisdom

Non-life insurance business in Japan began with the establishment of Tokio Marine Insurance[1] in 1879 as a marine insurance company and Tokyo Fire Insurance as a fire insurance company in 1888.[2]

Non-life insurance in Japan initially developed mainly for marine insurance and fire insurance, but with the post-war motorization, automobile insurance and automobile liability insurance have grown, and they are today's main insurance products.

Kenkichi Kagami is the person who made outstanding achievements in Japan's marine insurance history and created the foundation for the non-life insurance industry in Japan.

This chapter will reveal the characteristics of the non-life insurance business and the process of its development in Japan by looking at the various activities of Kagami, who implemented management reforms that reflected the essence of non-life insurance business and created the foundation for the Japanese non-life insurance industry.

Before looking back on Kagami's business and his achievements, this chapter looks at the history of marine insurance which originated in Europe. A leading view about the origin of marine insurance was that it developed from adventure (maritime) "bottomry"[3] in medieval Italy.

Although there was a system called maritime bottomry even in ancient Greek and Roman periods, it developed as a risk sharing method for ships and cargo primarily in Italy, along with the development of Mediterranean trade, where the risk of navigation was relatively small.

Unlike today, it was a story of an era when the probability of accidents could not be statistically grasped. As the name bottomry shows, it was a high-risk, high-return contract, and interest on the principal was a high level of 24% to 36% per voyage.

In 1230, bottomry was stopped under the Pope's order to ban interest. However, with the development of Mediterranean trade, the need to diversify the risks associated with maritime transport increased, and marine insurance began with the wealthy people in northern Italy serving as insurance underwriters.

Marine insurance began in northern Italy during a period of commercial revolution in the fourteenth to fifteenth centuries, and then further developed in the seventeenth century with the rise of the shipping industry centering on the UK, and it is said to have developed from the side businesses of merchants.

In the middle of the seventeenth century, many coffee shops were opened in London. A coffee shop that Edward Lloyd ran (Lloyd's Coffee House) was later developed into a non-life insurance mecca. Lloyd gathered various information and provided it to coffee shop customers to attract them to the shop. Lloyd's coffee shop, which was capable of quickly gathering and providing necessary information ahead of its rivals, became a merchant's information base. It was there that valuable information led to business opportunities and risk avoidance was exchanged. The information collected by Lloyd was mostly related to shipping and trade, such as weather, ocean currents, and international affairs, and this kind of information attracted many shipowners, shippers, and insurance agents. In 1713, Lloyd's was founded by coffee shop patrons, and personal marine insurance was undertaken there.[4]

In 1720, two companies, London Assurance and Royal Exchange Assurance, were established as licensed insurance companies. Since both companies were exclusively authorized to undertake marine insurance, other insurance companies in the corporate organization were completely unable to undertake marine insurance. Fortunately, as Lloyd's was an individual firm, it avoided the ban on underwriting, and since the licensed companies focused on marine insurance as well as fire insurance, Lloyd's grew to account for the majority of marine insurance in London. In the nineteenth century, many marine insurance companies were established in Western European countries in addition to the UK.

2 Birth of Non-life Insurance Business in Japan

2.1 A Similar System to Non-life Insurance

Trade lending was introduced to Japan by the Portuguese during the *Shuin-sen* trade era in the early seventeenth century.[5] It was called "nage-gane", and it was concluded between shippers and capitalists who had knowledge of trade and voyage, and the interest equivalent to insurance premiums was said to be 30–80% per voyage. However, "nage-gane" disappeared due to the Edo Shogunate's national isolation policy.

"Marine contract", which is a transaction similar to marine insurance, developed in Japan. This is a risk management method created by regular maritime transport, represented by the Higaki and Barrel ships in the Edo period. The maritime contract was a transportation contract in which the shipping wholesaler or shipowner bore the damage if the cargo was damaged due to marine accidents, and the compensation cost for the damage was added to the fare. In other words, it was a system in which the shipping wholesaler or shipowner was the carrier and, at the same time, an underwriter for marine insurance. Until Tokio Marine Insurance was established in 1879, this contract played a risk management function in commercial transactions.

After the Meiji Restoration, Japan introduced marine insurance and fire insurance based on the modern insurance system, which was developed mainly in the UK. Yukichi Fukuzawa, who established Keio University, lectured on Western insurance systems (contract systems) at Keio. Insurance was incorporated into school education curriculums relatively early; in 1878, insurance was adopted as a specialized subject at Mitsubishi Commercial School, and in 1879, a lecture on marine insurance law was started at the University of Tokyo.

2.2 Establishment of Tokio Marine Insurance Company

In 1879, the Tokio Marine Insurance Company was established as Japan's first insurance company. The company's establishment dates back to a railway construction project between Tokyo and Aomori, which was envisioned in 1872 by an influential figure named Kaemon Takashima.

The promoters of this project were influential former daimyos (Japanese feudal lords) who became kazoku (peerage) after the Meiji Restoration. However, the Meiji government decided that it was not suitable as a business of peerage because the new railway construction project required enormous financial resources and the business risk was high.

On the other hand, because the peerage needed business to achieve their economic independence, the Meiji government proposed a plan to sell off the existing railway (between Shinbashi and Yokohama), which had a more promising profit prospect, and a business union to work on this business was established with Eiichi Shibusawa as president. However, the implementation of the system of kinroku-kosai (hereditary pension bonds)[6] had an impact on the finances of the kazoku peerage, and eventually the railway disposal project was withdrawn.

The kazoku who were involved in this project sought a new business to replace the railway business. They came up with three candidates: (1) a marine insurance company, (2) the Stock Exchange, and (3) the construction of Nobiru Harbor at the estuary of Kitakami River. In those days, the railway was undeveloped, so the center of logistics was maritime transportation. Shibusawa, who realized the need to bear the risk of marine transportation, insisted on the establishment of a marine insurance company, and commissioned a survey to Katsunori Masuda, who later became the chief operating officer of Tokio Marine Insurance Company.

In order to catch up with developed countries in Europe and the USA, the Meiji government promoted the policy for encouragement of new industry. The development of non-life insurance in Japan cannot be discussed without noting this policy of industrial development. The increase in logistics with the development of industrialization promoted the growth of the shipping industry, and interest in marine insurance enhanced.

In the early Meiji era, Japan's international maritime logistics were dominated by American shipping companies. To counter this, a local kaiso (shipping) company was established in 1870 and the Japan Post Steamship Company was established in 1872; however, both companies lost business to foreign shipping companies. To deter foreign shipping companies, the Meiji government protected the Mitsubishi Company, led by Yataro Iwasaki, by granting the right of navigation in the waters near Japan, and eventually succeeded in eliminating the domination of foreign shipping companies.

Initially, Iwasaki's level of awareness about the importance of marine insurance was not necessarily high. However, as business with foreign countries expanded, he felt a strong need for marine insurance. In 1876, he applied to the Meiji government for the establishment of an insurance company and a license to operate the company. However, the application was rejected by opposition from Shigenobu Okuma, who was the Minister of Finance. Although no clear reason for rejecting the application was recorded, a conflict of interest in the establishment of an insurance company by a shipping company is considered to be one of the reasons for the rejection.

In 1878, a plan to establish the Tokio Marine Insurance Company started in full-scale with the aim to raise capital from kazoku (peerage). Eiichi Shibusawa, the actual leader of this project, requested that Iwasaki invest in the Tokio Marine Insurance Company. However, in order to avoid placing the new company under Mitsubishi's control, Shibusawa proposed to Iwasaki, the head of Mitsubishi, that the investment ratio of Mitsubishi be limited to 33% or less, and that the appointment of the company's officers be left to Shibusawa. Iwasaki felt strongly the need for the insurance business and accepted this condition. Although the Meiji government rejected the 1876 application of an insurance business license, it granted the license to the 1878 application. Thus, the history of Tokio Marine Insurance, the leading company in the non-life insurance industry in Japan, began.

3 The Occurrence of Management Crisis

3.1 Competition with Rival Companies

In 1893, the monopoly of Tokio Marine Insurance collapsed with the emergence of rival companies. Nippon Kairiku Insurance Co., Ltd., Teikoku Marine Insurance Co., Ltd. (a part of Yasuda Fire & Marine Insurance's predecessor) and Osaka Insurance Co., Ltd. (predecessor of Sumitomo Marine & Fire Insurance) were established one after another. In addition, the Tokyo Fire Insurance Company (a part of Yasuda Fire & Marine Insurance's predecessor) was established in 1887 as a specialized fire insurance company, followed by the Meiji Fire Insurance Company (a part of the Tokio Marine & Fire Insurance's predecessor) and the Japan Fire Insurance Company. For the Japanese non-life insurance industry in the Meiji period, companies specializing in marine insurance and companies specializing in fire insurance had their respective businesses. It was in 1914 that the Tokio Marine Insurance Company began its fire insurance business in addition to marine insurance.

At the time of establishment, Tokio Marine Insurance's main business territories were Tokyo, Osaka, Hokkaido, Niigata, Toyama, Ishikawa, and Fukui. In these areas, the company undertook insurance contracts for the transportation of goods such as rice and dried-pressed boiled herring (used as fertilizer). It was also fortunate for Tokio Marine Insurance that it was a business practice to contract insurance on trades between domestic remote locations. Until its competitors entered into the market, Tokio Marine Insurance was able to maintain a high insurance premium as the only insurance company in Japan that handled marine insurance.

However, the emergence of Nippon Kairiku Insurance Co., Ltd., led by Naoharu Kataoka,[7] threatened the monopoly of Tokio Marine Insurance. Both companies had almost the same business areas and insurance products, so the two companies fought a fierce battle to gain customers. In addition, with the establishment of Teikoku Marine Insurance, the dumping of insurance premiums became common under the names of "return for no claim" or "return at term end". Intense price competition was not suitable for insurance businesses that required public benefit. However, this fierce competition also promoted understanding of risk and insurance philosophy.

3.2 *Special Characteristics of Non-life Insurance Management*

Due to the emergence of domestic competitors and the worsening balance of overseas sales in the UK, Tokio Marine Insurance's business condition rapidly deteriorated. The failure of the insurance business in the UK was due to managers' poor understanding of the uniqueness of insurance management. Here, it is important to review the characteristics of accounting for non-life insurance business, which is an essential part of insurance business.

In non-life insurance management, the period of insurance contracts does not necessarily match the accounting period for calculating profit and loss. For example, for accidents that occurred during the current fiscal year, insurance payments may be paid during the current fiscal year, or payments may be delayed to the next fiscal year (Fig. 12.1).

If a loss is accounted for only insurance claims paid during the current fiscal year, and the insurance payments to be paid in the next fiscal year are not included in the current loss, it will not accurately reflect the profits and losses of the insurance company.

The profit and loss settlement and profit appropriation methods adopted by Tokio Marine Insurance divided all revenues into premium

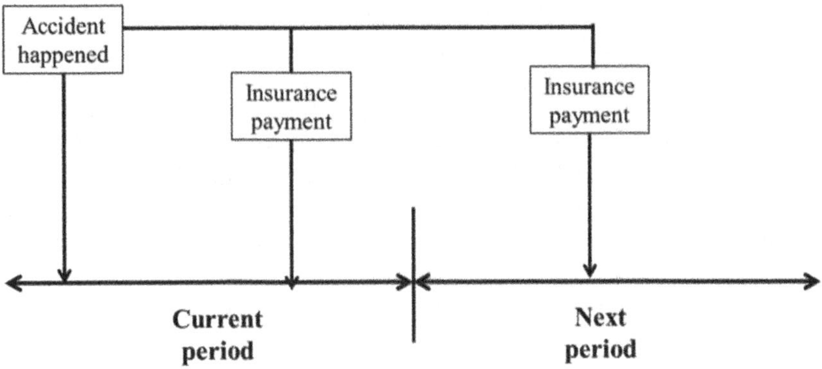

Fig. 12.1 Insurance claim payment. (Source: Created by the author based on Kogure 2010, page 107)

revenues and capital revenues, and operating income obtained by subtracting expenses from insurance revenues were spent on executive bonuses and reserves. Capital revenue was given to shareholders as dividends, and this method was called the "genkei" calculation method. It was a method of settling accounts in which only claims paid during the current period were recorded as a loss and claims to be paid in the next period were not recognized.

Due to the large deficit in UK business and the slowdown in insurance premium revenues in the domestic market, Tokio Marine Insurance fell to no dividends in the second half of 1895. However, from the second half of 1891 to the first half of 1894, the company paid a high dividend (16%). The Meiji government welcomed a rather high dividend rate without questioning the Tokio Marine Insurance's settlement method. Their high profit was a virtual image created by an accounting method that did not accurately reflect the actual state of profits and losses. The reason why such an apprehension of profits was overlooked was due to the lack of managers' knowledge about managing insurance business.

4 Kenkichi Kagami

4.1 History

Kenkichi Kagami was born in 1868, in Gifu City, Gifu Prefecture, as the second son of Shozo Kagami. In 1877, he moved to Tokyo due to his father's work, and in 1884, he graduated from the Tokyo Prefectural

Junior High School (later Tokyo Prefectural Daiichi Junior High School) with excellent grades.

His father operated a shop selling tea leaves in Kyobashi, Tokyo, after he retired from an organization called "Eki-Teiryo", which was in charge of postal and communications business. However, his father's amateur merchant business quickly became stuck. Although Shozo Kagami did not make enough money, he was eager to educate his children and did not stop the studies of Kenkichi and his brother Koichiro. As their family was not wealthy, the Kagami brothers did door-to-door sales while carrying tea boxes to help maintain the household.

Kenkichi Kagami had a strong will to go to school after graduating from junior high school. Among the three candidate schools, Tokyo Higher Commercial School, the Naval Academy, and the Army Academy (students did not have to pay tuition fees in these schools), he chose to go to the Tokyo Higher Commercial School (predecessor of Hitotsubashi University). Another reason why he decided to go to this school was because he had been good at English and arithmetic when he was in junior high school. At the Tokyo Higher Commercial School, he became a close friend of Hachisaburo Hirao[8] (who later became managing director of Tokio Marine Insurance), Tetsuya Mizushima (who later became the president of Kobe High School of Commerce), and Naotaro Shimono (who later became a professor of Tokyo University of Commerce).

In 1888, after graduating from Tokyo Higher Commercial School, Kagami started to work as a teacher at the Kyoto Prefectural Commercial School, where he taught book-keeping and commercial arithmetic. At that time, it was common for graduates of Tokyo Higher Commercial School, who did not join companies or banks, to find employment as local schoolteachers.

Kagami's reputation as a teacher was good, and if he had followed his teaching career, he might have risen to a high position such as principal. However, Kagami felt unsatisfied with academic life, and in 1890, he left the school and joined the Osaka Prefectural Commodity Display Office (predecessor of the Osaka Industrial Technology Laboratory) as an auditor.

The Osaka Prefectural Product Display Office introduced foreign buyers to domestic products and domestic companies. Kagami gained a good reputation for his high level of English communication skills, and many foreign buyers relied on him. Kagami's ability was highly regarded by Teigo Iba, then the president of Sumitomo Zaibatsu (industrial conglomerate), and Iba even asked Kagami to join Sumitomo. As Kagami had hopes to work at a trade-related job in the future, he read through many books on Western finance and economy that the Osaka Prefectural Commodity Display Office owned.

4.2 Joining Tokio Marine Insurance

Tokio Marine Insurance at that time was managed by Heigoro Shoda from Mitsubishi Zaibatsu (industrial conglomerate) as director, and Katsunori Masuda as manager. Masuda was dispatched by Eiichi Shibusawa as a person who was familiar with non-life insurance business because he studied marine insurance at commercial school. However, both men were amateurs in running an insurance company. In order to reconstruct Tokio Marine Insurance, which fell into a management crisis, it was urgent to recruit talented personnel from outside of the company.

At such a time, Kagami was recommended by Jiro Yano, principal of the Tokyo Higher Commercial School, to join Tokio Marine Insurance. Yano's younger sister was the wife of Takashi Masuda, the older brother of Katsunori Masuda, who was the manager at Tokio Marine Insurance. Probably the Masuda brothers asked Yano to introduce talented people to them.

In 1891, Kagami took the entrance examination of Tokio Marine Insurance. He was one of three candidates who took the exam. However, the result was that all three candidates failed. Kagami was re-examined as he had outstanding English communication skills and he was hired as a clerk. He experienced various insurance-related work such as customer relations, book-keeping, and telegraphing to London, and in his third year, he was assigned to London. Kagami was singled out as a person to rebuild the insurance business in London.

5 Rebuilding Insurance Business in London

5.1 Going to the UK (1894–1898)

Kagami went to the UK twice, in 1894–1898 and 1898–1899. He felt that the cause of the poor business performance in the UK was due to the time lag between the revenue of insurance premiums and occurrence of loss. The accounting method Tokio Marine Insurance adopted was called the "reserve for casualties" method. In this method, operating income and insurance money (loss) were calculated and accounted separately. In order to improve the shortcomings of this method, Kagami proposed that the settlement of operating revenue be delayed for six months and to use the revenue for insurance payments; however, this proposal was never adopted.

From 1882, the Liverpool Agency increased the number of requests for reverse exchange[9] and it began to place stress on Tokio Marine Insurance management. Management teams that lacked an essential understanding of insurance management also became aware of the importance of the matter. Shibusawa, who felt a sense of crisis, proposed that Kagami be dispatched to London to investigate the cause and plan for improvement. Director Heigoro Shoda and general manager Katsunori Masuda agreed with this proposal, and it was officially decided to dispatch Kagami to the UK. The future of Tokio Marine Insurance, which was an excellent company representing the Meiji era, was entrusted on the shoulders of a young employee.

5.2 *The Conditions of UK Insurance Business*

After arriving in London, Kagami started to investigate the actual conditions of the Liverpool Agency, whose loss ratio had deteriorated. He collected an old list of ships and tackled an enormous amount of work distinguishing the underwriting of ships and cargo since 1890. As a result, he discovered that there was a loss from the first year of operation in London and that insurance payments had increased since then. Kagami's rigorous investigations gradually revealed the UK underwriting problems.

Underwriting means the acceptance of risk, and insurance companies generally select and contract high-quality projects with low risk. On the other hand, insurance companies sometimes do not refuse a high-risk case and underwrite it by charging a premium corresponding to the risk. The important point of the insurance business is to determine the risk inherent in the applied contract and to determine whether to collect insurance premiums commensurate with the risk.

The Liverpool Agency commissioned by Tokio Marine Insurance had problems with underwriting. The majority of insurance contracts underwritten by this agency were high-risk contracts rejected by UK insurance companies. Even if it was a high risk, if an agency undertook the insurance contract, the agency would receive a commission fee. Payment of insurance money was a loss for an insurance company; however, agency revenue was not impacted. Kagami revealed that the Liverpool Agency was undertaking high-risk insurance contracts to earn commissions.

Kagami prohibited the Liverpool Agency from underwriting insurance and newly commissioned the Geratri & Company in London to underwrite. However, changing the agency alone did not improve the business balance in the UK. Since Geratri & Company adopted the "genkei" calculation method, Kagami changed its insurance balance to a yearly calculation method and recalculated the balance. As a result, he discovered a loss from the first year of operation.

Kagami was convinced of the structural flaws of the genkei calculation method based on the results of his survey, and he strongly recommended Tokio Marine Insurance management to change to the annual calculation method, and as a result, they adopted the annual calculation method from 1899. This method was already widespread in Western countries.

The British maritime magazine *Fairplay* criticized Japanese insurance companies' creation of such a strange balance sheet, where all premium revenues were earned and losses were paid out from another reserve. The magazine pointed out that those Japanese insurance companies would eventually fail. Also, there was criticism in Japan that insurance companies adopted the genkei calculation method in order to realize a high dividend policy.

The deficiency of the genkei calculation method was that only operating expenses and insurance losses that incurred in the current fiscal year were deducted from the revenue of insurance premiums within a single fiscal year, and no underwriting reserves were assumed for the remaining period of the following fiscal year. It was an unreasonable method of calculating profit and loss, ignoring the unique characteristics of the insurance business. In addition, in order to pay dividends to shareholders, regardless of the amount of operating revenue, the idea of separating capital revenue from the beginning had many problems from the viewpoint of safety. At that time, Tokio Marine Insurance was in severe financial difficulties due to continuous insurance payments. Kagami proposed that the Tokio Marine Insurance headquarters abolish the genkei calculation method and adopt a policy year calculation method that he had devised; however, he could not gain the understanding of the officers.

This calculation method is called policy year basis loss ratio. It calculates the final loss ratio by grasping all insurance payments for accidents that occurred in the current period against revenue of premiums during the current period, including all subsequent payments.[10]

In 1895, Katsunori Masuda and Heigoro Shoda went to the UK one after another. Kagami submitted his detailed report "Inspection Report on U.K. Insurance Business" to Masuda and Shoda. The problems he pointed out were summarized into two points: elimination of high-risk contracts through appropriate underwriting, and improvement of random sales by developing statistical data on various risks.

5.3 Enactment of Insurance Business Law and Change to Annual Calculation Method

Change began with the government regulation for insurance companies. Although the laws and regulations relating to insurance business were stipulated in commercial law, there was a strong opinion within the government that insurance business should be supervised by a single legislation independent from commercial law. In 1896, the Investigation Committee of Codes resolved the following three points:

1. The special law concerning insurance companies shall be drafted after deciding the provisions of insurance under commercial law.
2. Until the special law is enacted, the insurance company is required to be a stock company, with the exception of mutual companies.
3. A mutual company also needs a government license.

In 1898, Tsuneta Yano, who was the manager of Kyosai Life Insurance of the Yasuda conglomerate, was hired by the Ministry of Agriculture and Commerce as an insurance officer and worked on drafting insurance business law. Insurance business law, which was enacted in 1899, abolished the genkei calculation method and stipulated the introduction of a reserve system for insurance policy reserves. This provision played a major role in strengthening the insurance company's management base. When Kagami stayed in the UK, he had interacted with Yano, who had been dispatched to Germany for life insurance research.

When Yano asked Kagami how the policy reserves in marine insurance should be managed, he answered that it was an incorrect practice to record the profit immediately after deducting the insurance money paid and general operating expenses from insurance premiums. The entire amount should be deferred and used for the insurance money to be paid in the second year.[11] Kagami's view was reflected in the policy reserve funding system stipulated in the Enforcement Rules of Insurance Business Law.

Table 12.1 Loss due to shift to annual calculation method

	FY1896 account	*Amount (Yen)*
(1)	Loss (January 1, 1897 to December 31, 1898)	502,713
(2)	Reserve at the end of 1896	560.943
(3)	Net loss (1 - 2)	502,152
	FY1897 account	
(4)	Total loss (January 1, 1897 to December 31, 1898)	14,094
(5)	Reserves to cover claim to be paid during the unexpired insurance period	142,496
(6)	Total (4 + 5)	156,590
(7)	Capital revenue for the second half of 1898	10,907
(8)	Net loss (6 - 7)	145,682
	Total losses in FY1896 and FY1897 (3 + 8)	647,835

Source: Prepared by the author based on Tokio Marine Insurance [1979a], p. 194. Disregarded fractions of less than 1 yen

Tokio Marine Insurance adopted Kagami's proposal and worked on the disposal of loss and improvement of the settlement method. Its contents were (1) the genkei calculation method was changed to the annual calculation method after June 1899, (2) perform a capital reduction, and (3) request a government subsidy.

The loss that Tokio Marine Insurance incurred as a result of the shift to the annual calculation method reached 647,835 yen. This loss was compensated by a government subsidy of 259,134 yen, a capital reduction of 375,000 yen, an increase of 2770 yen in valuation of the Osaka branch building, and an increase in valuation of owned shares of 10,931 yen (Table 12.1).

In order to properly calculate profit and loss for the period, currently the loss ratio, called the earned basis loss ratio, is used as an indicator. This indicator is also used for management decisions as it is not affected by the increase or decrease in contracts but reflects insurance claims for accidents that occurred during the period (Fig. 12.2).

The insurance policy reserve at the end of the previous fiscal year is the sum of A paid in the current fiscal year and B paid in the next fiscal year (A + B). Insurance claims paid during the period are the sum of A incurred in the previous period and C incurred in the current period (A + C). The insurance reserve at the end of the current period is the sum of B and D scheduled to be paid from the next period (B + D). When the numerator is applied to the above formula, "(A + C) + (B + D) - (A + B) = C + D" is

$$\text{Earned Basis Loss ratio} = \frac{\text{Insurance claims paid(Incurred Loss)} + \text{Reserve for current year-end} - \text{Reserve for previous year-end}}{\text{Earned premiums}} \times 100\%$$

Fig. 12.2 Calculation of formula for earned basis loss ratio. (Source: Kogure 2010, p. 108, Author revised)

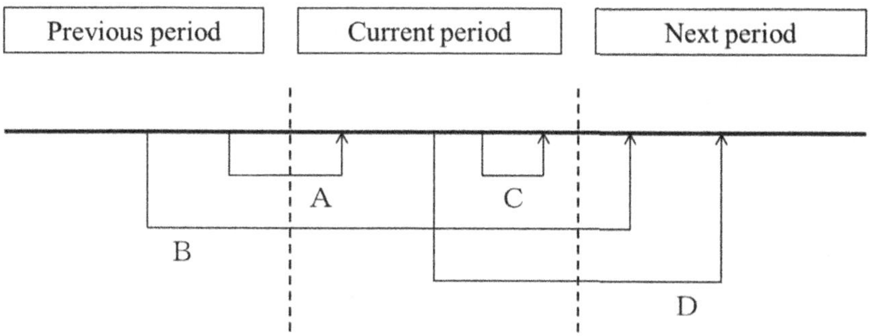

Fig. 12.3 Relationship between insurance claims paid and reserves for payment. (Source: Kogure 2010, p. 108, Author revised)

obtained, and [C + D] is recognized as the insurance money occurred in the current period.

Prior to the enforcement of the insurance business law, Tokio Marine Insurance shifted to the annual calculation method. However, there were some insurance companies, such as Nihon Kairiku Insurance, that were forced to dissolve due to an increase in losses as a result of the revision of the calculation method (Fig. 12.3).

5.4 *Kagami's Reform Concept*

In 1896, Kagami wrote the "Report and Recommendation on the U.K. Agency Business" and he made a proposal for management reform. He said that three elements were necessary in order for insurance business to succeed in the UK: (1) the company's own creditworthiness, (2) the company's supporters and sponsors, and (3) human resources.

Insurance companies in London were supported by people who had a deep understanding of underwriting, special knowledge, and experience.

For business matters offered to insurance companies, conditions such as whether the risk was good or bad, whether the insurance company should have undertaken the risk or not, and what insurance premium level the company needed to charge were finally judged by those experts.

After returning to Japan, Kagami thoroughly promoted human resource development at Tokio Marine Insurance based on his experience in the UK. The biggest factor in the failure of insurance business in London was that Tokio Marine Insurance selected a partner agent with poor underwriting capability. At that time, Tokio Marine Insurance had no human resources who could understand and practice underwriting correctly.

Kagami returned to Japan once in April 1898 and went to the UK again in August of the same year. The purpose of his second visit to the UK was to close the Tokio Marine Insurance London branch and find a leading agency to commission the company's insurance business. In 1899, he decided to commission Willis Faber & Company as a new partner for Tokio Marine Insurance. Willis Faber & Company was a marine insurance broker that joined Lloyd's and it had the largest premium revenue in the UK. Furthermore, this company had sufficient experience and insight into various risks and did not give Kagami the impression that they ran the risk of undertaking a high-risk contract just to earn commissions.

Fortunately, Tokio Marine Insurance signed an agency contract with Willis Faber & Company and also succeeded in signing a comprehensive reinsurance contract for cargo insurance. Japanese non-life insurance companies in those days did not have comprehensive reinsurance contracts with foreign insurance companies, and as a result they had to conclude a reinsurance contract for each individual contract. Generally, if insurance companies undertake a large insurance contract, they have to pay a substantial amount of insurance money if an accident occurrs. In this way, insurance companies always have factors that make their business results unstable. Therefore, minimizing the impact on financial performance, insurance companies need to have other insurance companies undertake some or all of the risks of the insurance contracts. This insurance contract is reinsurance, and reinsurance plays a major role for the stable management of insurance companies. Securing appropriate reinsurers in London, which could undertake Tokio Marine Insurance's risk, enabled Tokio Marine to actively expand business in Japan.

6 Kenkichi Kagami's Management Philosophy

In 1917, Kagami became managing director of Tokio Marine Insurance. He also served in many other important positions, including Chairman of Meiji Fire Insurance (1922), Chairman of Mitsubishi Marine and Fire Insurance (1925), Chairman of Mitsubishi Trust (1927), and President of Nippon Yusen Kaisha or NYK Line (1929). He also served as a member of Kizokuin (the House of Peers) (1930). Kagami also played an active part as an executive representing Mitsubishi Zaibatsu (industrial conglomerate) in those days.

Momosuke Fukuzawa, who was the husband of a daughter of Keio University founder Yukichi Fukuzawa, and was called the "King of Electric Power" for his success in the electric power business, described Kagami as a person who did not appeal to ordinary people but was a faithful servant of both the company and its shareholders.

Kagami was a typical office worker manager who joined Tokio Marine Insurance as an employee and climbed to the top of management by using his ability, and in that sense, he was a practitioner and a man of skill.

The Times in London published the following article when the news of Kagami's death was received:

> Along with his rare judgments, foresight and intelligence were integrated with his continuous efforts, courage, and patience, he was truly outstanding in any country and in every case of life.
>
> Throughout his five years of staying in London, he was deeply influenced by the insurers' high morality and cautious behavior in the London insurance market, and while there he made remarkable success as an underwriter for the Tokio Marine Insurance Company. Throughout his life, Mr. Kagami maintained his philosophy of integrity, fairness and deliberateness, and that would satisfy both parties in any business deal. (June 2, 1939 article)

Kenkichi Kagami also appeared on the cover page of the US *Time* magazine, following Heihachiro Togo and Emperor Showa.[12] This also indicates that he was highly respected overseas (Fig. 12.4).

Kagami emphasized that the foundation of an insurance company's management was trust. He said that trust was not based on the wealth of a company's assets, but on the personality and behavior of its employees. In addition, he insisted that trust in business was an intangible asset, and this intangible asset enabled the accumulation of tangible assets; therefore,

Fig. 12.4 Cover page of *Time* magazine. (Source: *Time* magazine archive)

managers should make every effort to gain trust from customers and society.

His management view was well described in his following remark: "I believe that no other business has to protect its trust, at the expense of everything, as the insurance business".[13]

Kagami was seen as a cold man because he had a clear mind and clear decision-making based on strong will. He never wasted company money. However, his essence was as an entrepreneur who had a selfless spirit, polished intelligence, and tremendous willpower in complete harmony.

The words that Kagami cherished throughout his life were, "how to say 'NO' gently". Insurance contracts that were unwillingly underwritten often resulted in significant losses. Anyone who can say NO gently, so that the other party is convinced, is a person who can do anything. The words that Kagami cherished in his life reveal his warm personality in caring for others even though he was a tough businessperson.

The features of Kagami as a corporate manager were (1) objective and rational decision-making based on actuarial analysis, (2) awareness of social responsibility as an insurance provider, and (3) a management philosophy based on trust. He investigated the cause of Tokio Marine Insurance's poor management by analyzing details of past data and he pushed the level of Japanese non-life insurance business to an international standard by introducing a modern accounting method. The truth the data told was the basis for his management judgment.

Kagami's attitude toward underwriting was a direct manifestation of social responsibility as an insurance provider and the spirit of service to policyholders. Insufficient analysis of the risks and expected damages may result in charging customers excessive premiums and not providing adequate compensation for damages. Recognizing that non-life insurance was closely linked to the socio-economic system, Kagami was fully aware that the responsibility of the insurer was fulfilled only by adequate underwriting.

In modern society, there is a growing interest in corporate social responsibility (CSR), and the central issue of CSR is who the company exists for. Corporate management is shifting to management that emphasizes the balance between social and economic returns to multi-stakeholders, including shareholders, in light of the fact that excessive profit-first policies have caused many corporate scandals.

Non-life insurance is responsible for mitigating business continuity risks and contributing to the sustainability of the economic system. Life insurance is responsible for mitigating risks of individual life continuity and contributing to the sustainability of social systems. The significance of insurance business is to support the sustainability of a socio-economic system composed of both individuals and companies.

Kagami stated that trust was the foundation of insurance business. He said that profit, which was a tangible asset, was built by trust, which was an intangible asset. It takes an enormous amount of time for a company to gain trust from society. Trust of an insurance company is generated from the actions of its managers and employees; therefore, they have to continue efforts to gain trust.

In Japan, non-insurance payment by insurance companies in 2005 became a major social problem. Many insurance companies did not pay the insurance money that they should have paid, based on their insurance policies. This problem continued until 2007. Under this circumstance, the Japanese Financial Services Agency issued an order to improve business operation to many life and non-life insurance companies including Tokio Marine. With the revelation of this faulty management system, that neglected customers, the trust the insurance companies built up in the past collapsed in a moment. Since then, Japanese insurance companies have been making continuous efforts to restore trust, but their managers are required to always remember the spirit and resolution Kagami had in mind when he was running Tokio Marine Insurance.

In 1970, Kagami, who led the development of Japanese insurance business, was inducted into the International Insurance Hall of Fame at the same time as Tsuneta Yano. The International Insurance Hall of Fame aims to honor those who have made significant contributions to the development of insurance business. Kagami and Yano were the first Japanese to receive this honor.

In May 1939, Kenkichi Kagami ended his 71-year-old life while serving as the chairman of Tokio Marine Insurance. His 48 years of service for the company was exactly the history of the development of the Japanese non-life insurance industry. Kagami's business life was solely dedicated to Tokio Marine Insurance and this was in contrast to Hachisaburo Hirao, Kagami's sworn friend, who expanded his field of activities to the political and industrial world after leaving the Tokio Marine Insurance Company.

Notes

1. Tokio Marine Insurance is currently the Tokio Marine & Nichido Fire Insurance Company.
2. Tokyo Fire Insurance later became Yasuda Fire and Marine Insurance, currently Sompo Japan Insurance Inc.
3. Bottomry was a monetary loan agreement in which the borrower borrows money from ships or cargo as collateral. If the collateral was completely lost in a maritime accident, both the principal and interest would be relieved.
4. The marine insurer based in Lloyd's Coffee House was called the Underwriters of Lloyd's Coffee House. In 1871, the Lloyd's Act was enacted, and it was reorganized into Lloyd's Insurance Association which had legal entity.
5. *Shuin-sen* was a ship that traded overseas with an overseas travel permit called Shuin-jo (a red stamp) issued by Japanese rulers from the end of the sixteenth century to the beginning of the seventeenth century.
6. Kinroku Kosai was the public bond issued for people in the class below aristocrats in compensation for the abolition of the Roku-rewarding system after the Meiji Restoration (Weblio: https://ejje.weblio.jp/sentence/content/%E9%87%91%E7%A6%84%E5%85%AC%E5%82%B5).
7. Naoharu Kataoka was involved in the establishment of Nippon Life Insurance in 1889 and he became president in 1904.
8. Hachisaburo Hirao became the managing director of Tokio Marine Insurance in 1917, after serving as the principal of Kobe Commercial School. He supported the management of Tokio Marine Insurance together with Kagami.
9. Reverse exchange is a way of settling a remittance. It was also called reverse remittance.
10. Kogure [2010], p. 110
11. Inagaki [1951], p. 83.
12. May 18, 1931 issue.
13. Inagaki [1951], p. 57.

References

Fukuzawa, Momosuke [1990] "Zaikai Jinbutsu Gakan (Personal view about businesspersons)" (Businesspeople Series) Tosho-shuppansha.

Fukuzawa, Yukichi and Yoshida, Kensuke [2008] "Western Travel Guide (Reprint Modern Japanese Literature)" National Literature Research Museum.

Hasegawa, Naoya [2008] "Japanese Entrepreneurs" Bunshindo.

Hasegawa, Naoya [2013] "History of financial business in Japan through entrepreneurial activities" Bunshindo.

Hoken Hyoron Sha [1973] "Directory of Insurance in Japan" Nihon Hoken Hyoron Sha

Inagaki, Suezaburo [1951] ""Mr. Kagami's notes" and "Reports and Opinions during his stay in the UK"" Tokio Marine and Fire Insurance.

Insurance Research Institute "Insurance: Non-life Insurance Statistics".

Insurance Research Institute [1982] "History of Japanese Insurance Business (Overview edition) (Company edition Vol. 1 and 2)" Insurance Research Institute.

Iwai, Ryotaro [1955] "The Biographies of Kenkichi Kagami and Takeo Kato" (The 9th volume, The Biographies of Japanese businesspersons) Toyoshokan.

Japan Insurance Newspaper [1968] "History of Insurance in Japan" Japan Insurance Newspaper.

Kobayashi, Tadashi [1991] "The Biographies of Insurance Thinkers" Insurance Mainichi Shimbun.

Kobayashi, Tadashi [2005] "Insurance Thought and Management Philosophy" Chikura Shobo.

Kogure, Masakazu [2010] "Mathematics of Insurance-Life Insurance/Non-life Insurance/Pension" Insurance Mainichi Shimbun.

Kojima, Hideki [2006] "Episode 11: Kenkichi Kagami" "Men's twilight years" Nikkei.

Suzuki, Sakae [1949] "Remembering Kenkichi Kagami" Kagami Memorial Foundation.

TIME Editorial Department [1997] "Japan's Real Face seen by TIME" Yohan Shuppan.

Tokio Marine and Fire Insurance [1964] "Eighty Year History of Tokio Marine".

Tokio Marine and Fire Insurance [1979a] "A hundred years history of Tokio Marine and Fire Insurance Co., Ltd.".

Tokio Marine and Fire Insurance [1979b] "100 Years of Tokio Marine".

Unoki, Tadashi [1940] "Kenkichi Kagami" Showa Shobo.

CHAPTER 13

Tsuneta Yano: Established a Life Insurance Business Through Mutualism

Tsuneta Yano (1866–1951). (Source: Tsuneta Yano Memorial Foundation)

Achievement of Tsuneta Yano and related SDGs

Economy	 	* Establishment of life insurance system * Reform of insurance sales system

(*continued*)

M. Takehara, N. Hasegawa, *Sustainable Management of Japanese Entrepreneurs in Pre-War Period from the Perspective of SDGs and ESG*, https://doi.org/10.1007/978-981-15-6507-6_13

(continued)

Society	 	* Stabilize society through life insurance * Reduce health risks * Research on life insurance system * Improve underwriting ability * Enhance employee education
Governance	  	* Management based on mutual company system * Promotion of non-for-profit management * Enactment of insurance business law

Source: Created by authors

1 Creation and Development of Modern Life Insurance

1.1 UK

The origins of life insurance are said to be the ancient Roman collegia tenuiorum and the British Friendly Society. Both were spontaneous organizations created for the purpose of mutual assistance and had strong regional and religious ties.

In 1698, the world's first life insurance company, the Mercers Company, was founded in the UK, but soon disappeared. In 1706, a mutual life insurance company, the Amicable Society for a Perpetual Assurance Office (Amicable Society), was founded, but the method of calculating claims and premiums was flawed. In 1721, marine insurance companies the Royal Exchange Assurance Corporation and the London Assurance Corporation entered the life insurance business.

Modern life insurance business began with the scientific life insurance of the Society for Equitable Assurance on Lives and Survivorship (Equitable) founded in 1762. The company developed a statistically rational premium based on mortality that enabled life insurance to grow exponentially.

Equitable created a new premium table based on death statistics in London, realizing their idea that life insurance premiums should be

Table 13.1 Trend of life insurance companies in the UK

	1800	*1824*	*1840*	*1855*
No. of companies	9	55	107	199

Source: Japan Institute of Life Insurance (1990, p. 15)

determined by the age of the insured. In addition, the company introduced various measures such as strengthening screening at the time of application, setting a limit on the total amount of insurance coverage, conducting periodic account settlement, and paying dividends to policyholders. The company adopted a mutual company system and did not deploy any sales staff. Though its performance was not significant, Equitable was credited for laying the foundation for the modern life insurance business.

In 1792, the Westminster Society was founded. The company was the first company to use outsiders (outside organizations) to sell life insurance. At that time, the need for life insurance was growing exponentially in the UK, as medical technology advanced, mortality rates declined, and many people working in commerce and industry gained a better understanding of life insurance (Table 13.1).

1.2 Germany

In Germany, negative ideas were dominant in assessing life monetarily. Widows' pensions were exceptionally permitted. Therefore, no life insurance company was established in Germany in the 1700s.

After that, on being influenced by the Industrial Revolution in the UK, development of industry in Germany was accelerated and the public's awareness of life insurance began to change. Germans who did not have domestic life insurers started contracting with UK life insurance companies.

In 1827, the first mutual life insurance company in Germany, Gothaer Lebensversicherungsbank auf Gegenseitigkeit, was established. The founder was Ernst Wilhelm Arnoldi, the founder of the Gothaer Fire Insurance and Bank. The company was a pioneer in adopting a mutual insurance system. Tsuneta Yano studied at Gothaer from September 1895 to December of the following year, learning how to manage the mutual insurance company.

2 History of the Life Insurance Business in Japan

The modern insurance system was introduced to Japan by Yukichi Fukuzawa. Fukuzawa introduced Western insurance system in his book *Seiyo Jijyo* in 1866, and conducted lectures on insurance at Keio Gijuku, a school he established. As a result, the wish to establish a life insurance company was growing, mainly among Fukuzawa's students. Among them was Heigoro Shoda, who later worked as a member of the board of directors at Tokio Marine Insurance Company.

In 1880, Heigoro Shoda, with the cooperation of Shinkichi Koizumi and Taizo Abe, both Fukuzawa students, drafted a proposal for establishing the Tokyo Life Insurance Company. It was modeled after the Tokio Marine Insurance Company founded in 1879. Their efforts led to the establishment of the Meiji Life Insurance Company in 1881.[1] Meiji Life, which was Japan's modern life insurance company, was established as a stock corporation. One year before Meiji Life was established, the Kyosai 500 company was established by Zenjiro Yasuda in 1880.[2] In 1902, Dai-ichi Life, the first mutual company in Japan, was established by Tsuneta Yano.

In fact, there was a mutual insurance company planned to be established in 1879, two years before the Meiji Life was established. The first mutual life insurance company in Japan was Dai-ichi Life Insurance established by Yano in 1902, but about 20 years before Dai-ichi Life was founded, a bureaucrat, Norikazu Wakayama, planned to establish the Nitto Hosei company.

Wakayama was born in Edo in 1840 as a child of a doctor. He studied at a private school of Koan Ogata, a famous scholar in medical science and Dutch studies in the Edo period. In the Meiji era, Wakayama joined a mission the new Meiji government dispatched to Western countries for two years from 1871 (the mission is called the Iwakura Mission). He stayed in Europe and the USA to continue his study on financial issues. After returning to Japan, Wakayama worked for the Ministry of Finance initially, but resigned from the Ministry of Finance in 1877, aiming to establish the Nitto Hosei Insurance Company.

The Nitto Hosei Insurance Company was modeled on an American mutual insurance company that Wakayama learned about during his stay in the USA. In September 1880, the Meiji government granted permission to establish the Nitto Hosei Insurance Company. Wakayama asked Zenjiro Yasuda to invest in the funding of the Nitto Hosei, which was equivalent of the capital of stock company, but Yasuda declined to invest because he could not understand the nature of the mutual company. As a result, the company faced financial difficulties from the outset, and also failed to acquire 100 contractors which was required by law by the time of its establishment. Eventually the company was dissolved without staring business.

On the other hand, the Kyosai 500 company established by Yasuda tried to realize Japan's unique life insurance philosophy by introducing a system to pay 1000 yen per person for death insurance, but eventually it was merged with another life insurance company named the Kyosai life which was established in 1894.[3]

Teikoku Life (the predecessor of the Asahi Life Insurance Company) was established in 1888, and the Nippon Life was established in 1889. Both Teikoku Life and Meiji Life used a table based on the mortality rate of seventeen British life insurance companies to calculate the mortality rate upon which the premium was calculated. On the other hand, the Nippon Life improved the accuracy of insurance premium calculation using the "Fujiwara Life Table" created based on Japan's demographic data for the seven years from 1881 to 1887 (Meiji 14 to 20).[4] In the early days of Japan's life insurance industry, these three companies, which were all stock companies, led the industry.

3 The History of Tsuneta Yano

Tsuneta Yano was born in 1865 in Higashi-ku, Okayama City, Okayama Prefecture, as the eldest son of a doctor, Mimasu Yano. In 1873, Yano entered a nearby elementary school and studied Yukichi Fukuzawa's "Gakumon no susume" (an encouragement of learning). Also, while attending elementary school, he studied Chinese writing at a private school. Later in his life, Yano published a book on the Analects of Confucius. His Chinese writing skills were nurtured during his childhood.

After graduating from elementary school, he served as an elementary school assistant for a while and then, in 1878, he entered the Okayama Medical School (the predecessor of the Okayama University School of Medicine) to take over his father's job. However, in 1880, Yano left the medical school without permission from the school and his parents and moved to Tokyo. Yano never divulged his reason for dropping out of Okayama Medical School.

After moving to Tokyo, Yano relied on his senior from his hometown, who was studying at the Tokyo Imperial University Law School, and was allowed to stay with him. With his parents' permission to study in Tokyo, Yano enrolled at a German language school to prepare to take an entrance exam for the School of Medicine at Tokyo Imperial University. Six months later, he passed the exam and was accepted from the preparatory school at the Tokyo Imperial University School of Medicine.[5]

However, he eventually returned to his hometown, Okayama, and re-entered the Okayama Medical School. In 1889, Yano graduated from the Okayama Medical school as a doctor at the age of 24.

4 Encounter with Life Insurance

In 1889, Yano went to Osaka, relying on his former teacher Isamu Kiyono. Yano planned to gain experience as a doctor. Kiyono served as director of the Osaka Medical School and director of the Osaka Hospital, and was also a consulting doctor of the Nippon Life Insurance Company established in 1889.

At that time, Nippon Life was recruiting physicians in anticipation of expanding its business. Yano joined Nippon Life in 1889, on the suggestion of Kiyono. This became his first encounter with life insurance. Yano had no interest in life insurance until he got a job as an insurance physician. However, he became interested in life insurance, so he enthusiastically engaged in research on life insurance theories and systems while conducting 500 medical examinations a year.[6] He also worked actively with sales employees to become familiar with the customer needs for life insurance.

In 1892, Yano delivered a congratulatory speech at the company's opening ceremony on behalf of the physicians. Meanwhile, he negotiated with Vice President Naoharu Kataoka for improving the working conditions of company doctors, and Kataoka promised to make this happen. It was Yano's initial plan that he worked for the Nippon Life for three years as an insurance physician and now the improvement of doctors' working condition was in sight, he determined the time had come to leave the company. Even though he was repeatedly persuaded by the company to stay in office, his determination did not change. However, the company subsequently hardened its attitude and fired Yano. Yano, who initially intended to leave the company voluntarily, was outraged. Yano's emotional resentment to Kataoka was so intense that Yano gave up returning to his family business and decided to concentrate on life insurance research.

The year after he resigned from Nippon Life, Yano compiled the research he began while working at Nippon Life Insurance and published it as a book titled *The New Life Insurance Regulations*. In the book, Yano criticized the situation in which too many life insurance companies at the time were doing business as profit-making corporations and lacked the spirit of mutual assistance and consideration for policyholders.

5 Establishment of the Dai-ichi Life Mutual Company

5.1 Encounter with Mutualism

After he was dismissed from Nippon Life, Yano spent the retirement allowance on living expenses and continued his research by reading various literature on life insurance and economics extensively. He discovered through German literature reviews that there was a mutual company system that did not seek profit as an organizational goal and returned all profits to the insurance policyholders. Yano understood that life insurance was an economic system based on the spirit of mutual assistance to maintain a society where people lived together. Yano came to think that an organization that realized his philosophy was a mutual company, and the establishment of a life insurance company with a mutual company system was his mission to achieve.

In 1893, Yano wrote 16 papers on life insurance. Of particular note was "the Mutual Life Insurance Company" (Japanese Commercial Magazine, August 1893) and the "Defects of the Japanese Life Insurance Business" (Tokyo Economic Magazine, July–October 1893).

The former paper stated that it was the result of the mutual company that made the public aware of the social significance of the insurance business, and concluded that the best life insurance company was the Gothaer Insurance Mutual Company in Germany. Later, Yano actually studied at Gothaer Mutual and learned about life insurance management based on mutualism.

In the latter paper, Yano pointed out the shortcomings of the mortality tables used by Japanese life insurance companies as the basis for calculating insurance premiums. He also noted that there were no non-profit insurance companies in Japan.

Yano self-published a series of his research results in *Toward Establishing a Non-Profit Life Insurance Company* (1893). Yano argued in the book that all life insurance companies established in Japan are for-profit corporations, but non-profit mutual companies were more appropriate for managing life insurance companies because of the following reasons:

- A mutual company operates in the same manner as a stock company, but it does not have to pay dividends to shareholders.
- Since dividends to shareholders are not required, a mutual life insurance company can provide insurance at a lower premium than a stock company.

Yano's articles drew the attention of Zenjiro Yasuda, who at that time ran the Kyosai 500 company founded in 1880.[7] When Yano met Yasuda, he suggested conducting a life insurance business based on mutualism. It is not clear to what extent Yasuda understood mutualism, but in response to Yano's advice, Yasuda dissolved the Kyosai 500 company and transformed it into a new company named "the Mutual Aid Life Insurance Partnership" in 1894. Yano himself became the manager of the company, and took over the sales department.

In 1895, with the permission of Yasuda, Yano visited the Gothaer Life Insurance Company in Germany and stayed there for about a year for research. The Gothaer was Germany's first life insurer and gained the immense trust as a leading life insurer.

A mutual company obtains earnings to be allocated to policyholders through competition in the market, which is similar to a stock company in that the stock company pays dividends to shareholders. However, in a mutual company, there is no conflict of interest between the policyholders and the mutual company that distributes earnings. That is, under a mutual company, a policyholder becomes an employee of the mutual company, and thus he or she is exclusively granted the right to receive company earnings. In this regard, mutual companies are superior to stock companies. Staying in the Gothaer for about a year, Yano became convinced of establishing and managing a life insurance company based on mutualism (Table 13.2 and Fig. 13.1).

Upon returning to Japan from Germany, Yano stopped by the UK, where he was fascinated with the business policy of Old Equitable (the Equitable Life Assurance Society), founded in 1762. The company had a

Table 13.2 Academic achievements of Tsuneta Yano (1893)

	Date of issue	*Publication*	*Article title*
1	1893.2	*Tokyo Economic Magazine*	Life insurance company's reserve
2	1893.2	*Ikai jiho*	New areas of applied medicine
3	1893.3	*Tokyo Medical Journal*	Insurance doctor Insurance medicine Duties of insurance doctor Difficulties insurance physicians face Examiner's challenges Responsibility of insurance doctors
4	1893.3	*Ikai jiho*	Insurance medicine Vo.1 & Vo.2
5	1893.3	*Ikai jiho*	Doctor, a lousy job
6	1893.4	*Forensic Journal*	Insurance medicine and forensic medicine
7	1893.4	*Japan*	Insurance for workers
8	1893.6	*Tokyo Economic Magazine*	Questions and Answers
9	1893.6	*Chugai Medical News*	Japanese life
10	1893.6	*Parliament*	Japanese fire insurance policy
11	1893.7	*Japan Journal*	Supervision of insurance company
12	1893.7	*Japan Journal*	Evaluation of life insurance business in Japan
13	1893.7	*Tokyo Medical Journal*	Final recommendation as an insurance physician
14	1893.7	*Ikai jiho*	A few point at issues in medical statistics
15	1893.8	*Japan Commercial Magazine*	Mutual life insurance company
16	1893.7–10	*Tokyo Economic Magazine*	Problems of the Japanese life insurance business

Source: Tsuneta Yano Memorial Committee (1957, pp. 34–35)

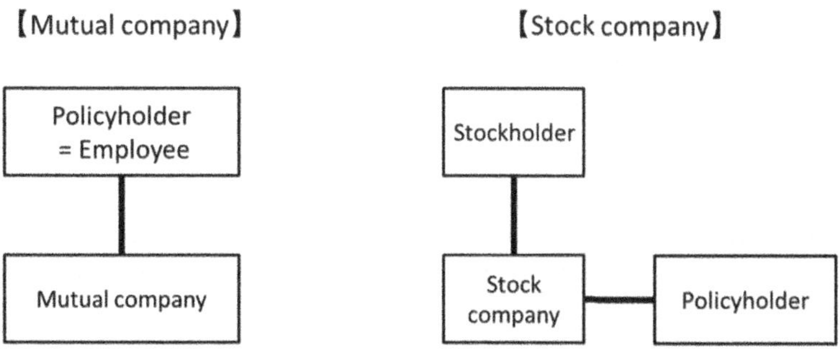

Fig. 13.1 Comparison of organizational forms of insurance companies. (Source: Toshiaki Tachibanaki and Chihiro Uematsu (1998) "Problems around Corporate governance of life insurance companies", Bunken Ronshu No. 123)

policy of not having agents that were considered indispensable for insurance sales. As a result, the expense ratio was kept low because the commission to be paid to agents was not necessary.

After returning to Japan, Yano planned to implement measures at Kyosai Life based on mutualism he learned in Germany and the UK. However, Kyosai Life executives opposed Yano's plan, as they believed that the profits gained from the insurance business should be invested in the businesses of Yasuda Zaibatsu (conglomerate led by Zenjiro Yasuda) rather than being returned to policyholders. Eventually, Yano left Kyosai Life in 1898.

5.2 *Drafting the Insurance Business Law*

Between 1893 and 1897, more than 30 life insurance companies were established in Japan. In addition, including quasi-life insurance companies and mutual aid associations, the life insurance market in Japan was in a state of disorder. Many of them were founded by people inspired by the success of Meiji Life and Nippon Life, and their main objective of doing business was making profit.

Initially, the Meiji government adopted a laissez-faire principle for the insurance business. Therefore, there was no law governing the insurance business, and no restrictions on establishing a company. As a result, many bubble and irresponsible insurance companies were established, and they had many negative effects on the development of the life insurance business.

Faced with these challenges, the Meiji government recognized the necessity of supervising insurance companies and started to draft an Insurance Business Law led by Keijiro Okano, a senior official for the Ministry of Agriculture and Commerce. Okano said, "It is not desirable that the profits be enjoyed only by shareholders and be hardly returned to policyholders. To eliminate this drawback, we need to create a mutual company as soon as possible to secure the insurance business. We have to enact the Mutual Company Law" (Tsuneta Yano Memorial [1957], p. 50).

After resigning from Kyosai Life, Yano asked Okano, who became acquainted with him while he was studying in Germany, for employment. Okano recruited Yano, who was familiar with the life insurance business, to the Ministry of Agriculture and Commerce and had him engage in drafting the Insurance Business Law. In addition to Okano, Yano worked with excellent legal scholars such as Kenjiro Ume and Kaoru Tanabe on drafting legislation, and he gave opinions on the management of the life insurance business from a practitioner's perspective.

In 1900, the Insurance Business Law was passed by the Diet and came into force in July of that year. The law, drafted by Yano and others, stipulated the following points:

1. To run a life insurance company, a license from a competent authority is required.
2. Insurance companies are limited to stock companies or mutual companies.
3. Insurance companies cannot do other businesses concurrently.

With the enforcement of the Insurance Business Law, supervision of life insurance companies was strengthened, insurers with weak management bases were restructured, and regulation on companies similar to life insurance progressed.

Yano planned to resign from the Ministry of Agriculture and Commerce and to establish a mutualism-based life insurance company when the Insurance Business Law was passed. However, he was persuaded to stay by the ministry as the ministry had limited officials who were knowledgeable about the practice of the insurance business. Yano remained in the ministry and served as the first manager of the insurance division from July 1900 to December 1901.

While Yano was in charge of the insurance division, it inspected about 70 insurance companies, both life and non-life, and ordered companies with poor financial performance to stop undertaking new contracts or to dispose of their properties. Among the poorly managed insurance companies that were forced to be dissolved by this inspection was the Nippon Kairiku Insurance Company. The company was headed by Masanao Kataoka, president of Nippon Life who virtually fired Yano.

The enforcement of the Insurance Business Law made it possible to establish a life insurance company in the form of a mutual company, but in reality, a new company was not established. The Kyosai Life Joint Partnership Company, managed by Zenjiro Yasuda, was expected to be transferred into a mutual company, but the company was eventually reorganized into a stock company. It seems Yasuda did not fully understand Yano's idea of mutualism.

Shareholders of a stock company can enjoy benefits such as shareholder dividends and capital increases through share issuance for shareholders if

Table 13.3 Difference between mutual companies and stock companies

	Mutual company	*Stock company*
Nature	Intermedíate Corporation established under the Insurance Business Law. It is not for profit.	For-profit Corporation established under the Company Act
Capital	Funds contributed by fund contributors	Capital invested by shareholders
Members	Policyholders (=Employees)	Stockholders
Decision-making body	Employees general meeting	General shareholders meeting
Attribution of profit and loss	Policyholders (=Employees)	Stockholders

Source: Created by authors based on minutes of the Fifth Meeting of the Financial Services Agency's Financial Council

business performance grows steadily. On the other hand, mutual company investors do not have the merit of stock company shareholders because the fund dividend rate is determined in advance. In addition, if the amount of retained earnings increases, there is a possibility that the capital will be redeemed successively to the investors. Therefore, mutual companies were considered to be relatively less attractive to investors seeking economic returns (Table 13.3).

5.3 *Establishment of Dai-ichi Mutual Life Insurance Company*

In 1901, Yano resigned from the Ministry of Agriculture and Commerce, and began to prepare the establishment of a mutualism-based life insurance company. He named the new company Dai-ichi Life Mutual Company, as it was Japan's first mutual company (Dai-ichi means first in Japanese). The new company's initial fund was set at 200,000 yen, and staff recruiting started to secure 100 employees, which was required under the Insurance Business Law.

Yano intended to establish a fire insurance company and a life insurance company as a mutual company, but the philosophy of the mutual company was not easily understood; therefore, it was extremely difficult for him to attract investors. Okano, a colleague of Yano at the Ministry of Agriculture and Commerce, could not overlook Yano's difficulties and introduced Kenzo Ikeda, director of the 100th Bank. Okano's help saved Yano. With the introduction from Ikeda, Rokuro Hara (president, Yokohama Shokin Bank), Ichizaemon Morimura (founder of the Morimura Zaibatsu [conglomerate]), Kintaro Hattori (founder of the Hattori Watch shop, Current Seiko Holdings), and Kichizaemon Sumitomo (owner of the Sumitomo Family [Conglomerate]) agreed to invest in Dai-ichi Life. As a result, trust for Dai-ichi Life increased drastically.

In 1902, the general meeting for establishment of the Dai-ichi Mutual Life Insurance Company was held, and Yasutoshi Yanagisawa was selected as the president. Yanagisawa was a typical intellectual in those days, serving as a member of Kizokuin (the House of Peers) and the chairman of the Tokyo City Assembly. Yano assumed the role of Managing Director.

Yano advocated a management philosophy that "Daiichi Life Insurance always aims to be the best company, not the largest company", and he set the company's code of conduct to be "reliable, reasonable and kind". Dai-ichi Life's business philosophy was strongly influenced by what Yano learned at the Gothaer Insurance Company and Old Equitable.

The mortality table and sales method adopted by Dai-ichi Life strongly reflected the company's unique policy. Many other life insurance companies, including Meiji Life, used the UK 17 company table to calculate life insurance premiums. However, Yano devised a mortality table based on the mortality rate of Japanese (it was called Yano's Table 13.2), and Dai-ichi Life adopted it in its insurance premium calculation.[8] Yano's Table 13.2 made it possible to calculate appropriate premiums that reflected the mortality rate in Japan.

The sales method also reflected Yano's philosophy. Many life insurance companies solicited insurance through their own agents and sales staff. Those companies adopted a method of commissioning local influencers to become their agents and sell life insurance to local people.

The insurance company paid their agent commissions which was around 5% of the premium. The company also had operating expenses including entertainment for agents. These commissions and operating expenses were added to the insurance premiums paid by the contractors.

Yano stated that Dai-ichi Life would ask customers to pay only insurance premiums and therefore did not use agents or sales staff. He made it clear that Dai-ichi Life would not buy a contract for agent commissions.

Yano adopted a progressive approach that did not seek rapid quantitative expansion. As a result, Dai-ichi Life's growth was slow. It was in 1909 that the total amount of insurance contracts reached 10 million yen, seven years after its foundation. On the other hand, Chiyoda Life Insurance, which was founded in 1904 as a second mutual life insurance company after Dai-ichi Life, had actively expanded sales through agents, reached 10 million yen in 1906, and exceeded 20 million yen in 1908.

As a result of efforts made by Yano and his team to achieve efficient management, such as breaking away from the high cost of insurance sales, Dai-ichi Life could make a small surplus since the first financial settlement. In 1906, the company paid the first employee dividend of 3% on paid premiums. As a result, life insurance companies began to pay dividends in order to compete with Dai-ichi Life.

The *Tokyo Asahi Shimbun*,[9] one of the major newspapers at the time, pointed out that many of the 29 life insurance companies had problems in managing expenses, such as operating expenses for agents, defects in insurance reserves, and inadequate asset management. The newspaper evaluated that Dai-ichi Life was the best life insurance company in Japan with the lowest expense ratio in the industry.[10]

6 Tsuneta Yano's Management Philosophy

6.1 Yano's Management Philosophy

In 1915, Yano assumed the post of president of Dai-ichi Life, becoming the Chief Executive Officer in both name and reality. The characteristics of his management philosophy are summarized in the following four points: (1) incrementalism, (2) no agents' policy, (3) high-priced contract, (4) strict underwriting. These are based on the management philosophy of the Old Equitable and the Gothaer Life Insurance Company that Yano learned throughout his career. Yano aimed to be the best company, not to expand its scale.

Incrementalism meant not pursuing quantitative expansion. Yano disliked the stupidity of competing with other companies by spending on substantial operating expenses. At that time, sales activities by agents were common, but Dai-ichi Life did not set up sales agents. Also, in order to avoid costly small insurances contracts, Dai-ichi Life only undertook insurances worth 500 yen or more per contract.

In order to secure dividends for policyholders, it is necessary to keep the loss ratio low. Dai-ichi Life focused on eliminating high-risk policies with strict underwriting. These measures were implemented for the benefit of policyholders, not for the company. Profit is partially returned to shareholders in a stock company, but, in a mutual company that has no shareholders, profits are returned to policyholders.

One thing to keep in mind when discussing Yano's view of corporate management is his policy of appointing directors. In "Our Management Policy" published in Toyo Keizai Shimpo Publishing (1930), Yano stated that he would not appoint an employee as an officer and a director. Banks and insurance companies in those days selected executives from their employees, but Yano criticized this practice as rewarding the subordinates according to their services, not the right criteria for appointment of officers and directors.

Yano thought that the life insurance company's business foundation was based on trust, so its executives must have absolute trust from outside the company. This idea is similar to the idea of outside directors employed by many modern companies. It is considered that Yano's attitude toward appointment of directors shows that the company must gain the trust of internal and external stakeholders in order to build the best mutual company.

As Dai-ichi Life grew, Yano felt the need for talent capable of managing the company. He asked Keijiro Okano, a colleague from his days of the Ministry of Agriculture and Commerce, to introduce the right person. The person whom Okano introduced was Taizo Ishizaka, who later became Dai-ichi Life's president. At that time, Ishizaka was manager in charge of the exchange and postal saving division of the Ministry of Communications, and he had a promising future. Ishizaka hesitated to join Dai-ichi Life, but after listening to opinions and suggestions of those around him, he finally joined in 1915 as a secretary. In 1938, Ishizaka took over the position of president from Yano and grew Dai-ichi Life from a medium-sized life insurance company to an industry-leading company. After World War II, Ishizaka left the company with Yano before the enforcement of the revised expulsion from public office, but subsequently held key positions such as president of Tokyo Shibaura Electric Company (currently Toshiba Corporation) and second chairman of Keidanren (Japan Business Federation).

6.2 *Yano's Management Philosophy Described in His Books*

Yano worked not only on the insurance business but also on improvement of statistical data and social education. He authored numerous books, including *The Interest Rate Review* (1904), *Pocket-sized Analects of*

Confucius (1907), *Geisha Theory* (1912), and *The Japan Census Chart* (1927).

The Japan Census Chart embodied Yano's desire for youth education. In the preface to the first edition published in 1927, Yano stated, "If the editor (Yano) was a young educator and had several students, I would like to teach what I wrote in this book to any student regardless their major".

Since its first publication in 1927, the book has been widely used as a valuable data collection for students, schoolteachers, and the general public to know the current state of the economy and industry.

Yano had a strong interest in statistical and numerical data such as creating a mortality table based on the Japanese mortality rate (Yano's first table) at Kyosai Life Insurance, which he joined per request from Zenjiro Yasuda. Also, the Dai-ichi Life's financial report was detailed. This was based on Yano's conviction that the actual state of management must be disclosed entirely by numbers. Rational management based on analysis of quantitative data using statistics and customer-first principle based on mutualism formed the basis of Yano's life insurance business.

Yano cited the "scientific validity of business plans" and the "importance of trust" as factors for successful corporate management. He said: "Japanese people tend to rush too quickly to be successful when they start a business. it is important that the business plan needs to be developed based on detailed calculations that encompassed all situations".

Regarding trust, and based on the fact that Dai-ichi Life took ten years to obtain trust from society, he stated that entrepreneurs should keep in mind that it would take a certain period of time to obtain trust, which is the foundation of business.

In 1951, five years after he retired from the chairmanship of Dai-ichi Life, Yano closed his 85-year-old life with his family.

In 1970, Yano was inducted into the International Insurance Hall of Fame. The International Insurance Hall of Fame aims to honor those who have made significant contributions to the development of the insurance business. Yano was the first member of the Japanese life insurance industry to enter the Hall of Fame.

7 Conclusion

This chapter examined Tsuneta Yano, who laid the foundation of Japan's life insurance business. The core elements of Yano's management were:

1. Objective and rational decision-making based on actuarial science.
2. Awareness of social responsibility as an insurance company.
3. Spirit of service to policyholders.
4. Management philosophy based on trust.

Yano made a pioneering achievement in the field of insurance research, such as presenting the Japanese Mortality Table he developed at the first International Actuary Conference. In order to promote the use of data in Japan, he also put his heart into publishing the aforementioned Japan Census Chart.

Yano thought that the management of insurance companies based on mutualism would fulfill their social responsibility as insurance companies. Yano criticized stock companies' mission of increasing shareholder value and claimed the superiority of mutual companies that prioritized returning profits to policyholders.

In today's society, companies are required to fulfill a wide range of corporate social responsibility (CSR). In light of the remorse that excessive profit-seeking behaviors caused many corporate scandals, the business is shifting to a management style that emphasizes the balance between social and economic returns to multi-stakeholders, including shareholders.

Yano stated, "Trust is the foundation of the insurance business. Profit, which is a tangible asset, is built by trust, which is an intangible asset". It takes an enormous amount of time for a company to gain trust from society. Trust for insurance company is derived from the behaviors of managers and employees, and to gain and maintain the trust, they are required to continue their efforts.

In Japan, non-payment of insurance claims by a number of life insurance companies was uncovered in 2005 and it became a big social problem. According to a survey conducted in 2007, Dai-ichi Life's number of non-payments was approximately 70,000 and amounted to ¥18.9 billion. The unpaid amount was the highest among 38 life insurance companies.

It was revealed that many Japanese life insurance companies had been doing faulty management, neglecting customers, and the trust they had accumulated was lost in a moment. Life insurance companies are required to return to the true aim of the insurance business that Yano was obsessed with and do their utmost to restore their lost trust.

Notes

1. Meiji Life was a predecessor of the current Meiji Yasuda Mutual Life Insurance Company.
2. Kyosai 500 also later became a part of the Meiji Yasuda Life Insurance Company.
3. The Kyosai 500 companies adopted a system in which policyholders were limited and the burden of insurance claims was evenly "imposed" on the policyholders. However, this system had the following problems: (1) policyholders were limited from the beginning; (2) additional sales was not possible unless some policyholders died; therefore, the business couldn't scale and earn profits. As a result, the company was reorganized into a mutual aid life insurance partnership in 1894.
4. Nippon Life completed its own insurance premiums table based on this Fujisawa Life Table (No. 2). However, at this point, it was not yet based on their insured's mortality rate. The calculation based on the company's insured mortality rate was not realized until 1911 when Meiji Life, Teikoku Life, and Nippon Life made the "Japan Three Companies Life Table".
5. Preparatory school is equivalent to the current university liberal arts program.
6. In 1892, though not completed, Yano attempted to write two papers.
7. In 1893, Zenjiro Yasuda took over Tokyo Fire Insurance, the first fire insurance company in Japan (later the company became the Yasuda Fire and Marine Insurance, the predecessor of the current Sompo Japan Insurance). In addition, Yasuda established a new Teikoku Marine Insurance.
8. The mortality table devised by Yano was based on the Cabinet Statistics Bureau Table on Japanese mortality. Yano was involved in compiling this statistic as a commissioned researcher.
9. *Tokyo Asahi Shimbun* was the former title of the Japanese daily newspaper *Asahi Shimbun* in the East Japan region.
10. *Tokyo Asahi Shimbun* ran stories titled "Dangerous Insurance Company" (May 16, 1910) and "Inner Curtain of Life Insurance Company" (from June 5 to July 11, 1910).

References

Dai-ichi Life [1958] "55th Anniversary of Dai-ichi Life", Dai-ichi Life Mutual Company.

Dai-ichi Life [1972] "Dai-ichi Life Seventy Year History", Dai-ichi Life Mutual Company.

Dai-ichi Life [1982] "The Origin of Mutualism (including Gothaer Story)" Dai-ichi Life Mutual Company.
Fukuzawa, Yukichi and Yoshida, Kensuke [2008] "Western Travel Guide (Reprint Japanese Modern Literature)" National Institute of Japanese Literature.
Hasegawa, Naoya [2008] "2. Innovators in the Insurance Industry" "Japanese Entrepreneurs" Bunshindo.
Hoken Hyoron Sha [1973] "Japan insurance directory" Nihon Hoken Hyoron Sha.
Inamiya, Matayoshi [1962] "Tsuneta Yano" Jiji Press.
Insurance Research Institute [1982] "History of the Japanese Insurance Industry (Overview) (Company Edition, Volume 1&2)" Insurance Research Institute (Hoken Kenkyujo).
Insurance Research Institute, "Insurance: Life Insurance Statistics" (each fiscal year) Insurance Research Institute (Hoken Kenkyujo).
Japan Institute of Life Insurance [1990] "New Life Insurance Lectures, Volume 1 Overview" Yuhikaku.
Kobayashi, Tadashi [1991] "The Biographies of Insurance Thinkers" Hoken Mainichi Shimbun.
Kobayashi, Tadasi [2005] "Insurance Thought and Management Philosophy" Chikura Shobo.
Nippon Insurance Shimbun [1968] "History of Insurance Business in Japan" Nippon Insurance Shimbun.
Tsuneta Yano Commemorative Society [1957] "Biography of Tsuneta Yano" Tsuneta Yano Commemorative Society.
Yamashita, Tomonobu [1988] "Modern Issues of Mutual Company Law" Tsuneta Yano Memorial Society.
Yano, Tsuneta [1927] "The Japan Census Chart (Showa 2 edition)" Nihon Hyoron Sha.
Yano, Tsuneta [1928] "If you want success, take this path" Jitsugyo no Nihon Vol. 31, No. 7.
Yano, Tsuneta [1929] "Life insurance" "Socio-Economic System Volume 5 Industry" Nihon Hyoron Sha.
Yano, Tsuneta [1965] "One word collection" Tsuneta Yano Memorial Society.

Index[1]

[1] Note: Page numbers followed by 'n' refer to notes.

M. Takehara, N. Hasegawa, *Sustainable Management of Japanese Entrepreneurs in Pre-War Period from the Perspective of SDGs and ESG*, https://doi.org/10.1007/978-981-15-6507-6

L

M

N

The manufacturer's authorised representative in the EU is Springer Nature Customer Service Centre GmbH, Europaplatz 3, 69115 Heidelberg, Germany. If you have any concerns regarding our products, please contact ProductSafety@springernature.com

Printed and bound by CPI Group (UK) Ltd, Croydon, CR0 4YY
30/09/2026
02225325-0003